STANDING AGAIN AT SINAI

Judaism from a Feminist Perspective

JUDITH PLASKOW

1817

Harper & Row, Publishers, San Francisco

New York, Grand Rapids, Philadelphia, St. Louis
London, Singapore, Sydney, Tokyo, Toronto

To my son,
Alexander Gideon Plaskow Goldenberg

What do we want for our sons? . . . We want
them . . . to discover new ways of being men
even as we are discovering new ways of
being women.

ADRIENNE RICH
Of Woman Born

Unless otherwise specified, Bible quotations come from the new Jewish
Publication Society translation or the Revised Standard Version.

Parts of chapter 2 appeared in condensed and earlier versions in *Tikkun*
vol. 1, no. 2 (November 1986) and *The Melton Journal* 22 (Fall 1987). Part
of chapter 5 appeared in somewhat different form in Christie Balka
and Andy Rose, eds., *Twice Blessed*, Beacon Press, 1989.

FIRST EDITION

Library of Congress Cataloging-in-Publication Data

Plaskow, Judith.
    Standing again at Sinai.

    Includes bibliographical references.
    1. Women in Judaism.   2. Feminism—Religious aspects—
Judaism.   I. Title.   II. Title: Judaism from a feminist—perspective.
BM729.W6P55   1990   296'.082   89-45559
ISBN 0-06-066683-8

---

90 91 92 93 94 HAD 10 9 8 7 6 5 4 3 2 1

Contents

Acknowledgments

No book is ever the work of a single author, and this is perhaps especially true of a Jewish feminist theology, which is necessarily grounded in a number of different communities. The community most important to this book is B'not Esh, the Jewish feminist spirituality collective I helped to found in 1981, which has been the center of my religious life for the last eight years. The work and ideas of several individuals in B'not Esh have been particularly important to me, and I acknowledge them at many points in this book. Above and beyond these special debts, however, it is what B'not Esh has accomplished as a community that has allowed me to write this theology of community.

Another group that has been crucial to my development as a feminist and a theologian is the Women and Religion Section of the American Academy of Religion. I see this work as in large measure a product of ideas and friendships sparked in the Section; and I see myself as trying to work through in a Jewish context questions and ideas that come out of and belong to a wider feminist community. The New York Feminist Scholars in Religion, which has been meeting for fifteen years, for me sustains the work of the Women's Section in between its annual meetings, providing a place for ongoing discussion and dialogue.

Other communities important to the genesis of this book are Havurat Ha-Emek in Northampton, Massachusetts, and Havurah Aliza in New York, both of which are year-round sources of support and community. The Havurah Institutes, particularly the first Institute in 1980, but also others after that, have given me places both to test and discuss ideas and also to work with other Jewish feminists.

Many individuals and small groups have read portions of this book and have given me important comments and feedback that I have tried to attend and respond to: the New York Feminist Scholars in Religion, especially Beverly Harrison, Karen Brown, and Anne Barstow; Frederick Brandfon and other faculty at the University of Southern California, where I visited in the spring of 1986; Elisabeth Schüssler Fiorenza, Alison Jordan, Marion Klotz, Richard Meirowitz, Florence Miale, Barbara Johnson, Donna Robinson Divine, Paula Rayman, Nira Yuval-Davis, Marcia Falk, and Denni Leibowitz. Three people read the entire manuscript: my editor Janice Johnson, who made many helpful suggestions for clarifications and revisions, and Martha Ackelsberg and Carol P. Christ. Martha read as one who has shared the experience of B'not Esh and all that led up to it, and Carol as a longtime friend, colleague, and sister thealogian. Martha's work on community, and spirituality and politics, has become part of my own thinking. Carol and I have moved in different directions in the course of the last decade, but our differences have made her work all the more important to me and her comments and questions all the more what I needed to hear.

A Mary Ingraham Bunting Fellowship in the spring of 1986 and a Manhattan College sabbatical grant for 1987–1988 allowed me to write much of this book. I am grateful for both for giving me the time to pursue my work at a point when I was ready to do so.

Introduction: It's Feminist, But Is It Jewish?

The subject of this book is feminist Judaism. Exploring the implications of women's increasing involvement in naming and shaping the Jewish tradition, it asks what might happen to the central categories of Jewish thought as women enter into the process of defining them. The book comes out of and draws on twenty years of Jewish feminist work—in synagogues and study groups, *havurot* and Rosh Hodesh groups, and many communities around the country. It seeks to apply this work to the theological sphere, to rethink key Jewish ideas and experiences from one feminist perspective. As Jewish women recognize ourselves as heirs to and shapers of Judaism, as we explore our own experiences and integrate them into the tradition, we necessarily transform the tradition and shape it into something new. How, then, might the central Jewish categories of Torah, Israel, and God change as women appropriate them through the lens of our experience?

Since the project of transforming Judaism through a feminist vision is new and far-reaching, it is important to confront at the outset some of the fears and questions it raises. For many people—from secular feminists to observant Jews—the notion of a feminist Judaism is an oxymoron. Feminists often see Judaism as irredeemably patriarchal, attachment to it as incomprehensible and retrogressive. Jews often perceive feminism as an alien philosophy, at odds with Jewish self-understanding in important ways. On either view, Jewish feminists dwell in a state of self-contradiction that can be escaped only by choosing between aspects of our identity.

This either/or view of Jewish feminism is well illustrated by an incident at a Jewish theology conference I attended several years ago, at which a prominent left-wing Orthodox rabbi told a moral tale for the benefit of the feminists present. In the Bialystok Ghetto, he said, women were the primary gunrunners because they could pass as non-Jews more easily than men. In the last days of the Ghetto, the women staged a brief rebellion, refusing to hand over the guns they had smuggled and arguing that it was better to join the Partisans in the forest than to make a last, fruitless stand against the Nazis. But the women finally surrendered the weapons when the men insisted, he continued, because as Jews first and women second, they realized they needed to remain in solidarity with their men. "What would you have done?" he asked us. "Which side are you on?" His underlying question hung unasked in the ensuing silence: "Are you a feminist or are you a Jew?"[1]

It is not only outsiders who share this story's assumption that Judaism and feminism are in conflict; that suspicion also finds echoes in Jewish feminists ourselves. At the first National Jewish Women's Conference, in 1973, I delivered a paper entitled "The Jewish Feminist: Conflict in Identities." The paper explored both the sexism of the Jewish tradition and the tensions I felt between Judaism and feminism as alternative communities.[2] I wrote the speech at a time in my life when I was exploring traditional Judaism and concurrently becoming increasingly involved in feminist activity and research. I was developing a new consciousness of myself as a woman at the same time I was learning more and more about the the ways in which Judaism excluded me, and I was sometimes overwhelmed by the contradictions between the two identities.

Not all of traditional Jewish attitudes toward women were new to me in the early 1970s. I was educated in a classical Reform congregation in which the rabbi opposed the ordination of women as "against tradition," so the conflicts between the promise of liberal Judaism and women's actual roles were long familiar. I saw that the rhetoric of Reform, while it held out the hope of equality, masked the reality of women's exclusion from religious leadership. I also knew that the educational opportunities available to friends in the Conservative movement had similarly conveyed contradictory messages: For example, while a girl could be bat mitzvah, this event marked the end, rather than the beginning, of her participation in congregational life.

As I became more involved with traditional practice, other starker disabilities of women presented themselves. The legal inability of women to initiate divorce, for instance, entails that a woman with an obstinate or missing husband must remain unmarried for the rest of her life. The fact that, in traditional Judaism, women are not counted in a *minyan* (quorum required for public prayer) or called to the Torah amounts to our exclusion from the public religious realm. I experienced the issue of minyan not as a theoretical problem, but as a pressing reality demanding feminist response. In one moment of epiphany my (former) husband and I were standing outside the Yale chapel on a Sabbath morning, chatting with a friend before going in for services. While we were talking, a member of the congregation came out and asked my husband to come in right away because they needed a minyan. I suddenly realized that, while I had attended services regularly for a year and a half and my husband was a relative newcomer, I could stay outside all day; my presence was irrelevant to the purpose for which we had gathered. Such experiences—and they are part of the lives of thousands and thousands of Jewish women—did and do make me feel that there are aspects of Jewish and feminist identity that are irreconcilable.

In the main, however, the process of coming to write this book has been for me a gradual process of refusing the split between a Jewish and a feminist self. I am not a Jew in the synagogue and a feminist in the world. I am a Jewish feminist and a feminist Jew in every moment of my life. I have increasingly come to realize that in setting up Judaism and feminism as conflicting ideologies and communities, I was handing over to a supposedly monolithic Jewish tradition the power and the right to define Judaism for the past and for the future. "Judaism" was a given that I could fit myself into or decide to reject. It was not a complex and pluralistic tradition involved in a continual process of adaptation and change—a process to which I and other feminist Jews could contribute. Like the wicked child of the Passover Seder, I was handing over Judaism to *them*, denying my own power as a Jew to help shape what Judaism will become.

I am no longer willing to relinquish that power. I reject the rabbi's dilemma of whether to hand over the guns to the men and be a Jew or keep the guns and be a woman who denies my people. As I intuited when I first heard his story but now see more clearly, the choice is a false one. The women of the Bialystok Ghetto were acting as Jews, but they understood the meaning of Jewish action differently from the men. Had they held to their position, the story would have had a different ending—but still a Jewish one. Perhaps some of the inhabitants of the Ghetto might have survived instead of all of them being destroyed. The rabbi's moral tale may thus be read as having a different lesson from the one he intended. When Jewish feminists allow Judaism and feminism to be defined by others in oppositional ways, then we are stuck with two "givens" confronting each other, and we are fundamentally divided. When, however, we refuse to sever or choose between different aspects of our identity, we create a new situation. If we are Jews not despite being feminists but *as feminists*, then Judaism will have to change—we will have to work to change it—to make a whole identity possible. This change, moreover, may lead to new life for us and for the tradition.

The commitment that underlies this book is precisely a commitment to creating a new Jewish situation, to making a feminist Judaism a reality. Since I assume this commitment but do not defend it elsewere in the text, my decision to remain within a patriarchal tradition requires some explanation. The important decisions we make in our lives are seldom rooted in rational calculation or easily analyzable, so the sources of this commitment are difficult for me to articulate. Especially in the American context where religious traditions are often viewed as selections in a great smorgasbord from which we pick and choose, the place of upbringing, community, and identity in adult religious decisions is often neglected or devalued. For me, the move toward embracing a whole Jewish/feminist identity did not grow out of my conviction that Judaism is "redeemable," but out of my sense that sundering Judaism and feminism would mean sundering my being. Certainly, I did not become a feminist Jew by adding up columns of sexist and nonsexist passages in the Bible and tradition and deciding the nonsexist side had won. Judaism is, I shall argue, a deeply patriarchal tradition. To change it will require a revolution as great as the transition from biblical to rabbinic Judaism precipitated by the destruction of the Second Temple. I do not believe there is some nonsexist "essence" of Judaism in the name of which I struggle, nor do I believe that success is assured.

The factors that make up my commitment to change, and particularly to religious change, are more complex and intertwining. First, from childhood, I have been drawn to and fascinated by questions of ultimate truth and meaning so that I cannot put aside the peculiar difficulties of religious sexism to struggle against male domination on some less charged ground—even the ground of Jewish secularism. Second, if Judaism is patriarchal, I do not believe there is any *non*patriarchal space to which I can go to create a new religion. It is true that women who move outside traditional religions dispense with the need to deal with certain arguments and institutions that drain feminist energy. Still, as I see it, the creativity, imagination, and risks involved in creating a feminist Judaism (or Christianity) are in many ways similar in nature and substance to the work and risks involved in creating a purely feminist spirituality.

These are arguments for Judaism by default, however, and they would not be sufficient, were it not that I find value and meaning in Judaism and in my own Jewish identity, and that

Judaism has been an important and nourishing part of my life. Many Jewish feminists, alienated by the sexism of the tradition, are making their way back to Judaism because of anti-Semitism in the women's movement. Learning about anti-Semitism had a profound effect on my sense of Jewish identity as I early immersed myself in literature about the Holocaust. And growing up as part of a minority in American culture contributed to my sense of connection to Judaism and to my sense of Jewish loyalty. But I never experienced minority status as simply negative; it came to me as both burden and gift. It gave me a different lens for looking at the world, the lens of the outsider who has access to questions the majority does not see. Moreover, anti-Semitism, while it reverberated with the central Jewish experience of slavery in the land of Egypt, was never the whole of my Jewish identity. Judaism was also lighting candles on Friday night and observing the cycle of the year; it was the stories of my ancestors, the words of the prophets calling us to justice and social engagement—the ethical monotheism we learned about in religious school and in which I deeply believed.

In *Beyond God the Father*, Mary Daly talks about the fact that feminists always live and work "on the boundaries" of particular institutions in our patriarchal world.[3] I have chosen to work with other Jewish feminists on the boundary of Judaism because that is where the different aspects of my identity most fully come together. In 1980, when I taught a course on Jewish feminist theology at the first National Havurah Summer Institute, it was my first opportunity to grapple with issues of theology and spirituality in a Jewish feminist context. Talking with other Jewish feminists about our relation to tradition, I felt it as a coming home. Out of that Institute, several women started B'not Esh, an ongoing Jewish feminist spirituality collective that has tried to create a space in which feminist Judaism is a reality.[4] I have found in that collective a community of vision and struggle that I believe has much to offer toward the transformation of the wider Jewish community as well as the transformation of our society and our world. It is this vision—a vision shared by many others inside and outside the Jewish feminist community—that I hope to articulate and explore.

While it will take the rest of this book to develop the substance of my Jewish feminist vision, here I can indicate at least the direction of my thinking. Jewish feminism has emerged as a diverse and complex religious and social movement, as diverse and complex as Jewish identity itself. Just as Jewishness encompasses religious, ethnic, national, and communal elements, so Jewish feminists have addressed a range of inequalities in Jewish life.[5] Feminists have fought for women's ordination and created new Jewish rituals. We have addressed the absence of female leadership in Jewish communal institutions and examined images of women in Jewish literature. We have scrutinized the Jewish family and the family-centeredness of Judaism, looked at the roles of women in Israel, struggled with anti-Semitism in the culture and the women's movement, and started to unearth Jewish women's contributions to Jewish and secular culture.[6]

Through this diversity, the Jewish feminist movement has experienced some of the same tensions that have divided the women's movement as a whole. Whether in analyzing women's communal roles, dissecting the image of the Jewish princess, or studying aspects of Jewish law, different Jewish feminists have written and worked out of fundamentally different feminist visions. Without nullifying the plurality of issues addressed or the diversity of perspectives brought to them, a basic question has asserted itself: Is the goal of Jewish feminism equal rights for women or communal and religious transformation? Is the purpose of feminism to provide women equal access to all the privileges and responsibilities of Jewish men or to integrate women's experience into Jewish life, and in doing so, to begin a far-reaching and open-ended process of reformation?

Like many Jewish feminists of differing specific concerns, I was initially drawn to feminism through issues of equal access.

Since women's subordination in Jewish law and exclusion from public ritual life are obvious and painful, the focus on equal access was a natural beginning stage. The issues first at the center of feminist discussion were not ones that feminists chose, but issues that, in a sense, chose us; problems like divorce and minyan that, in their concreteness and urgency, clamored for remedy. The process of living with these questions for a while gradually made clear, however, that problems of equal rights are only symptoms of a broader patriarchal worldview. The fight for specific reforms led to a thicket of fundamental questions with implications far beyond the particular problems that gave rise to them. Thus Jewish feminists might agree that it is a matter of simple justice for Jewish women to have full access to the riches of Jewish life. But when a woman stands in the pulpit and reads from the Torah that daughters can be sold as slaves (Ex. 21:7–11), she participates in a profound contradiction between the message of her presence and the content of what she learns and teaches. It is this contradiction feminists must address, not simply "adding" women to a tradition that remains basically unaltered, but transforming Judaism into a religion that women as well as men have a role in shaping.

The importance of this deeper transformation is highlighted by the changes in non-Orthodox Judaism in the last twenty years: Most of women's civil and religious disabilities have been eliminated. But these changes have not turned Judaism into a feminist tradition. They have simply meant that, as women take our place in Jewish life—as we are called to the Torah, as we are counted in the minyan and lead services, as we act as rabbis and cantors—we function as participants in, teachers, and preservers of a male religion. We become full members of a tradition that women played only a secondary role in shaping and creating. We appear to be equals, but we leave intact the history, structures, images, and texts that exclude and testify against us. When we act as though equal access were the whole feminist agenda, we do not touch the roots of our marginality or the foundations of our subordination.

For me, then, feminism is not about attaining equal rights for women in religious or social structures that remain unchanged, but about the thoroughgoing transformation of religion and society. Feminism is a process of coming to affirm ourselves as women/persons—and seeing that affirmation mirrored in religious and social institutions. As women begin to share with each other our pain as women, we start to see the systematic ways in which social ideologies and institutions have kept us from ourselves.[7] We begin—or should begin—to make connections between our oppression as women and other forms of oppression from which women and men suffer. Feminism, I believe, aims at the liberation of all women and all people, and is thus not a movement for individual equality, but for the creation of a society that no longer construes difference in terms of superiority and subordination. The project of creating a feminist Judaism fits into a larger project of creating a world in which all women, and all people, have both the basic resources they need to survive, and the opportunity to name and shape the structures of meaning that give substance to their lives. In the Jewish context, this means re-forming every aspect of tradition so that it incorporates women's experience. Only when those who have had the power of naming stolen from us find our voices and begin to speak[8] will Judaism become a religion that includes all Jews—will it truly be a Judaism of women and men.

The notion of feminism as a process of radical transformation raises, as a last point, the issue of boundaries. For many Jews, Jewish feminists among them, the notion of women taking power to shape the Jewish tradition provokes not just a sense of contradiction but a feeling of dislocation and chaos. Once women begin radically altering Judaism, where will change stop? How much of what lies rooted in childhood memory, of what many Jews love and value, will be eroded by criticism and destroyed? At what point in the reinterpretation of Judaism does the Jewish tradition cease being Jewish and become something else?

While the question of boundaries is one Jewish feminists are frequently asked and that we ask ourselves, it rests on assumptions and anxieties that require careful scrutiny. Often the question of boundaries identifies Judaism with its elite, mainstream rabbinic expression; and further, with certain aspects of rabbinic Judaism that are assumed to be unchanging and essential. The question leaves out of account or assumes as un-Jewish the many ancient and modern competitors of the rabbis, as well as the various and changing forms of popular Judaism that have existed side by side with rabbinism.[9] Moreover, insistence on predetermined boundaries disguises the fact that rabbinic Judaism itself was the product of enormous changes—a shift from Temple sacrifice as the center of worship, to study and prayer as the dual foci of Judaism. This profound change was perceived as a transition rather than a break only because the Jewish community willed it so, and undertook to reinterpret the past to meet the needs of a radically different present. Focusing on boundaries, however, serves to prevent further change, preserving the status quo in the name of some disaster that experimentation might bring. It simultaneously delegitimates Jewish feminism and accords it enormous power. It implies that if feminists persist in transforming tradition, three thousand years of historical development may be uprooted.

But such anxieties misunderstand the nature of fundamental religious change, which is both slower and less manipulable than the question of limits assumes. Boundaries evolve over time in the context of changing circumstances; they cannot be erected in the abstract. The Jews of the past, drawing on the religious forms available to them, created and recreated a living Judaism, reshaping tradition in ways consonant with their needs. What determined the "Jewishness" of their formulations was not a set of predetermined criteria, but the "workability" of such formulations for the Jewish people: the capacity of stories and laws and liturgy to adapt to new conditions, to make sense and provide meaning, to offer the possibility of a whole life. Feminist changes may seem more threatening than the changes of the past because they are proposed with the consciousness and deliberation that mark our modern sensibility. Moreover, women's experiments may feel intrinsically un-Jewish simply because they represent women taking initiative within the religious sphere. In this sense, Jewish feminism does involve a radical discontinuity with the tradition: It constitutes a first attempt to make Jewish religiosity reflect the Jewish people as a whole. But the mechanisms that will decide the success or failure of Jewish feminism are old and tried. Some feminist changes will endure because they are appropriate, because they speak to felt needs within the community and ring true to the Jewish imagination. Others will fall by the wayside as eccentric, mechanical, or false. To try to decide in advance which will be authentic is to confine our creativity and resources; it is to divert energy needed to shape the kind of Jewish community in which we want to live.

Because much of this book will be concerned with transforming Judaism, however, it seems important to put aside my suspicion of boundary questions, to mention some of the many aspects of Judaism I take for granted. I do not intend this list as a set of limits—though parts of it do represent *my* limits—but as an attempt to clarify my own Jewish givens as they enter into my Jewish feminist identity.

First of all, in the face of sometimes contrary evidence, I assume that Jewish women past and present are part of the Jewish people. I affirm my own Jewishness as a central part of my identity. I affirm the value of Jewish identity alongside other particular identities. Being part of a community with its own history, convictions, customs, and values can add richness and meaning to life; I believe these things are worth preserving—not as frozen forms, but as elements in dialogue with changing social and historical reality.

Second, I assume that, for better and for worse, Jewish history is my history, the texts that record that history are my texts. Abraham and Sarah are my ancestors, as are Elijah and the women who worshiped the Queen of Heaven (Jer. 44:15–19). I went forth from Egypt and danced with Miriam at the shores of the sea. Even where I dissent from biblical or rabbinic teaching, where I find it problematic, unjust, or simply wrong, I still see it as part of a past that has shaped and formed me. As mine, it is a past for me to struggle with, not a past on which I am willing to turn my back.

Third, aside from general discussion of the language of liturgy, I say little in the book about the Sabbath, the holidays, the cycle of the year, or the cycles of individual life. If I leave out of account particular holidays and rituals, it is not because I consider them unimportant but because I take for granted their continuation. Certainly, women need many new rituals for events in our lives and histories that have hitherto gone unmarked. But I assume that these new rituals are additions to rhythms of work and rest, seasons of self-examination, mourning, and rejoicing that Jews have always observed.

Fourth, and on a more strictly theological level, I assume there is a God and that God is one. I devote considerable space to discussing the need to transform the traditional picture of God, including the nature of God's unity, because I believe it is important to find ways of speaking to and about God that reflect feminist experience and make sense in the modern world. I am convinced that a feminist Judaism can restore the viability of God-talk within Judaism, providing the tradition with a language it has lost and sorely needs. The history of the Jewish people is intelligible only as a history of response to the encounter with God in Jewish experience. The question of God is central to Jewish theology and Jewish self-understanding.

Fifth, I assume that to have been a slave in the land of Egypt is the basis of a profound religious obligation to do justice in the world. I assume that one finds God in the world, in acts of love and justice, and not beyond or outside the world. As a Jew, one enters into relationship with God through membership in the Jewish people. Relationship with God is mediated through community and expresses itself in community. The word of God is not far off; "it is not in heaven" (Deut. 30:12), but in our daily choices, the things we undertake and do. Thus I assume a deep relation between the spiritual and the everyday, between what we say about God and the way we structure our lives.

My last assumption is somewhat different from the others. It specifies my religious location rather than a conscious decision, and marks a limitation rather than a choice. I know that I write as a North American Ashkenazi Jew, beyond that, even as a New York Jew with a certain upbringing. I know that the Orthodox woman in my own city experiences Judaism very differently from me, not to mention the Ashkenazi woman in Israel or the woman from India or Turkey or Iraq. A feminist analysis of Judaism from any one of their perspectives would look very different from this one. I am aware of the danger of specifying my location as a feminist and then continuing to write as if that location were universal. This danger is compounded by the fact that Israeli feminists of all backgrounds, and Sephardic feminists wherever they live, are just beginning to speak up about their lives, and then rarely on religious issues, so that there is not yet a range of voices with which I can be in dialogue.[10] I embrace my own perspective insofar as it is what enables me to write and to express ideas that may be recognizable to others whatever their backgrounds. But I am also aware of the particularity of my perspective—and aware that I will understand the contours of that particularity only as it calls forth correction and discussion from others.

These assumptions, some tacit, some to be elaborated, will find their way into the rest of the book. There, interwoven with discussion of central aspects of Judaism and feminist experience, they provide part of the foundation for a vision of what Judaism might become.

1. Setting the Problem, Laying the Ground

The need for a feminist Judaism begins with hearing silence. It begins with noting the absence of women's history and experiences as shaping forces in the Jewish tradition. Half of Jews have been women, but men have been defined as normative Jews, while women's voices and experiences are largely invisible in the record of Jewish belief and experience that has come down to us. Women have lived Jewish history and carried its burdens, but women's perceptions and questions have not given form to scripture, shaped the direction of Jewish law, or found expression in liturgy. Confronting this silence raises disturbing questions and stirs the impulse toward far-reaching change. What in the tradition is ours? What can we claim that has not also wounded us? What would have been different had the great silence been filled?

Hearing silence is not easy. A silence so vast tends to fade into the natural order; it is easy to identify with reality. To ourselves, women are not Other. We take the Jewish tradition as it has been passed down to us, as ours to appropriate or ignore. Over time, we learn to insert ourselves into silences.[1] Speaking about Abraham, telling of the great events at Sinai, we do not look for ourselves in the narratives but assume our presence, peopling the gaps in the text with women's shadowy forms. It is far easier to read ourselves into male stories than to ask how the foundational stories within which we live have been distorted by our absence. Yet it is not possible to speak into silence, to recover our history or reclaim our power to name without first confronting the extent of exclusion of women's experience. Silence can become an invitation to experiment and explore—but only after we have examined its terrain and begun to face its implications.

This chapter has two purposes: to chart the domain of silence that lies at the root of Jewish feminism and to take up the methodological presuppositions that inform my thinking. While it is not my primary intention in this book to set out an indictment of Judaism as a patriarchal tradition, criticism is an ongoing and essential part of the Jewish feminist project. Not only is criticism a precondition for imagining a transformed Judaism; without a clear critique of Judaism that precedes and accompanies reconstruction, the process of reconstruction easily can be misconstrued as a form of apologetics. In exploring the territory of silence and describing my methodology, I mean to prevent this misunderstanding by clarifying the stance and intent that underlie my constructive thinking.

Exploring the Terrain of Silence

In her classic work *The Second Sex*, Simone de Beauvoir argues that men have established an absolute human type—the male—against which women are measured as Other. Otherness, she says, is a pervasive and generally fluid category of human thought; I perceive and am perceived as Other depending on a particular situation. In the case of males and females, however, Otherness is not reciprocal: men are always the definers, women the defined.[2] While women's self-experience is an experience of selfhood, it is not women's experience that is enshrined in language or that has shaped our cultural forms. As women appear in male texts, they are not the subjects and molders of their own experiences but the objects of male purposes, designs, and desires. Women do not name reality, but rather are named as part of a reality that is male-constructed. Where women are Other, they can be present and silent simultaneously; for the language and thought-forms of culture do not express their meanings.

De Beauvoir's analysis provides a key to women's silence within Judaism, for, like women in many cultures, Jewish women have been projected as Other. Named by a male community that perceives itself as normative, women are part of the Jewish tradition without its sources and structures reflecting our experience. Women are Jews, but we do not define Jewishness. We live, work, and struggle, but our experiences are not recorded, and what is recorded formulates our experiences in male terms. The central Jewish categories of Torah, Israel, and God all are constructed from male perspectives. Torah is revelation as men perceived it, the story of Israel told from their standpoint, the law unfolded according to their needs. Israel is the male collectivity, the children of a Jacob who had a daughter, but whose sons became the twelve tribes.[3] God is named in the male image, a father and warrior much like his male offspring, who confirms and sanctifies the silence of his daughters. Exploring these categories, we explore the parameters of women's silence.[4]

In Torah, Jewish teaching, women are not absent, but they are cast in stories told by men. As characters in narrative, women may be vividly characterized, as objects of legislation, singled out for attention. But women's presence in Torah does not negate their silence, for women do not decide the questions with which Jewish sources deal. When the law treats of women, it is often because their "abnormality" demands it. If women are central to plot, the plots are not about them. Women's interests and intentions must be unearthed from texts with other purposes, for both law and narrative serve to obscure them.

The most striking examples of women's silence come from texts in which women are most central, for there the normative character of maleness is especially jarring. In the family narratives of Genesis, for example, women figure prominently. The matriarchs of Genesis are all strong women. As independent personalities, fiercely concerned for their children, they often seem to have an intuitive knowledge of God's plans for their sons. Indeed, it appears from the stories of Sarah and Rebekah that they understand God better than their husbands. God defends Sarah when she casts out Hagar, telling Abraham to obey his wife (Gen. 21:12).[5] Rebekah, knowing it is God's intent, helps deceive Isaac into accepting Jacob as his heir (Gen. 25:23; 27:5–17). Yet despite their intuitions, and despite their wiliness and resourcefulness, it is not the women who receive the covenant or who pass on its lineage. The establishment of patrilineal descent and the patriarchal family takes precedence over the matriarch's stories.[6] Their relationship to God, in some way presupposed by the text, remains an undigested element in the narrative. What was the full theophany to Rebekah, and how is it related to the covenant with Isaac? The writer does not tell us; it is not sufficiently important. And so the covenant remains the covenant with Isaac, while Rebekah's experience floats at the margin of the story.

The establishment of patrilineal descent and patriarchal control, a subtext in Genesis, is an important theme in the legislation associated with Sinai. Here again, women figure prominently, but only as objects of male concerns. The laws pertaining to women place them firmly under the control of first fathers, then husbands, so that men can have male heirs they know are theirs. Legislation concerning adultery (Deut. 22:22, also Num. 5:11–31) and virginity (Deut. 22:13–21) speaks of women, but only to control female sexuality to male advantage. The *crime* of adultery is sleeping with another man's wife, and a man can bring his wife to trial even on suspicion of adultery, a right that is not reciprocal. Sleeping with a betrothed virgin constitutes adultery. A man who sleeps with a virgin who is not betrothed must simply marry her. A girl whose lack of virginity shames her father on her wedding night can be stoned to death for harlotry. A virgin who is raped must marry her assailant. The subject of these laws is women, but the interest behind them is the purity of the male line.

The process of projecting and defining women as objects of male concerns is expressed most fully not in the Bible, however, but in the Mishnah, an important second-century legal code.

Part of the Mishnah's Order of Women (one of its six divisions) develops laws discussed in the Torah concerning certain problematic aspects of female sexuality. The subject of the division is the transfer of women—the regulation of women who are in states of transition, whose uncertain status threatens the stasis of the community. The woman who is about to enter into a marriage or who has just left one requires close attention. The law must regularize her irregularity, facilitate her transition to the normal state of wife and motherhood, at which point she no longer poses a problem.[7] But it is not even the contents of the order, male-defined as they are, that trumpet most loudly women's silence. In a system in which a division of Men would be unthinkable nonsense, the fact of a division Women is sufficient evidence of who names the world, who defines whom, in "normative" Jewish sources.

Thus Torah—"Jewish" sources, "Jewish" teaching—puts itself forward as *Jewish* teaching but speaks in the voice of only half the Jewish people. This scandal is compounded by another: The omission is neither mourned nor regretted; it is not even noticed. True, the rabbis were aware of the harshness of certain laws pertaining to women and sought to mitigate their effects. They tried to find ways to force a recalcitrant husband to divorce his wife, for example. But the framework that necessitated such mitigations went unquestioned. Women's Otherness was left intact. The Jewish passion for justice did not extend to Jewish women. As Cynthia Ozick puts it, one great "Thou shalt not"—"Thou shalt not lessen the humanity of women"—is missing from the Torah.[8]

For this great omission, there is no historical redress. Indeed, where one might expect redress, the problem is compounded. The prophets, those great champions of justice, couch their pleas for justice in the language of patriarchal marriage. Israel in her youth is a devoted bride, subordinate and obedient to her husband/God (for example, Jer. 2:2). Idolatrous Israel is a harlot and adulteress, a faithless woman whoring after false gods (for example, Hos. 2,3). Transferring the hierarchy of male and female to God and his people, the prophets enshrine in metaphor the legal subordination of women.[9] Those who might have named and challenged women's marginalization thus ignore and extend it.

The prophetic metaphors mark an end and a beginning. They confront us with the injustice of Torah; they link that injustice to other central Jewish ideas. If exploring Torah means exploring a terrain of women's silence, this is no less true of the categories of Israel or God.

Israel, the bride, the harlot, the people that is female (that is, subordinate) in relation to God is nonetheless male in communal self-perception. The covenant community is the community of the circumcised (Gen. 17:10), the community defined as male heads of household. Women are named through a filter of male experience: that is the essence of their silence. But women's experiences are not recorded or taken seriously because women are not perceived as normative Jews. They are part of but do not define the community of Israel.

The same evidence that speaks to women's silence in the tradition, to the partiality of Torah, also reflects an understanding of Israel as a community of males. In the narratives of Genesis, for example, the covenant moves from father to son, from Abraham to Isaac to Jacob to Joseph. The matriarchs' relation to their husbands' God is sometimes assumed, sometimes passed over, but the women do not constitute the covenant people. Women's relation to the community is also ambiguous and unclear in biblical legislation. The law is couched in male grammatical forms, and its content too presupposes a male nation. "You shall not covet your neighbor's wife" (Ex. 20:17). Probably we cannot deduce from this verse that women are free to covet! Yet the injunction assumes that women's obedience is owed to fathers and husbands, who are the primary group addressed.

The silence of women goes deeper, however, than who defines Torah or Israel. It also finds its way into language about God. Our language about divinity is first of all male language; it is selective and partial. The God who supposedly transcends sexuality, who is presumably one and whole, comes to us through language that is incomplete and narrow. The images we use to describe God, the qualities we attribute to God, draw on male pronouns and experience and convey a sense of power and authority that is clearly male. The God at the surface of Jewish consciousness is a God with a voice of thunder, a God who as lord and king rules his people and leads them into battle, a God who forgives like a father when we turn to him. The female images that exist in the Bible and (particularly the mystical) tradition form an underground stream that occasionally reminds us of the inadequacy of our imagery without transforming its overwhelmingly male nature.

This male imagery is comforting and familiar—comforting because familiar—but it is an integral part of a system that consigns women to the margins. Since the experience of God cannot be directly conveyed in language, imagery for God is a vehicle that suggests what is actually impossible to describe. Religious experiences are expressed in a vocabulary drawn from the significant and valuable in a particular culture. To speak of God is to speak of what we most value. In attributing certain qualities to God, we both attempt to point to God and offer God's qualities to be emulated and admired. To say that God is just, for example, is to say both that God acts justly and that God demands justice. Justice belongs to God but is also ours to pursue. Similarly with maleness, to image God as male is to value the quality and those who have it. It is to define God in the image of the normative community and to bless men—but not women—with a central attribute of God.

But our images of God are not simply male images; they are images of a certain kind. The prophetic metaphors for the relation between God and Israel are metaphors borrowed from the patriarchal family—images of dominance softened by affection. God as husband and father of Israel demands obedience and monogamous love. He repays faithfulness with mercy and loving-kindness, but punishes waywardness, just as the wayward daughter can be stoned at her father's door (Deut. 22:21).

When these family images are combined with political images of king and warrior, they reinforce a particular model of power and dominance. God is the power over us, the One out there over against us, the sovereign warrior with righteousness on his side. Family and political models of dominance and submission are recapitulated and rendered plausible by the dominance and submission of God and Israel. The silence and submission of women becomes part of a greater pattern that makes it appear fitting and right.

What emerges then is a "fit," a tragic coherence between the role of women in Jewish life, and law, teaching, and symbols. Women's experiences have not been recorded or shaped the contours of Jewish teaching because women do not define the normative community; but of course, women remain Other when we are always seen through the filter of male interpretation without ever speaking for ourselves. The maleness of God calls for the silence of women as shapers of the holy, but our silence in turn enforces our Otherness and a communal sense of the "rightness" of the male image of God. Moreover, if God is male, and we are in God's image, how can maleness *not* be the norm of Jewish humanity? If maleness is normative, how can women not be Other? And if women are Other, how can we not speak of God in a language of Otherness and dominance, a language drawn from male experience?

Confronting these interconnections is not easy. But it is only as we hear women's silence as part of the texture of Jewish existence that we can place our specific disabilities in the context in which they belong. Women's exclusion from public religious life, women's powerlessness in marriage and divorce are not accidental; nor are they individual problems. They are pieces of a system in which men have defined the interests and the rules, including the rules concerning women. Manipulating the system to change certain rules—even excision of many of them—will not of itself restore women's voices or women's power of naming. On the contrary, without awareness of the broader context of women's silence, attempts to redress concrete grievances may perpetuate the system of which they are part. Thus, as feminists demand that women be allowed to lead public prayer, the issue of language is often set aside. Traditional modes of liturgical expression are assumed to be adequate; the only issue is who has access to them. But women's leadership in synagogue ritual then leaves untouched the deeper contradictions between formal equality and the fundamental symbols of the service, contradictions that can be addressed only through the transformation of religious language. Similarly, attempts to solve particular legal (*halakhic*) problems often assume the continued centrality and religious meaningfulness of *halakhah* (law). But halakhah is part of the system that women did not have a hand in creating. How can we presume that if women add our voices to tradition, law will be our medium of expression and repair? To settle on halakhah as the source of justice for women is to foreclose the question of women's experience when it has scarcely begun to be raised.

Clearly, the implications of Jewish feminism reach beyond the goal of equality to transform the bases of Jewish life. Feminism demands a new understanding of Torah, Israel, and God. It demands an understanding of Torah that begins by acknowledging the injustice of Torah and then goes on to create a Torah that is whole. The silence of women reverberates through the tradition, distorting the shape of narrative and skewing the content of the law. Only the deliberate recovery of women's hidden voices, the unearthing and invention of women's Torah, can give us Jewish teachings that are the product of the whole Jewish people and that reflect more fully its experiences of God.

Feminism demands an understanding of Israel that includes the whole of Israel and thus allows women to speak and name our experience for ourselves. It demands we replace a normative male voice with a chorus of divergent voices, describing Jewish reality in different accents and tones. Feminism impels us to rethink issues of community and diversity, to explore the ways in which one people can acknowledge and celebrate the varied experiences of its members. What would it mean for women *as women* to be equal participants in the Jewish community? How can we talk about difference without creating Others?

Feminism demands new ways of talking about God that reflect and grow out of the redefinition of Jewish humanity. The exclusively male naming of God supported and was rendered meaningful by a cultural and religious situation that is passing away. The emergence of women allows and necessitates that the long-suppressed femaleness of God be recovered and explored and reintegrated into the Godhead. But feminism presses us beyond the issue of gender to examine the nature of the God with male names. How can we move beyond images of domination to a God present *in* community rather than over it? How can we forge a God-language that expresses women's experience?

Methodological Underpinnings

Although I intend to devote the rest of this book to exploring the implications of feminism for the transformation of Jewish life, I must touch first on another foundational aspect of my feminist reconstruction of Judaism. My basic critique of Judaism as a male-defined religion rests on a number of assumptions concerning texts, sources, experience, and authority, assumptions that inform my efforts at construction as much as they do my critique. My perspective as a Jewish feminist is shaped not simply by the personal experiences I delineated in the introduction, but also by a series of theological and methodological presuppositions that are influenced by my experiences but cannot be reduced to them. These presuppositions are as essential to my argument as my understanding of Judaism as a patriarchal tradition.

Women's Experience

"Women's experience" is an important and problematic phrase I mention repeatedly in the preceding pages. At several points in discussing women's silence, I turn to this term to name an element missing in Jewish sources and Jewish communal life. The phrase is sufficiently obvious to be overlooked, and at the same time fraught with significant difficulty. It conceals a number of problems and comprehends a major methodological decision.

On one level, the term "women's experience" is quite straightforward. I mean it to refer to the daily, lived substance of women's lives, the conscious events, thoughts, and feelings that constitute women's reality. To say that women's experience is not part of the Jewish tradition is to say that we do not know the world as women have perceived it. We do not have women's account of Jewish history in its large and small moments, filtered through women's perceptions and set in a framework of their making.

On this definition, "women's experience" is not an essence or abstraction. It does not refer to some innate capacity of women, some eternally female mode of being that is different from male being. If women's experience is distinct from men's—and I believe it is—the reasons are primarily historical and social. The different socialization of men and women, present in different ways in every culture, nurtures divergent capacities and divergent experiences of the world. But also, insofar as women are projected as Other, women's experience is doubled in a peculiar way. Knowing she is just herself, a woman must nonetheless deal with the imposition of Otherness. She must forever measure herself against a standard that comes from outside. If she would act against prevailing stereotypes, she must do so being aware of their existence, and this adds an extra burden to whatever she undertakes.[10] Like the Jew, who is always a Jew in the eyes of the world, a woman is assessed in terms of her particularity. The social and historical situation of the Other is not the same as the situation of one who takes identity for granted.

If "women's experience" is primarily a product of culture rather than of some innate female nature, however, then it is also not unitary or clearly definable. The problem with the phrase "women's experience" is that it implies uniformity where—even if we restrict ourselves to Jewish women—there is great diversity. One can delineate certain common elements to women's situation: shared biological experiences, common imposition of Otherness, exclusion from the encoding of cultural meanings. But women have appropriated, interpreted, and responded to these elements very differently, both as individuals and as members of different (Jewish) cultures. It is too easy for one dominant group—in this case, the North American Ashkenazi Jew—to define women's experience for all women, forgetting that even Jewish women's experience is a great tapestry of many designs and colors. Since no woman's work can ever include the whole tapestry, each must remember she speaks from one corner, the phrase "women's experience" qualified by a string of modifiers that specify voice.

Yet despite the real danger of defining it monolithically, the phrase "women's experience" can hardly be avoided. It is indispensable both for signifying a terrain of silence—no group of Jewish women has had the privilege of defining Jewish reality—and for signaling an important methodological choice. In a system in which women have been projected as Other, there is no way within the rules of the system to restore women to full personhood. The conviction that women are fully human is a critical and disruptive principle that comes from outside. Commitment to "women's experience" marks precisely an a priori commitment to women's humanity. It is the fundamental feminist methodological move. Without the presupposition of women's full humanity, there is no bridge from the male Jewish tradition to a feminist Judaism. All one can do is manipulate the rules of the system to alleviate women's disabilities, without altering the assumptions from which those disabilities arise. To commit oneself to recovering women's experiences within Judaism, on the other hand, is to say that women as well as men define Jewish humanity and that there *is no Judaism*—there is only male Judaism—without the insights of both. This is the starting point for a feminist Judaism, and it represents a basic realignment of the feminist's relationship to tradition.

Suspicion and Remembrance

If insistence on the full humanity of women represents a deliberate and important break with Jewish tradition, it clearly has important implications for the feminist's relationship to Jewish sources. Insofar as Jewish sources assume women's Otherness, are they simply evidence for women's oppression? Do they have anything of value to teach Jewish women? How does one sort out the oppressive from the nonoppressive elements in Jewish sources? How does one decide that a certain fundamental presupposition—like the presupposition of woman's Otherness—must be disavowed? These questions are part of the critical issue of authority that commitment to women's experience raises. Since this is an issue with many ramifications, it needs to be approached deliberately and from several sides.

Attitude toward sources is one dimension of the issue of authority. In discussing the deep-rooted sexism of the Jewish tradition, I use the *Tanakh* (Hebrew Scriptures) to demonstrate women's silence in Jewish writings. In doing so, I presuppose a dual and paradoxical relationship to the biblical text. I take for granted my critical freedom in relation to the Bible; but I also take for granted my connection to it, the value of examining its viewpoint and concerns. I pronounce the Bible patriarchal; but in taking the time to explore it, I claim it as a text that matters to me. This double relation is not unthinking. It stems from my belief that the Jewish feminist must embrace with equal passion (at least) two different attitudes to Jewish sources. These are described by Elisabeth Schüssler Fiorenza, who in developing feminist principles of interpretation for the study of the New Testament, distinguishes between a "hermeneutics of suspicion" and a "hermeneutics of remembrance," both of which must inform a feminist appropriation of religious texts.[11]

A hermeneutics of suspicion "takes as its starting point the assumption that biblical texts and their interpretations are androcentric and serve patriarchal functions."[12] Since both the Tanakh and rabbinic literature come from male-dominated societies and are attributed to male authors, they need to be examined for androcentric assumptions and content, and for their attention, or lack of it, to women's experiences and concerns. While mainstream sources may have much to say to women, they cannot be accepted uncritically.[13] All too often, they serve to consolidate or reinforce patriarchal values or to inculcate models of power that are destructive or oppressive.

Moreover, it is not just a few obviously patriarchal texts that must be subjected to critical examination and judgment. Feminists cannot assume that any traditional source is entirely free from sexism. Some years ago, referring to Phyllis Trible's project of "depatriarchalizing" the Bible, Mary Daly quipped that a depatriarchalized Bible would make a nice pamphlet.[14] While the comment is clever, it could have gone further: a depatriarchalized text would not exist. Biblical insights are formulated in a patriarchal culture and expressed in patriarchal terms. The husk and the kernel interpenetrate; each can be named, but they cannot be divided. Thus the fact that the prophets expressed their concern for justice in the language of patriarchal marriage does not make that concern trivial or unreal. But it does mean that, in different contexts, the very same texts can be liberating or oppressive. To ignore this fact—to talk about justice without reference to the patriarchal metaphors in which justice is described—is to leave the oppressive aspects of texts to do their work in the world.

At the same time Jewish sources must be viewed with mistrust, they are, however, the sources we have. If suspicion is one side of the feminist's relationship to tradition, the other side is remembrance. Jewish sources have formed us for good and for ill, and they remain our strongest links with the Jewish historical experience. Since, in Schüssler Fiorenza's words, "the enslavement of a people becomes total when their history is destroyed and solidarity with the dead is made impossible," feminists must appropriate Jewish sources not simply as witnesses to women's oppression but as testimonies "of liberation and religious agency." A "hermeneutics of remembrance" insists that the same sources that are regarded with suspicion can also be used to reconstruct Jewish women's history. Just as no source, however neutral or liberating it may seem, is exempt from feminist scrutiny, so even the most androcentric text can provide valuable information about Jewish women's past.[15] Biblical legislation concerning menstruation, for example, can serve as the basis for reconstructing women's understanding of menstruation taboos. Prophetic injunctions against idolatry can furnish clues concerning women's participation in polytheistic traditions.[16] Read with new questions and critical freedom, traditional sources can yield "subversive memories" of past struggles for liberation within and against patriarchy, memories that link contemporary women to a transformative history.[17]

Critical Method and Religious Unity

The distinction "suspicion/remembrance" suggests a dual attitude toward Jewish texts that is central to a feminist critical appropriation of Jewish sources. Other aspects of the problem of authority and textual interpretation plague modern readers more generally and thus enter into feminist interpretation without emerging specifically from feminist concerns. Modern scientific criticism, for example, has left many people with a divided relationship to religious texts different from the division "suspicion/remembrance." The same religious sources that claim to give overarching significance to life, and that may indeed provide frameworks of meaning, are simultaneously seen as human creations, culture-bound expressions of past religious values. The distinction "critical method/religious unity" points to a second tension in attitudes toward religious texts, a tension not unique to feminism but with which feminists must grapple.

On the one side, modern scientific thought and historical scholarship have eroded the sacred authority of traditional sources. Religious texts, they tell us, are not a transcript of divine revelation but the work of human beings living in partic- ular social and historical contexts and responding to historical and cultural needs. The same critical tools, literary and histor- ical, that one would bring to reading any text are appropriate to religious sources. We cannot understand either "biblical at- titudes" toward women or women's roles in "the biblical peri- od," for example, without taking into account that biblical texts span a thousand years of history and come from very different cultures. We should not expect that the roles of women in the period of early Israelite settlement would be the same as wom- en's roles under the monarchy or in the postexilic period. Sim- ilarly, a rabbinic midrash on a biblical text reflects the questions and concerns of the rabbinic period. It does not give us the meaning of the Tanakh for biblical times. Thus, in my earlier discussion of the narratives of Genesis as an instance of wom- en's silence, I did not consider the ways later midrash takes up and elaborates the themes of the stories, sometimes shifting their emphasis or meaning. That is not relevant to the changing *biblical* silence concerning women, which can be examined in its own right.

But while religious texts can be broken down literarily and historically, as received tradition, they come to us whole. One may divide and analyze for purposes of criticism or historical reconstruction. The religious meaning of a work, however, may lie in its historical impossibilities, the tensions of the final ed- iting, or the rhythm of the narrative heard as a totality.[18] Schol- ars may debate, for instance, whether there was an Exodus from Egypt, what proportion of the future Israelite community dwelt in Egypt, and how the Exodus narrative became part of Jewish experience. Whatever they decide, however, the Exodus story, *as a story*, is constitutive for Jewish self-understanding. As such, it has a claim on contemporary Jews, who must wres- tle with its meaning. An analogous point can be made for rab- binic midrash. Midrash may not tell us what the Bible meant in its own time, but it often tells us how particular narratives are comprehended by the Jewish community, and therefore how certain texts have shaped communal values. It may therefore be appropriate sometimes to consider the midrashic meaning of a text as if it were its true meaning, for it may be through the midrash that a text is read and known.

Suspicion/remembrance and critical method/religious unity are aspects of textual appropriation that, on first consideration, may appear to correspond. Critical methods are appropriate to suspicion, for they allow us to see sources in their patriarchal contexts; while to remember our history, we seem to need texts whole. In fact, however, the categories are interwoven. Critical methods are necessary both in analyzing androcentric texts and in historical reconstruction. They can help us recover both the patriarchal setting of our sources and the religious possibilities the sources conceal. Similarly, a text may be considered as a unity or in the light of later interpretation both in order to scrutinize its sexism and in order to get at its religious meaning. Traditional stories may be mediated to us through androcentric midrash, but midrash can also unveil in a text religious import that would otherwise go unseen.

A complex view of texts, then, can be part of any reading. Indeed, a multilayered consciousness can be difficult to avoid. The modern reader may find it hard to look for religious meaning without a critical view of sources intruding in the background.[19] This divided awareness is both burdensome and liberating. A critical reading can yield results that are disturbing to religious faith, but it can also free texts for deeper appropriation. To approach texts critically is not to dismiss them. On the contrary, it can be part of what it means to take sources seriously as a modern person. When we understand the meaning of a religious text in and for its time, we are freer to take the text and apply it to our own time. Seeing how particular sources answered the religious needs of some people in the period in which they were written allows us to look at contemporary needs and to interpret for today. Thus awareness of how midrash dealt with rabbinic questions might lead us to write midrash that deals with women's questions. Awareness of women's silence in the narratives of Genesis might lead us to restore women's voices, connecting to the text in fresh ways.

Authority

To use Jewish texts as a basis for historical reconstruction and to take them seriously as literary units is nonetheless different from investing them with final authority. Particularly since neither the intent nor direction of feminist reconstruction is derived from Jewish sources, the issue of the authority of these sources for feminist thought needs to be pressed further. How do a "hermeneutics of suspicion" and the use of critical methods accord with the authority of traditional texts? In the process of interpretation, where does authority finally reside? While this question intersects with a number of issues to be considered in other chapters, it is too central to any project of religious transformation to be treated only piecemeal. It will be necessary to anticipate some later discussion, therefore, to take it up in this context.

Modernity has brought increasing awareness of both the global diversity of religious beliefs and practices and the cultural location and historical development of individual religious traditions. This awareness has undermined the authority of traditional religions and weakened their claims to universality or to eternal truth. Feminists have participated in confronting the breakdown of old authority structures, and have responded to the problem of authority in several different ways. While some religious feminists have used the weakening authority of the western traditions to criticize and move outside them entirely, others have sought within their traditions authority structures consonant with their beliefs. A number of Christian feminists, for example, have sought to find a "real (that is, nonsexist) Paul" or a feminist Jesus who can function as models for Christians today.[20] This nonsexist strand of the tradition is identified with "true" Christianity, while sexist Christianity is false and must change. Other feminist thinkers have acknowledged the basic androcentrism of biblical thinking, but have found within Scripture minority themes that submit the Bible to self-criticism. Some have focused on the prophetic tradition—not necessarily as a set of texts, but as an ongoing process of criticizing the status quo. Others have pointed to the equality of the original creation or to the presence of female God-language throughout the Bible.[21] While such themes are not statistically the norm, they may function as *normative* in that they provide a scriptural basis for feminist faith.

The problem with attempting to ground feminist (or any contemporary) conviction in Scripture, however, is that it denies or disguises the authority of the reader. When one element of a text is declared true or normative, where does authority actually lie? Do biblical texts themselves provide a sure basis for judging between their conflicting perspectives? The contrary uses to which the Bible has been put suggest that the needs and values of a community of readers are as much a source of norms as the texts themselves. Different communities have different stakes in maintaining and defending the authority of the Bible, but the selection of particular texts or passages as central or normative can seldom be justified on purely textual grounds.

If it is not the Bible itself that tells us which parts are authoritative, authority must rest in some outside source. In our individualistic American culture, this source is often identified as the individual, who picks and chooses among texts according to "personal preference." If we do not have the divine word, ostensibly we are left with only our own words, words that are changeable and subject to sway.[22] From a feminist perspective, however, human choices are not reducible to God/text or whim. Human beings are fundamentally communal; our individuality is a product of community, and our choices are shaped by our being with others.[23] Scripture itself is a product of community. It may be revelatory or communicate lasting values, but revelation is communally received and molded. Revelation is the experience of a reality that transcends language, that cannot be captured or possessed in words. The communal experiences of

God's presence and power that lie at the origins of Jewish existence were crystalized by certain sensitive individuals, and recreated in language to be stored in memory. Language bears witness to revelation. It allows the possibility that, centuries after the original event, one may find reverberating in a text the extraordinary experience in which it was formed.[24]

But language bears witness to the enduring in words that are limited. Not only must it suggest rather than chronicle the revelatory experience, it does so within the cultural framework that language itself inscribes. Revelation may surprise us and destroy our preconceptions, but it must compete with language already in place. The Bible emerged in a context in which patriarchal modes of social organization were being consolidated and justified. The record of revelation is for the most part assimilated to this task and never decisively breaks with it.[25] As we have seen, women's revelatory experiences are largely omitted from the sources; narratives are framed from an androcentric perspective; the law enforces women's subordination in the patriarchal family. Insofar as biblical texts silence women and serve to oppress them, they must be criticized as "revealing" patriarchy.

The authority that grounds this criticism, however, is not individual experience or some private intuition. It is rather the experience of particular communities struggling for religious transformation.[26] For example, the community that is my central authority is the Jewish feminist community, for it is in this community my identity finds fullest expression. But beyond it lie the *havurah* and broader feminist communities, the wider Jewish community, and the communities of all those working for religious and political change. Just as Jews of the past experienced God and interpreted their experiences in communal contexts that shaped what they saw and heard, so we also read their words and experience God in communities—communities in continuity with, but different from, theirs. It is the contemporary feminist community that has taught me to value and attend to women's experience. It is this community that has taught me that Jewish sources have been partial and oppressive, occasionally ugly and simply wrong.

It is true that through and behind the androcentrism of Jewish teaching may lie profound and important insights and frameworks of meaning. Jewish sources have a claim on me to be read and heard and taken seriously. But the claim is not final. I am responsible first to the Jewish feminist community and its struggle to create a Judaism that includes all Jews. To say that this community is my central source of authority is not to deny the range of ideas or disagreements within it, or the other communities of which I am part. It is simply to say that I have been formed in important ways by Jewish feminism; without it I could not see the things that I see. It is to say that my most important experiences of God have come through this community, and that it has given me the language with which to express them. To name this community my authority is to call it the primary community to which I am accountable. It is to claim that its vision enhances life beyond itself—that it can enhance Jewish life and life on this planet.

To locate authority in particular communities of interpreters is admittedly to make a circular appeal. Yet it is also to acknowledge what has always been the case: that in deciding what is authoritative in sacred texts, deciding communities take authority to themselves. When the rabbis said that rabbinic modes of interpretation were given at Sinai, they were claiming authority for their own community—just as other groups had before them, just as feminists do today.

A Word about Theology

In the last several pages, I have addressed certain of my theological presuppositions, but not my reasons for writing a theology. Yet it may seem that if my goal is a feminist Judaism, feminist theology is a peculiar place to begin. Theology, after all, has had only a limited role in Jewish religious life.[27] Reflection on God, the mission of Israel, the nature of human life has more often been confined to the interstices of rabbinic discussions or dealt with midrashically than considered independently in works on such subjects. While there is a history of Jewish philosophy from Philo to the present, philosophy is generally left to a marginal few with the interest in and inclination to such things. The main energy of Jewish intellectual life has gone into the elaboration of the law, and it is observance of the law, rather than adherence to theological principles, that marks one a religious Jew. Law takes precedence over beliefs and feelings, which are expected to flow from action rather than to ground it.

But if the law maintains its primacy in Jewish self-understanding, theology affects Jewish practice in important, unseen ways. Indeed, there is a mutually reinforcing relationship between Jewish theology and Jewish religious practice and institutions. Patriarchal theology, while it cannot of itself give rise to patriarchal structures, supports patriarchy as a religious and legal system. When Torah is thought of as divinely revealed in its present form, the subordination of women is granted the seal of divine approval. When God is conceived of as male, as a king ruling over his universe, male rule in society seems appropriate and right. The correlate of this relationship between patriarchal theology and religious structures is that feminist theology may help to undermine patriarchal institutions, and at least will no longer support them. When Torah embraces the experience of women and men as full members of the Jewish people, it will no longer be possible to base women's subordination on appeals to the divine will. When we think of God as male/female friend and lover, or as the ground and source of being, new images of human relating will be fostered in our imaginations, and we will not be able consciously or unconsciously to appeal to metaphors for God to justify male social domination.

So long as theology is dismissed as unimportant, the sexism built into certain basic Jewish ideas is aided and abetted by the neglect of theology. It is difficult to confront the structural implications of God's maleness, for example, if the community is not really interested in thinking about God anyway. The issue of the gender of God can always be jettisoned on the grounds that theology is trivial, at the same time old images continue to work their effects. Only when the basic categories of Jewish thought are reconstructed in the light of women's silence will unexamined theological assumptions cease to operate at women's expense.

The fact that theology surreptitiously affects many aspects of Jewish practice may make theology relevant even to secular Jewish feminists. Jewish literature and communal life, radicalism and ethnic identity are governed by a host of presuppositions concerning which Jews are normative, what constitutes Jewish values, the proper ways to order community, and the proper tasks of life. Many of these presuppositions have infiltrated from the theological sphere but remain doubly hidden when religion as well as theology is rejected. Theological analysis, because it lays bare some of the assumptions that operate unnamed in secular Jewish movements, can provide secular feminists with more power to transform these assumptions.

But there is another reason why theology is important. When a religious system has become established and its structures self-perpetuating, it often loses contact with the experiences at its root. Rabbis need not stand at Sinai with the first generation to make legal decisions. They must read the works of their predecessors and follow the appropriate rules. Moreover, insofar as Jewish identity is based on orthopraxis, there is no necessary relation between practice and religious experience; practice is self-justifying, it makes one a Jew. But for those who would transform the tradition, the situation is different: Reform always begins in conviction and vision. Jewish feminism, like all reform movements, is rooted in deeply felt experience and a powerful image of religious change. Wherever the individual feminist locates her active interests—in liturgy, theology, midrash, law—she acts out of commitment to an animating vision that has important repercussions for community life and practice. My central reason for writing a Jewish feminist theology, then, is to articulate one version of this vision and to foster its growth. If feminist theologies help to reanimate the connection between practice and belief in the Jewish world more generally, they will have made another important contribution to Jewish religious life.

2. Torah: Reshaping Jewish Memory

Entry into the covenant at Sinai is the root experience of Judaism, the central event that established the Jewish people.[1] Given the importance of this event, there can be no verse in the Torah more disturbing to the feminist than Moses' warning to his people in Exodus 19:15, "Be ready for the third day; do not go near a woman." For here, at the very moment that the Jewish people stands at Sinai ready to receive the covenant—not now the covenant with individual patriarchs but with the people as a whole—at the very moment when Israel stands trembling waiting for God's presence to descend upon the mountain, Moses addresses the community only as men. The specific issue at stake is ritual impurity: An emission of semen renders both a man and his female partner temporarily unfit to approach the sacred (Lev. 15:16–18). But Moses does not say, "Men and women do not go near each other." At the central moment of Jewish history, women are invisible. Whether they too stood there trembling in fear and expectation, what they heard when the men heard these words of Moses, we do not know. It was not their experience that interested the chronicler or that informed and shaped the Torah.[2]

Moses' admonition can be seen as a paradigm of what I have called "the profound injustice of Torah itself."[3] In this passage, the Otherness of women finds its way into the very center of Jewish experience. And although the verse hardly can be blamed for women's situation, it sets forth a pattern recapitulated again and again in Jewish sources. Women's invisibility at the moment of entry into the covenant is reflected in the content of the covenant which, in both grammar and substance, ad-

dresses the community as male heads of household. It is perpetuated by the later tradition, which in its comments and
codifications takes women as objects of concern or legislation
but rarely sees them as shapers of tradition and actors in their
own lives.

It is not just a historical injustice that is at stake in this verse,
however. There is another dimension to the problem of the Sinai passage without which it is impossible to understand the task
of Jewish feminism today. Were this passage simply the record
of a historical event long in the past, the exclusion of women at
this critical juncture would be troubling, but also comprehensible for its time. The Torah is not just history, however, but
also living memory. The Torah reading, as a central part of the
Sabbath and holiday liturgy, calls to mind and recreates the past
for succeeding generations. When the story of Sinai is recited
as part of the annual cycle of Torah readings and again as a
special reading for Shavuot, women each time hear ourselves
thrust aside anew, eavesdropping on a conversation among
men and between men and God.[4] As Rachel Adler puts it, "Because the text has excluded her, she is excluded again in this
yearly re-enactment and will be excluded over and over, year
by year, every time she rises to hear the covenant read."[5] If the
covenant is a covenant with all generations (Deut. 29:13ff), then
its reappropriation also involves the continual reappropriation
of women's marginality.

This passage in Exodus is one of the places in the Tanakh
where women's silence is so deeply charged, so overwhelming,
that it can provoke a crisis for the Jewish feminist. As Rachel
Adler says, "We are being invited by Jewish men to re-covenant,
to forge a covenant which will address the inequalities of wom-
en's position in Judaism, but we ask ourselves, 'Have we ever
had a covenant in the first place? Are women Jews?'"[6] This is a
question asked at the edge of a deep abyss. How can we ever
hope to fill the silence that shrouds Jewish women's past? If
women are invisible from the first moment of Jewish history,
can we hope to become visible now? How many of us will fight

for years to change the institutions in which we find ourselves only to achieve token victories?[7] Perhaps we should put our energy elsewhere, into the creation of new communities where we can be fully present and where our struggles will not come up against walls as old as our beginnings.

Yet urgent and troubling as these questions are, there is a tension between them and the reality of the Jewish woman who poses them. The questions emerge out of a contradiction between the holes in the text and the felt experience of many Jewish women. For if Moses' words come as a shock and affront, it is because women have always known or assumed our presence at Sinai; the passage is painful because it seems to deny what we have always taken for granted. Of course we were at Sinai; how is it then that the text could imply we were not there?

It is not only we who ask these questions. The rabbis too seem to have been disturbed at the implication of women's absence from Sinai and found a way to read women's presence into the text. As Rashi understood Exodus 19:3—"Thus shall you say to the house of Jacob and declare to the children of Israel"—"the house of Jacob" refers to the women and "the children of Israel" refers to the men. The Talmud interprets Exodus 19:15 ("Do not go near a woman") to mean that *women* can purify themselves on the third day after there is no longer any chance of their having a discharge of live sperm.[8]

Apparently, women's absence was unthinkable to the rabbis, and this despite the fact that in their own work they continually reenact that absence. How much more then should it be unthinkable to us who know we are present today even in the midst of communities that continue to deny us? The contradiction between the Torah text and our experience is crucial; for, construed a certain way, it is a potential bridge to a new relationship with the tradition. To accept our absence from Sinai would be to allow the male text to define us and our connection to Judaism. To stand on the ground of our experience, on the other hand, to start with the certainty of our membership in our own people is to be forced to re-member and recreate its history, to reshape Torah. It is to move from anger at the tradition, through anger to empowerment. It is to begin the journey toward the creation of a feminist Judaism.

Give Us Our History

Jewish feminists, in other words, must reclaim Torah as our own. We must render visible the presence, experience, and deeds of women erased in traditional sources. We must tell the stories of women's encounters with God and capture the texture of their religious experience. We must expand the notion of Torah to encompass not just the five books of Moses and traditional Jewish learning, but women's words, teachings, and actions hitherto unseen. To expand Torah, we must reconstruct Jewish history to include the history of women, and in doing so alter the shape of Jewish memory.

The idea that Jewish feminists need to reenvision the Jewish past requires some explication, for it is by no means generally accepted. There are many Jewish feminists who feel that women can take on positions of authority, create new liturgy, and do what we need to do to create communities responsive to our needs in the present without dredging around in sources that can only cause us pain or lifting up little sparks of light as if they were sufficient to guide us. As the simple daughter asks in Esther Broner's Passover Seder, "If Miriam lies buried in sand,/ why must we dig up those bones?"[9] On this view, we need to acknowledge and accept the patriarchal character of the Jewish past and Jewish sources and then get on with issues of contemporary change. Studying our past can only cause us bitterness. "Mother, asks the wicked daughter,/ if I learn my history,/ will I not be angry?"[10]

But while the notion of accepting women's past invisibility and subordination and attending to the present has some attractiveness, it strikes me as untenable. If it is possible within any historical, textual tradition to create a present in dramatic discontinuity with the past—and I doubt that it is—it certainly seems impossible within Judaism. For the central events of the Jewish past are not simply history but living, active memory that continues to shape Jewish identity and self-understanding. In Judaism, memory is not simply a given but a religious obligation incumbent on both Israel and God.[11] "Remember this day, on which you went free from Egypt, the house of bondage, how the LORD freed you from it with a mighty hand" (Ex. 13:3). "I will remember my covenant which is between me and you and every living creature among all flesh" (Gen. 9:15). "We Jews are a community based on memory," says Martin Buber. "The spiritual life of the Jews is part and parcel of their memory." Many versions of the past feed and sustain Jewish existence, but memories expanded and slightly reshaped with each generation have for centuries been handed down from parent to child, and with them a certain set of attitudes toward the past and toward the world.[12] It is in telling the story of our past as Jews that we learn who we truly are in the present.

Perhaps the best example of the significance of memory in Jewish life is the Passover Seder. On this most widely celebrated of Jewish holidays, families gather together not to memorialize the Exodus from Egypt but to relive it. As the climactic words of the Seder say (slightly transformed!), "In every generation, each Jew should regard her or himself as though she or he personally went forth from Egypt. . . . It was not only our ancestors which the Holy One redeemed from slavery, but us also did God redeem together with them." But even this reliving would be pointless, or simply a matter of momentary experience, were it not meant to shape our wider sense of identity and obligation. Indeed, the experience and memory of slavery and redemption are the very foundations of Jewish religious obligation. "You shall not wrong or oppress a stranger, for you were strangers in the land of Egypt" (Ex. 22:20, altered). "I the LORD am your God who brought you out of the land of Egypt, the house of bondage" (Ex. 20:2). All the commandments follow. In the modern era, the memory of slavery in Egypt has also taken on more specifically political meaning. It has fostered among some Jews an identification with the oppressed that has led to involvement in a host of movements for social change—and has fueled the feminist demand for justice for women within Judaism.[13]

The past as depicted in Jewish sources can be used not simply as a warrant for change, however, but also as a bulwark against it. If we need any further proof of the power of memory in Jewish life, we need only consider the ways in which the past is used against the possibility of innovation. Arguments against the ordination of women as rabbis, for example, are rooted not so much in any real legal impediment to women's ordination as in the fact that historically rabbis have been men. The notion of a woman as rabbi feels "un-Jewish" to many Jews because it is perceived as discontinuous with a Jewish past that makes certain claims upon its present bearers. On question after question, the weight of tradition is thrown at women as an argument for keeping things the way they are.

It is because of the past's continuing power in the present that, when the rabbis profoundly transformed Jewish religious life after the destruction of the second Temple, they also reconstructed Jewish memory to see themselves in continuity with it. So deeply is the Jewish present rooted in Jewish history that changes wrought in Jewish reality continually have been read back into the past so that they could be read out of the past as a foundation for the present. Again and again in rabbinic interpretations, we find contemporary practice projected back into earlier periods so that the chain of tradition can remain unbroken. In Genesis, for example, Abraham greets his three angelic visitors by killing a calf and serving it to them with milk (Gen. 18:7–8), clearly a violation of the laws of kashrut which forbid eating milk and meat together. As later rabbinic sources read the passage, however, Abraham first served his visitors milk and only then meat, a practice permitted by rabbinic law.[14] Not only did Abraham and the other patriarchs observe the law given at Sinai, according to the rabbis, they actually founded rabbinic academies. *Genesis Rabbah* interprets Genesis 46:28, "And he sent Judah before him unto Joseph, *to teach* the way," to mean that he prepared an academy for the teaching of Torah.[15] The point is not that such rereadings were a conscious plot to strengthen rabbinic authority—though certainly they would have served that function—but that it was probably unimaginable to the sages that the values they lived by could not be taught through the Torah. The links between past and present were felt so passionately that any important change in the present had to entail a new understanding of history.

All this has an important moral for Jewish feminists. We too cannot redefine Judaism in the present without redefining our past, because our present grows out of our history. The Jewish need to reconstruct the past in the light of the present converges with the feminist need to recover women's history within Judaism. Knowing that women are active members of the Jewish community in the present, even though large sectors of the community continue to define themselves in male terms and to render women invisible,[16] we know that we were always part of the community—not simply as objects of male purposes but as subjects and shapers of tradition. To accept androcentric texts and contemporary androcentric histories as the whole of Jewish history is to enter into a secret collusion with those who would exclude us from full membership in the Jewish community. It is to accept the idea that men were the only significant agents in Jewish history when we would never accept this (still current) account of contemporary Jewish life. The Jewish community today is a community of women and men, and it has never been otherwise. It is time, therefore, to recover our history as the history of women and men, a task that will both restore our own history to women and provide a fuller Jewish history for the Jewish community as a whole.[17] Again to quote from Broner's Seder, "Mother, asks the clever daughter,/ who are our mothers?/ Who are our ancestors?/ What is our history?/ Give us our name. Name our genealogy."[18]

History, Historiography, and Torah

It is one thing to see the importance of recovering women's history, however, and another to accomplish this task in a meaningful way. First of all, qua historian, the Jewish feminist faces all the same problems as any feminist historian trying to recover women's experience: Both her sources and the historians who have gone before her record male activities and male deeds in accounts ordered by male values. What we know of women's past are those things men considered it significant to remember, seen and interpreted through a value system that places men at the center.[19] The Bible, for example, focuses on war, government, and the cult, all male spheres.[20] It describes women and their activities primarily as they aid or hinder the plans of men or, in rare cases, as they perform roles usually reserved for men.[21] The Talmud records the discussions of male rabbis in male academies, discussions that touch on women mainly as they pose some problem for male control.

But second, beyond these large issues, the Jewish feminist faces additional problems raised by working with religious sources. The primary Jewish sources available to her for historical reconstruction are not simply collections of historical materials but also Torah. As Torah, as sacred teaching, they are understood by the tradition to represent divine revelation, patterns of living adequate for all time. In trying to restore the history of Jewish women, the Jewish feminist historian is not only trying to revolutionize the writing of history but is also implicitly or explicitly acting as theologian, claiming to amplify Torah, and thus questioning the finality of the Torah we have. Indeed, to rewrite Jewish history to include women is to alter the boundaries of Torah and thus to transform it. It is important, therefore, in seeking to recover women's history in the context of a feminist Judaism to confront the view of Torah that this implies.

I understand Torah, both in the narrow sense of the five books of Moses and in the broader sense of Jewish teaching, to be the partial record of the "Godwrestling" of part of the Jewish people.[22] Again and again in the course of its existence, the Jewish people has felt itself called by and accountable to a power not of its own making, a power that seemed to direct its destiny and give meaning to its life. In both ordinary and extraordinary moments, it has found itself guided by a reality that both propelled and sustained it and to which gratitude and obedience seemed the only fitting response.

The term "Godwrestling" seems appropriate to me to describe the written residue of these experiences, for I do not imagine them à la Cecil B. deMille as the boomings of a clear (male) voice or the flashing of tongues of flame, publicly visible, publicly verifiable, needing only to be transcribed. I imagine them as moments of profound experience; sometimes of illumination but also of mystery, moments when some who had eyes to see understood the meaning of events that all had undergone. Such moments might be hard-won, or sudden experiences of clarity or presence that come unexpected as precious gifts. But they would need to be interpreted and applied, wrestled with and puzzled over, passed down and lived out before they came to us as the Torah of God.[23]

I call this record partial, for moments of intense religious experience cannot be pinned down and reproduced; they can only be suggested and pointed to so that readers or listeners may from time to time catch for themselves the deeper reality vibrating behind the text. Moreover, while moments of revelation may lead to abandonment of important presuppositions and openness to ideas and experiences that are genuinely new, they also occur within cultural frameworks that can never be escaped entirely, so that the more radical implications of a new understanding may not even be seen. I call Torah the record of part of the Jewish people because the experience and interpretation found there are for the most part those of men. The experience of being summoned and saved by a single power, the experience of human likeness to the creator God, the experiences of liberation and God's passion for justice were sustained within a patriarchal framework that the interpretation of divine revelation served to consolidate rather than to shatter.[24]

There is a strand in the tradition that acknowledges this partialness of Torah and that thus indirectly allows us to see what is at stake in the recovery of women's past. According to many ancient Jewish sources, the Torah preexisted the creation of the world. It was the first of God's works, identified with the divine wisdom in Proverbs 8. It was written with black fire on white fire and rested on the knee of God. It was the architectural plan God consulted in creating the universe.[25] For the Kabbalists, this preexistent or primordial Torah is God's wisdom and essence; it expresses the immensity of God's being and power. Our Torah of ink and parchment is only the "outer garments," a limited interpretation of what lies hidden, a document that the initiate must penetrate more and more deeply to gain momentary glimpses of what lies behind. A later development of the idea of a secret Torah asserted that each of the 600,000 souls that stood at Sinai had its own special portion of Torah that only that soul could understand.[26] Obviously, no account of revelatory experience by men or women can describe or exhaust the depths of divine reality. But this image of the relation between hidden and manifest Torah reminds us that half the souls of Israel have not left for us the Torah they have seen. Insofar as we can begin to recover women's experience of God, insofar as we can restore a part of their history and vision, we have more of the primordial Torah, the divine fullness, of which the present Torah of Israel is only a fragment and sign.[27]

What is the connection, however, between recovering Torah and recovering women's history? Retrieving primordial Torah is a large task to ask "history" to perform. And in fact, in the foregoing discussion, I have been slipping back and forth between different meanings and levels of the term "history." The rabbinic reconstruction of history, which I used as an example of rewriting Jewish history, by no means involved "doing history" in our modern sense. On the contrary, it was anachronistic and ahistorical. Taking for granted the historical factuality of the momentous events at Sinai and their essential congruence with their own religious perspective, the rabbis turned their attention to mining the eternal significance of these events. As they expanded Scripture to make it relevant to their own times, they clothed later traditions with authority and connected them to the original revelation. Reshaping Jewish memory did not involve discovering what "really happened," but projecting later developments back onto the eternal present of Sinai, and in this way augmenting and reworking Torah.[28]

Recovering women's history through modern historiography, that is, through a careful and critical sifting of sources, is a second meaning of history I have used implicitly. It is not just different from rabbinic modes of thinking but in many ways in conflict with them. Modern historiography assumes precisely that the original "revelation," at least as we have it, is not sufficient, that there are enormous gaps both in tradition and in the scriptural record, that to recapture women's experiences we need to go behind our records and *add* to them, acknowledging that that is what we are doing. As Yosef Yerushalmi points out in his book on Jewish history and Jewish memory, historiography stands in a radically different relation to the past from the kind of remembering rabbinic thought represents. Modern historical writing "brings to the fore texts, events, processes, that never really became part of Jewish group memory." It challenges and relativizes those memories that have survived.[29] It is not explicitly concerned with creating a living history for a particular people but rather with correcting memory to achieve a broader view of "what happened" in the past. While Yerushalmi's discussion of modern Jewish historiography takes no note of feminist history, it is especially the purpose of the feminist historian to challenge tradition in the way he describes. Surfacing forgotten processes and events, nameless persons and discarded sources, the feminist calls Jewish memory to the bar, accusing it of partiality and distortion, of defining Jewish women out of the Jewish past.

Insofar as feminists use the techniques of modern historiography, the tensions between feminist and traditional approaches to Jewish history are important and real, and the theological relevance of feminist history is not immediately obvious. And yet, like the rabbis, feminists too are not simply interested in acquiring more knowledge about the past but in uncovering what has been revealed—this time, to women. We want to incorporate women's history as part of the living memory of the Jewish people, and thus create a history that functions as Torah. Information about women's past may be instructive and even stirring, but it is not transformative until it becomes part of the community's collective memory, part of what Jews call to mind in remembering Jewish history. Historiographical research is crucial to a new understanding of Torah because it both helps recover women's religious experiences and relativizes the Torah we have, freeing our imaginations to consider religious possibilities neglected or erased by traditional sources. Historiography is not sufficient, however, to create a living memory. The Jewish feminist reshaping of Jewish history must proceed on several levels at once. Feminist historiography can open new questions to be brought to the past and can offer a broader picture of Jewish religious experience. It must be combined, however, with feminist midrash and feminist liturgy before it can shape the Jewish relationship to God and the world and thus contribute to the transformation of Torah.

Feminist Historiography and the Recovery of Women's History

Historiography as one aspect of the feminist reconstruction of Jewish memory challenges the traditional androcentric view of Jewish history and opens up our understanding of the Jewish past. In the last two decades, feminist historians have demanded and effected a far-reaching reorientation of the presuppositions and methods of historical writing. Questioning the assumption that men have made history while women have stayed home and had babies, they have insisted that women and men have lived and shaped history together. Any account of a period or civilization that does not look at the roles of both women and men, their relation and interaction, is "men's his-

tory" rather than the universal history it generally claims to
be.[30] The great silence that has shrouded women's history testifies not to women's lack of historical agency but to the androcentric bias that has shaped historical writing. In seeking to
recover women's history, feminist historians have mined androcentric sources for clues to women's lives and leadership, and
interpreted and filled in the gaps and silences that erase wom-
en's activity. They have made gender a central category of historical analysis, seeing it not just as a biological given but as
itself subject to historical development and change.[31] Feminist
historians have moved from writing the history of women's
oppression or women's contributions to significant movements
or events as men define them to trying to understand women's
history in women's own terms. Looking at history from a woman-centered perspective, they have tried to reconstruct independent women's cultures developed within or over against the
prevailing assumptions of patriarchal society. They have tried
to shift our view of the past, to enable us to see how the past
changes when "seen through the eyes of women and ordered
by the values they define."[32]

All the issues raised by feminist historians are relevant to
Jewish women's history; yet their insights and methods have
just begun to be applied. Whole areas of our past remain entirely unexamined, and there is scarcely a question on which there
is not important work left to do. At this point, not only is it
impossible to give a comprehensive account of the changes in
Jewish women's roles, status, and experience over time and in
different communities, even the interpretation of data from specific periods is incomplete and disputed. My primary interest in
historiography, however, is theological rather than historical. I
am concerned with the ways in which feminist historiography
can open up our understanding of Torah by offering as Torah a
new range of sources. Insofar as my focus is on the *implications*
of women's history for reconstructing Jewish memory and the
sense of God's presence in Jewish life, it is possible, through a
few concrete examples, to raise some questions about what it

might mean to recover women's history, both as this recovery would affect our present and our view of the past.

Traditional apologetic accounts of the role of women in Judaism often begin with Miriam, Deborah, or Huldah as luminous examples of Jewish womanhood proving the dignity and equality of Jewish women throughout the ages.[33] Feminist historians too are concerned with the significance of these women in biblical history; but for feminists, the existence of female judges and prophets proves both less and far more than the apologist would allow. On the one side, while the activities of women leaders tell us little about the lives of ordinary women during the same historical periods, accounts of exceptional women indicate the accessibility to women of charismatic leadership roles. Women may have been barred from established, inherited religious office, but when, in the biblical period, "the mantle of the Lord" fell upon a particular woman, she could judge or prophecy with authority, and was accorded communal recognition and respect.[34] While women's "Otherness" is the norm in biblical writing, important religious roles were sometimes available to individual women.

On the other side, however, whatever they tell us of women's religious power, the stories of exceptional women also allow us to glimpse a process of textual editing through which the roles of women are downplayed and obscured. Miriam, for instance, is called prophetess. As the one who leads the women in a victory dance on the far shores of the Red Sea (Ex. 15:20–21), she is clearly an important religious figure in the preconquest Israelite community.[35] During the sojourn in the wilderness, she and Aaron challenge Moses' authority, claiming that the Lord speaks through them as well as through their brother (Num. 12:2). When Miriam is punished by God for her temerity and is shut out of the camp for seven days, the community waits for her before continuing on its desert journey (Num. 12:15). Moreover, the Torah records the place of her death and burial (Num. 20:1), another attestation to her communal significance. The same passages that hint at Miriam's importance, however, at the same time undercut it. The dance at the Sea links Miriam with a foundational event of Israelite history, but she appears in the narrative with no introduction and no account of her rise to religious leadership. This surprising silence suggests that there were other Miriam traditions that were excluded from the Torah.[36] In the incident in which Miriam and Aaron speak against Moses, God strikes Miriam white with leprosy and forces her to remain outside the camp, while Aaron is simply reprimanded (Num. 12:5–15). Moreover, although the later midrashic tradition assumes the greatness of Miriam alongside Aaron, the actual narrative space accorded Miriam in the Torah is only a fraction of what Aaron receives.[37] The Torah leaves us, then, with tantalizing hints concerning Miriam's importance and influence and the nature of her religious role, but she is by no means accorded the narrative attention the few texts concerning her suggest she deserves.[38]

The example of Huldah similarly illustrates the scant attention important women receive in the Bible. In her case, 2 Kings offers only a brief and isolated account of an obviously influential prophetess. In the time of King Josiah, Hilkiah, the high priest, discovers an important scroll in the Temple (identified by scholars as the book of Deuteronomy). At the king's instruction, his servants bring the scroll to the prophetess Huldah to inquire about its implications and significance. When she tells them that the book is indeed the word of God and that the kingdom of Judah will be destroyed because its prescriptions have gone unheeded, Josiah immediately accepts her words and calls for general repentance and rededication (22:8–23:3). The question then becomes why we know nothing else of a prophet who was sufficently well-known and respected that the king's servants would turn to her at this critical juncture. Why is there no book of Huldah along with the books of the other prophets? What was her word of God to the people of Israel? Can it be because she was a woman that she left no school to record her prophecies and pass them on to succeeding generations?

Thus as important as references to exceptional women are in allowing us to reconstruct the range of women's roles, they are equally important clues to the silences in our sources. Stories of powerful women point to a history of women's participation in Jewish life that is much richer and fuller than extant sources imply. The same texts that indicate that women were religious leaders at various points in the biblical period, and that suggest that they too encountered God and responded to that encounter, also point to the fact that the Bible's writers and redactors were ambivalent toward or simply lacked interest in women's leadership and insights. As Elisabeth Schüssler Fiorenza has demonstrated for the New Testament, biblical traditions concerning women are "selected, redacted, and reformulated" by men living in a patriarchal world and sharing its mentality. The disparagement of Miriam's authority and the brevity of the narrative concerning Huldah suggest an androcentric selection process that saw traditions about women as either threatening or unimportant. Thus scarcity of information about women's leadership cannot be assumed accurately to reflect women's actual influence or importance in a particular period. On the contrary, the fact that centuries of androcentric sifting and editing left any traditions concerning women suggests that these may represent only a fraction of what we have lost.[39]

Recovering the stories of exceptional women, however, even where this is done not in an apologetic spirit but with full attention to the complexities of both the androcentric transmission process and of women's relationship to a wider patriarchal religious context, is only part of the task of the feminist historian. Stories of outstanding women are important to our understanding and appreciation of women's religious agency, but they can also distract attention from the fate of ordinary women and from seemingly undramatic but far-reaching changes in gender relations. Feminist scholars, mindful of the paucity of clues resulting from a long and interested editing process, have nonetheless sought in religious texts evidence of shifting patterns and ideologies of sex roles, evidence that might shed some light on the social and religious situation of the mass of women in a given time.

Archeologist Carol Meyers, for instance, has begun to reconstruct the roles of women in early Israel through a combination of biblical and archeological evidence. Although the details of her model are speculative, she asks important new questions about the changing roles of women in biblical society, questions that point to the social construction of gender in biblical culture. She points out that skeletal remains from the period of early Israelite settlement reflect the presence of both endemic disease and periodic plague. This suggests, she argues, that the ancient Israelites would have desperately needed large families to offset the effects of a high death rate, particularly since they were also trying to cultivate newly acquired territory and subdue part of the population. In this precarious situation, women's biological contribution would have been very important and highly valued, as would have been their contribution to agricultural production. Meyers speculates that the exclusion of women from other roles—that is, the priesthood—might have been rooted in the exigencies of this early period when women's energies were required for agricultural work and childbearing. Initially, the restriction of women's roles might have been practical and carried no opprobrium. Indeed, given the importance of women in reproduction and production, Meyers thinks early Israelite society may have been relatively egalitarian. Later, however, in the very different cultural context of the monarchy, a functional restriction became the basis for "ideologies of female inferiority and subordination."[40]

Other feminist scholars, focusing more narrowly on biblical narrative, have found in the accounts of origins and in the family stories of Genesis evidence of shifts in patterns of social organization from matrilineal descent and matrilocal residence to patrilineal/patrilocal social forms.[41] According to this view, the early Israelite period, however egalitarian compared to later times, was a period in which patriarchal structures were being consolidated and older cultural patterns destroyed. In her imaginative and speculative book, *Sarah the Priestess*, Savina Teubal argues that many puzzling features of the patriarchal narratives can be explained by the assumption that the matriarchs were struggling to maintain traditions and customs different from those of their husbands. Sarah's "incestuous" marriage to Abraham, for example, becomes comprehensible in a matrilineal system in which siblings with different mothers would not be considered blood relatives.[42] Rebekah's concern that Jacob marry according to the matrifocal traditions of her homeland reflects her attempt to maintain her own customs against the profound changes symbolized by Esau's Hittite wives (Gen. 27:46).[43] The creation narratives in Genesis 2–3, as ideological justifications for patriarchy, reflect both a protest against these old ways and acknowledgment of a once different order. Eve, seeker of wisdom and the "mother of all the living," is created from Adam's rib in a clear "patriarchal inversion" of biological reality.[44]

The Bible provides fragmentary evidence not just of women's leadership and of changing family patterns but also of women's religious lives outside of "normative" structures. Biblical evidence suggests that polytheistic worship, for all that the prophets called it idolatry and whoredom, was nonetheless attractive to large numbers of Israelites. Indeed, if one reads the prophetic accounts carefully, it seems clear that an indigenous polytheism flourished in Israel up until the exile.[45] The biblical material supporting this position is buttressed by startling ninth- to eighth-century B.C.E. inscriptional references to "Yahweh and his Asherah," as well as by archeological discovery of numerous female images in Israelite houses over centuries of settlement.[46]

While such worship was attractive to Israelites of both sexes, a specific connection between women and goddesses is mentioned in the Bible on several occasions. When Jeremiah, after the destruction of the Temple, harangues the exiles in Egypt for worshiping the Queen of Heaven, the text specifically mentions women's involvement five times (Jer. 44). "Thereupon they answered Jeremiah—all the men who knew that their *wives* made offerings to other gods; all the *women* present, a large gathering" (v. 15, emphasis mine). Ezekiel, in a vision of the Temple's defilement, sees in the corner of the courtyard "women bewailing Tammuz" (8:14). Tammuz, son of the goddess Ishtar, was a Babylonian god of vegetation whose death each summer was ritually mourned by women.[47]

If polytheism had a particular hold on women, this might be partly explained by the numerous roles open to women in the polytheistic rites of the pre- and non-Israelite Ancient Near East. Women functioned as singers and dancers, diviners, and dream interpreters, mourners and priestesses.[48] With the prophetic rejection of pagan deities and the consolidation of the all male priesthood of Yahweh, women were barred from any leadership role in Israelite worship. Their involvement in worship was voluntary and limited by menstrual taboos that would have rendered them unclean a good part of their adult lives. It would not be surprising, then, if women showed special reluctance to abandon polytheistic worship, particularly devotion to goddesses. Perhaps they were unwilling to accept a conception of deity that excluded them from full participation in religious life. While the prophets, of course, condemned polytheistic practices as "whoring after false gods," such traditions remained a significant part of Israelite devotion—especially women's devotion—through the end of the monarchy.

Women's religious leadership, the biblical construction of gender, and women's participation in polytheistic rite could all be explored at far greater length. Yet even the briefest consideration of these topics serves to indicate that women's experience is obscured and erased in biblical writing and that such writing is selected and edited from a highly tendentious perspective. Women of power are downplayed or disparaged, and we are left wondering about the actual roles and teachings of numerous women who flit through biblical narratives. Patriarchal prerogatives are spelled out as divine commands in biblical legislation, but the shifts they represent from older forms of gender relations must be reconstructed from subtle clues. Polytheistic worship is condemned as utterly foreign and other, when the very span and passion of the condemnations bespeak the tenacity of that worship in the history of Israel. Through all this, we see a larger Torah behind the Torah, a Torah in which women's experience is rendered visible, and the social and religious forms to which they adhered are depicted in their complexity and power.

Looking at ancient Israel through feminist lenses thus entails a shift in perspective with potentially profound religious implications. A feminist perspective opens up the Tanakh, revealing both its historical/cultural context and the religious possibilities its editing conceals. A feminist approach widens our historical and religious vision by bringing to the fore material concerning women's religious history and experience that previously had gone unnoted. More important, it introduces another standard of *value* by which we might judge and appreciate what we see.[49] Feminism forces us to look at who defines certain developments as normative, to what end and with what implications. Insofar as feminism is characterized by concern and sympathy for women's experience, it demands we take seriously the religious forms that have spoken to women and attempt to reevaluate their place in, and relation to, the wider tradition.

It is not just Torah as traditionally understood, moreover, that can be sifted and mined for information about women. Feminist work expands the concept of Torah further by finding material on Jewish women's lives far outside the traditional canon. The process of reevaluation so fruitful in studies of the Tanakh has also been carried out in relation to other sources and periods. Bernadette Brooten's work on the inscriptional evidence for women's leadership in the ancient synagogue underscores issues that emerge from the biblical material and raises new problems and questions. Brooten has uncovered information on women's roles in the rabbinic period that challenges traditional rabbinic sources. She has also shown how androcentric scholarship can interpret material to fit its presuppositions, writing women out of history even where their presence is clear.

Her material is nineteen Greek and Latin inscriptions, ranging in date from the first century B.C.E. to the sixth C.E., that refer to women as "president of the synagogue," "leader," "elder," "mother of the synagogue," and "priestess."[50] A number of these inscriptions have been known to scholars for some time, but they have generally interpreted the titles as honorific when applied to women. Researchers have reasoned that since women could not have played a leadership role in the synagogue, such titles must belong to them as leaders' wives. As one scholar puts it, "Rufina herself bears the title *archisynagogos* [leader, head of the synagogue] which in the case of a woman is, of course, just a title."[51]

Brooten claims that there is absolutely no internal evidence supporting this much-argued position. Aside from the fact that honorific titles may not even have existed in the ancient synagogue, a number of women leaders are mentioned without reference to husbands, and other wives of synagogue leaders are mentioned without being given titles. Brooten, therefore, assumes that the titles were functional and tries to reconstruct the nature of each role. Heads of synagogues, she says, are amply attested in the literary sources as important functionaries. They seem to have been responsible for seeing to the reading of the law, inviting people to preach, collecting money from congregations to be sent to the patriarch, and helping in synagogue building and restoration.[52] While the women mentioned in the inscriptions may have been exceptional—some were possibly women who owned property and were able to make donations to synagogues—the inscriptions challenge the view that women were a priori excluded from leadership in Jewish religious life.[53]

Shaye Cohen, another scholar who accepts the functional significance of these titles, argues that they demonstrate the "pluralistic nature of ancient Judaism." Archeology, he says, "allows us to see the full range of Jewish expression in late antiquity," better than literary sources. But Cohen also argues that, since modern Jews accept rabbinic authority, and these women came from communities that were not under rabbinic authority, the titles are not a useful historical precedent.[54] I would contend, however, that if we assume that the history of Judaism is the history of women and men, we cannot dismiss women's leadership as simply a historical curiosity. The importance of the titles is precisely that they lead us to question rabbinic authority as the sole arbiter of authentic Judaism. Just as certain biblical materials force us to reevaluate received judgments about Israelite religion, in this case too, women's participation in what came to be defined as nonnormative worship must lead us to question how normative practice came to be defined and who had the right to do the defining.[55]

Evidence like these inscriptions is not simply material on the periphery of tradition waiting for an interpretive framework that can bring it in. Information on women's roles gleaned from literary and nonliterary sources may help us understand the social context of "normative" Jewish literature and thus allow us to challenge its world-construction. Indeed, feminist historians have come to recognize that religious, literary, and philosophical works setting forth women's nature or tasks are often prescriptive rather than descriptive of reality. So far from giving us the world "as it is," "normative" texts may reflect the tensions within patriarchal culture, seeking to maintain a particular view of the world over against social, political, or religious change.[56] Thus, in our own time, the rise of a strong and vocal "pro-family" lobby in both the political and religious spheres must be understood as a reaction to profound changes in women's roles and in the nature of family life. But if religious texts can be reacting against social and religious innovation, no particular religious system can be said to give us an accurate view of women's roles until it is set against careful analysis of other available materials from the same time.[57] In Brooten's words, "Non-literary materials should be a challenge, and not a simple complement, to the view of reality emerging from literature." Evaluation of the range of sources for Jewish women's history will make it "impossible to mistake male Jewish attitudes toward women for Jewish women's history."[58]

The material Brooten has studied, both these inscriptions and other documents, may shed light on the context of the Mishnah, a second-century code of Jewish law that forms the basis of the Talmud, the central text of rabbinic Judaism. Jacob Neusner, in his monumental work on the Mishnah's Order of Women, points out that the Mishnah does not reflect the reality of what women did or experienced but the relationship of women to men as men defined it. The Mishnah's focus is the regulation of those potentially dangerous moments when a woman leaves the house of one man to enter into a relationship with another.[59]

If the Mishnah is accepted as normative and perceived simply as "Torah," then its definition of women as Other is incorporated into Jewish life, and its patriarchal perspective is assumed to reflect the divine will. Any changes in women's situation with regard to marriage and divorce must then be worked out within the framework of a system that assumes men are at the center. If, however, we ask *why* the authors of the Mishnah created this particular system, taking the code in its social and religious context, the Mishnah is opened up as we see it against the background of other worldviews current at the time.[60] For, as the inscriptional evidence indicates, in the same period the Mishnah was written, the women it depicts as entirely under male control were taking on religious leadership in a number of corners of the Jewish world. Moreover, as Brooten makes clear in another article, these inscriptions are not the only materials that throw into question the view of women the Mishnah provides. While the Mishnah depicts women as unable to divorce their husbands, other evidence suggests that some women exercised the right of divorce. A number of documents from the first centuries C.E. indicate that, while the right of women to initiate divorce may have been controversial, individual women did divorce their husbands or reserve the option to do so in their marriage contracts.[61] Recovering women's history, then, both puts "normative" works into a context that may help us to understand their preoccupations, and at the same time expands our sense of Jewish religious possibilities.

But if ancient documents and artifacts provide us with important materials for reconstructing women's history, none that we know of comes directly from women's hands. Women's experience must be deduced from works that are filtered through a male perspective or that are largely impersonal so that we always stand at some remove from the reality of women's lives.

In the modern period, however, we have Jewish texts that actually come to us from women, giving us a more intimate view
of women's perceptions and spirituality. While these sources
often have been dismissed as "women's literature" or relegated
to casual reading, in fact they give us important glimpses of
women's religious experiences. In offering us access to the religious lives of women in the past, such texts provide resources
for a contemporary women's spirituality. Yet they also pose
problems arising from the relation of women's experience to its
larger patriarchal framework.

Chava Weissler's work on the *tkhines*, or petitionary prayers
of Eastern European Jewish women, provides a fascinating
glimpse of the rich spiritual world of Ashkenazic (Eastern European) women in the early modern period. While not all the
tkhines were written by women, some did have female authors
and reflect both the constraints and color of women's lives. The
tkhines by and large convey a spirituality structured by private
events and experiences. While the prayers in the *siddur* (prayerbook) are written in Hebrew and address God in the collective
voice of Israel, the *tkhines* are written in the Yiddish vernacular
and speak in the singular, each woman addressing God in her
own name. The subjects of many of the *tkhines* are private rituals or moments: women's three special commandments—lighting the Sabbath candles, taking the hallah dough, and ritual
immersion; Rosh Hodesh, the celebration of the new moon on
which women were exempted from work; important biological
events in women's lives like pregnancy and childbirth; visiting
the graves of the dead and personal or family problems and
occasions.[62] The titles of a few of the *tkhines* convey their intimate nature: "A prayer for an orphan to say on her wedding
day," "A prayer to say when a child is ill, God forbid," "A prayer
to say after giving birth," " A prayer for a woman to bring up
children well."[63]

What emerges from the *tkhines* is a sense of the emotionality
and intimacy of women's piety, its concreteness and relation to
everyday. The God of the *tkhines* is a God who is very near to
women, a God involved in the trials and tribulations of ordinary

family life. The *tkhines* make clear that at the same time women participated in the established cycle of the Jewish year, they also sought and discovered God in domestic routines and in the biological experiences unique to women. Women were obviously able to find great meaning in their limited number of commandments. They were deeply involved with their families, a sphere of connection that extended to the dead. They also felt deeply connected to the matriarchs, whose experience and merit they invoked.[64] The *tkhines* testify to the importance of relationship in women's spirituality. They provide models for celebrating many areas of women's experience the male tradition has ignored, filling in some of the gaps in the Hebrew blessings that sanctify aspects of everyday life but do not include important turning points in the lives of women.[65]

But the *tkhines* also suggest the limits of the range of women's concerns. Cynthia Ozick says they "reflect exactly the religious situation of women. . . . Half of them are biological; the other half concern themselves with the limited religious space offered to women." She compares them to the songs of a bird written in a steel cage in the middle of a desert.[66] The image is a bit dramatic, for the *tkhines* also reflect acquaintance with a considerable range of Jewish literature, and occasionally transform traditional sources in ways that affirm women's power and dignity.[67] The strengths and weaknesses of the *tkhines*, however, are two sides of the same coin. In giving vivid expression to the concrete realities of women's lives, they also reflect the confines of those lives. Thus they make clear the extent to which patriarchal boundaries affect women's religious expression even when those forms of expression are woman-made. Before we can adapt past forms of women's spirituality for ourselves, we must be aware of the subtle interplay between the ways women have found to express themselves within and against patriarchy and the ways patriarchal religion shapes and defines women's religious expression.

These glimpses of Jewish women's past are not meant to restore to us our history or to offer a particular reconstruction of

Jewish women's past, but to indicate the potential contribution of feminist historiography to the feminist reconception of Torah. That contribution has two aspects. First, reclaiming women's history reveals another world around and underneath the textual tradition, a world in which women are historical agents struggling within and against a patriarchal culture. The existence of this world does not alter the fundamentally androcentric perspective of "normative" texts or prove that Judaism is really egalitarian. It does, however, show that patriarchy had a history, that it developed in relation to demographic, economic, and religious factors, and that women resisted its encroachment in both the social and religious spheres. In the matriarchal period, women may have tried to maintain matrilineal and matrilocal social customs, resisting the new patrilineal descent associated with Abraham. During the monarchy, women worshiped goddesses and performed rituals to them. In antiquity, individual women functioned as leaders of synagogues, and others reserved the right to divorce their husbands, despite rabbinic teaching that this right was reserved for men. In the modern period, texts by women shed light on women's spirituality as it expressed itself within a patriarchal tradition. This world of women's experience is part of the Jewish world, part of the fuller Torah we need to recover.

Second, awareness of this neglected world "opens up" and challenges so-called normative texts. By this I mean that, in the light of women's history, we cannot see the Torah, the Tanakh, the Mishnah, or any Jewish text simply as given, as having emerged organically from an eternal, unambiguous, uncontested religious vision. We cannot see traditional sources simply as revelation, as representing the full Jewish experience of either the nature or commands of God. "Normative" sources reflect the views of the historical winners, winners whose victories were often achieved at the expense of women and of religious forms that allowed women some power and scope.[68] Insofar as women's religious and social self-expression and empowerment are values we bring to these texts, the texts are relativized, their normative status shaken. We see them against the background of alternative religious possibilities, alternatives that must now be taken seriously, because without them we have only the Judaism of a male elite and not the Judaism of all Jews.

This challenge to normative sources is as important, perhaps more important, than the particular contours of women's experience in any given time. It is true that groups of Jewish feminists, placing themselves in solidarity with the women of our history, have sought in the practices of our foremothers direct models for their own spirituality. The proliferation of Rosh Hodesh groups is an important example of an attempt to ground contemporary feminist spirituality in forms used by women in the past. So are rituals of casting circles, invoking the names of goddesses, or practicing ancient prayer postures, all of which—some feminists argue—our mothers may have done. But the simple fact that certain forms of religious expression were practiced by women does not make them intrinsically more appropriable than forms practiced by men. Some of women's past beliefs and traditions may prove meaningful to contemporary women. Others may not, either because of their embeddedness in a patriarchal tradition, or because of a changed social, economic, and religious situation. To sort out the historically interesting from the enduring will require deliberation and experimentation.

One benefit of recovering women's experience is indisputable, however. Reconstructing women's history enables us to see that "Judaism" has always been richer, more complex, and more diverse than either "normative" sources or most branches of modern Judaism would admit. It permits us to see that Torah embraces many patterns and variations of religious experience, that its boundaries are far broader than traditionally allowed. Awareness of women's presence and participation in Jewish history within and outside of mainstream Jewish forms frees us to explore our own experiences, even in directions that may extend the limits of contemporary Jewish theology and practice. Laboring to find our own voices in a patriarchal religion, we know we do so in solidarity with the women who went before us—women whose full Torah we have yet to recover.

Reshaping Jewish Memory

Reclaiming women's history is integrally connected to rebuilding contemporary Jewish life. We seek the history of Jewish women out of our need for a Jewish community in which women are present. In expanding Torah, in writing women into Jewish history, we extend the realm of the potentially usable Jewish past, grounding a Jewish community that can be a community of women and men. Women's experiences increase the domain of Jewish resources on which we can draw in recreating Judaism in the present, inspiring us to find our own forms of expression as the women and men of the past found theirs.

But historiography by itself cannot reshape Jewish memory. The gaps in the historical record alone would prompt us to seek other ways of remembering. However sensitively we read between the lines of mainstream texts seeking to recapture the reality of women's lives, however carefully we mine nonliterary and non-Jewish materials using them to challenge "normative" sources, many of our constructions will remain speculations and many of our questions will go unanswered. The androcentric bias of our sources and the patriarchal nature of the cultures from which they sprang means that much important information about women has simply been lost or was never recorded. Part of what we need to know we may with skilled probing recover, but the rest will need to be imagined.

But even if it were not the case that the sources are sparse and unconcerned with our most urgent questions, feminist historiography would still provide only a fragile grounding for the feminist transformation of Torah. For as I suggested earlier and the historical examples underscore, historiography recalls events that memory does not recognize.[69] It challenges memory, tries to dethrone it; it calls it partial and distorted. History provides a more and more complex and nuanced picture of the past; memory is selective. "We were slaves in the land of Egypt. The LORD our God with a mighty hand and outstretched arm. . . ." How do we recover the parts of Jewish women's history that are forgotten, and how do we then ensure that they will be *remembered*—incorporated into our sense of communal identity?

The answer to these questions is partly connected to the wider reconstruction of Jewish life. We turn to the past with new questions because of present commitments, but we also remember more deeply what a changed present requires us to know. The issue of reinterpreting the past is preamble to but also follows from issues of contemporary Jewish women's experience. Significant changes in contemporary Jewish communal and religious structures cannot but affect our perceptions of the past.

Midrash

Yet Jewish feminists are already entering into a new relationship with history based not simply on historiography but also on more traditional strategies for Jewish remembrance. The rabbinic reconstruction of Jewish history, after all, was not historiographical but midrashic. Assuming the infinite meaningfulness of biblical texts, the rabbis took passages that were sketchy or troubling and wrote them forward. They brought to the Bible their own questions and found answers that showed the eternal relevance of biblical truth.[70] Why was Abraham chosen to be the father of a people? What was the status of the law before the Torah was given? Who was Adam's first wife? Why was Dina raped?[71] These were not questions for historical investigation but imaginative exegesis and literary amplification. The sages gave the meaning of a text for the present and declared that meaning its meaning in all times.

The open-ended process of writing midrash—simultaneously serious and playful, imaginative, metaphoric—has easily lent itself to feminist use. Feminist midrash shares the uncomfortable self-consciousness of modern religious experimentation: elaborating on the stories of Eve or Dina, we know the text is partly an occasion for our own projections, that our imaginative reconstructions are a reflection of our own beliefs and experiences. But if its self-consciousness is modern, the root conviction of feminist midrash is utterly traditional. It stands on the rabbinic insistence that the Bible can be made to speak to the present day. If it is our text, it can and must answer our questions and share our values; if we wrestle with it, it will yield up meaning. Listening to the traditional sources, we wait for the words of women "to rise out of the white spaces between the letters in the Torah" as we remember and transmit the past through "the experience of our own lives."[72]

Together and individually then, orally and in writing, women are creating poetry, exploring and telling stories that connect our history with present religious experience. Perhaps the favorite subject for feminist midrash is Miriam. The courage she showed in saving her brother from Pharaoh's decree that all newborn Hebrew males must be killed, her ecstasy by the shores of the Sea, her eager presence at Sinai, the agony and injustice of her punishment with leprosy have all become subjects for feminist reflection. The feminist Miriam is the woman we glimpse through the gaps in the biblical story, the one who refuses to be "a forgotten flute, a broken harp." This is the Miriam who "dared be like a man, a prophet," who stands on the shores of the Red Sea singing forever "until the lands/ sing to each other." This is the Miriam who knows the validity of her own revelation. It is the Miriam who insists to her brother, "We have both been chosen./ What you witness on the mountain/ cannot live without the miracles/ below."[73]

Other feminist midrashim deal with a range of biblical and extrabiblical women.[74] My retelling of the Eve and Lilith story attempts to mine the ambiguity of the traditional midrash that, seeking to reconcile the creation stories in Genesis 1 and 2, describes Lilith as Adam's first wife.[75] I retain the rabbinic idea that Lilith was banished for demanding equality with Adam but refuse to judge her an evil demon, perceiving in that label the whole history of male naming of women who refuse to yield to

male authority. My story seeks to expose the patriarchal perspective of the midrash, at the same time exploring the question
it leaves open: What would happen, what is happening, as
women's power begins to be freed and defined by women? Ellen
Umansky, retelling the story of the sacrifice of Isaac from Sarah's perspective, explores the dilemma of a woman in patriarchal culture trying to hold on to her sense of self. Isaac was
God's gift to Sarah in her old age. She has no power to prevent
Abraham's journey to Moriah; she can only wait wailing and
trembling for him to return. But she is angry; she knows that
God does not require such sacrifices. Abraham cannot deprive
her of her own religious understanding whatever demands he
may make upon her as his wife.[76] Lynn Gottlieb, in dance,
song, and story, combines traditional midrashic themes with
her own religious experience in order to "find the female voices
of the past and receive them into our present."[77] Miriam seeking
healing in the wilderness, Esther whose experience as a secret
Jew in the court of King Ahasuerus was lived by Marrano wom-
en—an endless litany of names and voices comes to life and
dances before us as she reaches back into the past and "give[s]
us our name[s]. Name[s] our genealogy."[78]

While midrash can float entirely free from historiography, as
it does in some of these examples, the latter can also feed the
former so that midrash plays with historical clues but extends
them beyond the boundaries of the fragmentary evidence.
When this happens, feminists expand Torah not just through
midrash on the five books of Torah, but through midrash on
history understood as Torah. In her midrash on the simple
verse, "And Dina . . . went out to see the daughters of the land"
(Gen. 34:1), Lynn Gottlieb explores the possible relations between Dina and Canaanite women based on the presumption
of Israelite women's historical attachment to a plurality of gods
and goddesses.[79] A group of my students once used the same
historical theme to write their own midrash on the sacrifice of
Isaac as experienced by Sarah. In their version, Sarah, finding
Abraham and Isaac absent, calls to Yahweh all day without

avail. Finally, almost in despair, she takes out her small image of Asherah and prays to the Goddess, only to see her husband and son over the horizon wending their way home.[80]

Moving from history into midrash, Jewish feminists follow the advice of Monique Wittig in her mythic novel *Les Guérillères:*

There was a time when you were not a slave, remember that. You walked alone, full of laughter, you bathed bare-bellied. You say you have lost all recollection of it, remember. . . . Make an effort to remember. Or, failing that, invent.[81]

This passage, evocative and haunting, names a distinction to be both honored and ignored. Certainly there is a difference between an inscription about Yahweh and his Asherah or an ancient Aramaic divorce document written by a woman, and a modern midrash on Miriam or Sarah. The first provides us with information that can be ignored or variously interpreted, but that also confronts and challenges, inviting us to find a framework for understanding the past broad enough to include data at odds with selective memory. The second is more fully an expression of our own convictions, a creative imagining based on our own experience, albeit developed in dialogue with traditional texts. To be sure, all historical reconstruction also involves conviction and imagination, but still it tries to accommodate itself to data that midrash feels free to skip over or reshape.

Yet, in the realm of Jewish religious expression, invention is permitted and even encouraged. Midrash is not a violation of historical canons but an enactment of commitment to the fruitfulness and relevance of biblical texts. It is partly through midrash that the inscription or document, potentially integrable into memory but still on the periphery, is transformed into narrative the religious ear can hear. The discovery of women in our history can feed the impulse to create midrash; midrash can seize on history and make it religiously meaningful. Remembering and inventing together help recover the hidden half of Torah, reshaping Jewish memory to let women speak.

Liturgy

There is also a third mode of recovery: speaking/acting. Historically, the primary vehicle for transmission of Jewish memory has been prayer and ritual, the liturgical reenactment and celebration of formative events. Midrash can instruct, amuse, edify, but the cycles of the week and year have been the most potent reminders of central Jewish experience and values. The weekly renewal of creation with the inauguration of the Sabbath, the entry of the High Priest into the Holy of Holies on the Day of Atonement, the Exodus of Israel from Egypt every Passover—these are remembered not just verbally but through the body and thus doubly imprinted on Jewish consciousness.

Liturgy and ritual, therefore, have been particularly important areas for Jewish feminist inventiveness.[82] Feminists have been writing liturgy and ritual that flow from and incorporate women's experience, in the process drawing on history and midrash but also allowing them to emerge from concrete forms. The celebration of Rosh Hodesh as a woman's holiday, for example, one of the earliest and most tenacious feminist rituals, represents both a restoration of a traditional women's observance and an opportunity to experiment with new spiritual forms. The association of women with the moon at the heart of the original ceremony provides a starting point for exploring women's symbols within Judaism and cross-culturally. At the same time, the simplicity of the traditional ritual leaves ample space for invention. Penina Adelman's *Miriam's Well* provides a compendium of Rosh Hodesh rituals developed by feminists over the last twenty years. Suggesting a theme for each month that emerges out of the Jewish calendar, the book offers recipes for combining the stories and life events of contemporary Jewish women with those of Jewish women of the past. The month of Sivan, for example, coming in the late spring at the time of the biblical barley harvest, includes the festival of Shavuot on which the book of Ruth is read. Linking the themes of human fertility and fertility of the earth central to Ruth, the ritual for the month celebrates a girl's menarche. Participants tell the stories of their own first periods, devise a midrash about the biblical namesake of the girl being honored, and offer the girl gifts and blessings that mark her accession to Jewish womanhood.[83]

Feminist Haggadot (Passover liturgies) and Seder celebrations seek to bring women's experience to the central Jewish story and central ritual enactment of the Jewish year. Using history, midrash, and poetry, they build on the theme of liberation to make women's experience and struggle an important issue for the Passover holiday. The range of Haggadot reflects a range of feminist attitudes and situations. Some integrate women's stories into the established Passover ritual, dwelling, for instance, on the two midwives Shiphrah and Puah whose names are absent from the traditional Haggadah but who made Passover possible by disobeying Pharaoh's command to kill Hebrew males at birth (Ex. 1:15–21). Other Haggadot incorporate women's continuing quest for liberation as a distinct theme in the Seder—setting aside one of the traditional four cups of wine, for example, to honor contemporary women's struggles against oppression. Some women have developed a tradition of women's Seders held before or during the holiday and have created for them Haggadot that make women's liberation the center of Passover.[84]

A third area for feminist ritual creativity is birth ceremonies for girls. These are rooted in neither a historical nor a continuing ritual but in a desire to assert and celebrate the value of daughters, welcoming them into the community with a ceremony parallel to *Brit Milah* (circumcision). The absence of any traditional form but a simple naming in synagogue again leaves plenty of room for exploration, with some women borrowing traditional midrashim and blessings, others seeking symbols particularly appropriate to females, and others combining old and new ideas, all in ceremonies of their own making. My ritual for the birth of a daughter tries to place newborn girls in the context of Jewish women's history by telling the stories of some biblical women who form part of the covenant the baby girl now enters. Many other ceremonies have suggested physical symbols or acts that might conceivably carry the weight of circumcision in initiating girls into the covenant. Proposals have ranged from washing a baby's feet as a concrete and ancient symbol of welcome, to offering her central ritual symbols like a kiddush cup or prayer shawl, to breaking her hymen or immersing her in a *mikveh* (ritual bath) as a symbol of women's sexuality.[85]

Jewish feminist ritual creativity is not limited to these three areas. I mention them because they have provided basic structures around which a great deal of varied experimentation has taken place. But from reinterpretations of mikveh, to major reworkings of Sabbath blessings, to simple inclusion of the *imahot* (matriarchs) in daily and Sabbath liturgies—which, however minimally, says, "We too had a covenant; we too were there"—women are seeking to transform Jewish ritual so that it acknowledges our existence and experience.[86] In the ritual moment, women's history is made present.

We have then an interweaving of forms that borrow from and give life to each other. Women's history challenges us to confront the incompleteness of what has been called "Jewish history," to attend to the hidden and hitherto marginal, to attempt a true Jewish history that is a history of women and men. It restores to us some of women's voices in and out of the "normative" tradition, sometimes in accommodation and sometimes in struggle, but the voices of Jews defining their own Jewishness as they participate in the communal life. Midrash expands and burrows, invents the forgotten and prods the memory, takes from history and asks for more. It gives us the inner life history cannot follow, building links between the stories of our foremothers and our own joy and pain. Ritual asserts women's presence in the present. Borrowing from history and midrash, it transforms them into living memory. Creating new forms, it offers them to be remembered.

Thus, through diverse paths, we remember ourselves. Moses' injunction at Sinai—"Do not go near a woman"—though no less painful, is only part of a story expanded and reinvigorated as women enter into the shaping of Torah. If, in Jewish terms, history provides a basis for identity, then out of our new sense of identity we are also claiming our past. Beginning with the conviction of our presence both at Sinai and now, we rediscover and invent ourselves in the Jewish communal past and present, continuing the age-old process of reshaping Torah as we reshape the community today.

Torah as Law in a Feminist Judaism

Thus far, in discussing the feminist transformation of Torah, I have made no reference to halakhah or Jewish law. From a traditional perspective this omission is odd to say the least. "Torah" is often translated simply as "law." And even where Torah is understood in the broader sense in which I have used it—as living Jewish teaching—law certainly constitutes an important part of Jewish teaching, if not its center. Two considerations, however, have led me to place the issue of law at the end of this chapter. First, I want to indicate through form as well as content that, while halakhah has been a central focus of Jewish feminist attention, the task of reshaping Torah involves far more than reforming the law. Second, the role of halakhah in a feminist Judaism is so complexly problematic, and so few of its aspects have been addressed, that I can only unravel some questions relevant to a feminist exploration of halakhah as one part of the issue of Torah.

What makes the topic of halakhah so murky and difficult for feminists is partly the fact that it evokes and gets caught in denominational differences. Disagreements among the branches of modern Judaism come into play in feminist writing about the law far more than they do in relation to broader issues of recovering women's history. Discussions of halakhah easily polarize along denominational lines, with Orthodox feminists deeply concerned about the mechanisms of halakhic change and non-Orthodox feminists seeing such change either as relatively straightforward or as irrelevant. Orthodox feminists have focused their quarrels with Judaism largely on halakhic issues.[87] Non-Orthodox feminists, myself among them, have often expressed impatience with narrowly halakhic feminist analysis.[88] But when non-Orthodox feminists criticize Orthodox attention to halakhah, it is difficult to sort out specifically *feminist* issues from general discomfort with or lack of interest in Jewish law.

The issue of halakhah is problematic beyond its denominational divisiveness, however. Arguments about the value of a halakhic approach, and the many feminist attempts to grapple with particular legal problems, both have the effect of distracting attention from deeper questions concerning the law. Setting aside the issue of content that has captured feminist energy, are there feminist reasons why law as law should or should not be a central religious category in a feminist Judaism? What considerations are relevant to the question of whether, when "women add our voices to tradition, halakhah will be our medium of expression and repair?"[89] So little has been done by way of examining this difficult subject that I will simply try to peel away the layers of the question, indicating the many levels on which halakhah might pose problems for feminists.

The first layer of feminist objection to the law is objection to the content of (many) particular laws. It is this layer that has virtually monopolized feminist attention. Indeed, the subject has been considered so often that there is little purpose in discussing it at length here.[90] Basically, feminist analyses of halakhah have focused on two areas: laws pertaining to women's roles in public worship and laws pertaining to women's status in the family. Women's relation to the public religious sphere is shaped by a double exemption: exemption from study and exemption from positive commandments (that is, "Thou shalts") that must be performed at a particular time. These exemptions are explained in a number of different ways, and there are specific positive time-bound commandments women are expected to perform; but basically the exemptions ensure that no legal obligation interferes with women's domestic functions.[91] Since, according to Jewish law, one who is not obligated to perform an action does not have the same status as one who is obligated, the nonobligated person cannot perform that action on behalf of the obligated individual. Thus, even when women choose to attend synagogue, they are not counted in a minyan and cannot publicly read from the Torah.[92] Insofar as prayer and study are the heart and soul of traditional Judaism, the net effect of these laws is to render women peripheral Jews. As Rachel Adler argued in her classic essay on women and halakhah, the characteristic posture of the peripheral Jew is negative rather than positive. The fact that women must observe the negative commandments ("Thou shalt nots") prevents them from undermining Jewish life, but they are not permitted to participate fully in the religious life of the Jewish people.[93]

With regard to laws of family status, feminists have addressed a range of issues but focused most attention on the difficult and sometimes life-destroying problem of divorce.[94] Jewish divorce law, rooted ultimately in Deuteronomy 24, gives a husband the nonreciprocal right to divorce his wife by writing her a bill of divorce (*get*). The rabbis were keenly aware of the injustice of this lack of reciprocity and tried to mitigate its effects on women through legislation protecting them from rash divorce and miserable marriage.[95] Since the rabbis acted only within the framework of Deuteronomy's fundamental inequality, however, divorce remains open to abuse by angry or punitive husbands who either refuse to write a *get* or use a wife's need for one to extract money or other concessions. Moreover, if a husband disappears without witnesses to his death, his widow or abandoned wife, unable to divorce him, can never remarry. The casualty of this system is the *agunah*, the "chained wife," the woman essentially no longer married but unfree to remarry due either to tragic circumstance or the vindictiveness of her husband.

Feminists have addressed other specific legal disabilities of women. Criticism of particular laws, however, is not the most significant level of feminist objection to halakhah. If we strip away this layer of discourse we find underneath specific legislation an assumption of women's Otherness more fundamental than the particular laws in which it finds expression. Halakhah in its details discriminates against women because the world of law is male-defined and places men at the center. Women are objects of the law but neither its creators nor agents. Halakhot concerning the religious sphere assume a world in which women are "enablers." Women create the preconditions for men and male children to worship and study Torah, but women cannot do these things themselves without becoming less effective in their relational role. Laws concerning family status assume the essential passivity of women. Women are "acquired" in marriage and are passive in the dissolution of marriage, so that the law deprives them of control in important areas of their lives.[96]

But the presupposition of women's Otherness affects the content of the law well beyond the concrete instances of women's subordination. It shapes the very boundaries of the legal system, the questions that are raised and the questions that are never considered. Rachel Adler cites the discussion in Talmudic Tractate *Ketubot* of whether a woman should be considered a virgin for purposes of her marriage contract, if a man had intercourse with her when she was under three years old.[97] Since the rabbis rule in the woman's favor that she should be considered a virgin, the case would not fall under the category of halakhic disability. Yet the real problem with the discussion is not *how* they answer the question but the fact the question is raised at all. Surely, from a woman's perspective, the important questions have to do not with whether the little girl is tainted but with how such things can happen, "how the man [will] be held morally accountable for his behavior, and what compensation [is] due the child." From the perspective of a legal system in which women's sexuality is the possession of father or husband, however, such questions cannot arise.[98]

The first layers of criticism of halakhah, then, examine what the law has done to women, how it has disabled them, marginalized them, and passed over their concerns. Once the thoroughly patriarchal character of halakhah is understood and criticized, however, other levels of exploration emerge that put women back at the center. Thus, to begin with, what is the changing historical relationship of women to this androcentric system? The assumption of women's Otherness that shapes halakhah is no less present in traditional Jewish histories. In narrative as well as halakhah, women's roles are downplayed or undermined; women's questions and concerns are relegated to silence. Yet by reading between the lines of historical narratives or supplementing them with other material, we can partially recover a broader historical context in which women functioned as subjects and agents. What is women's history in relation to halakhah? How have women shaped the law, observed or responded to it, undermined or cherished it, used it to their own ends?

With respect to women as direct sources of legislation, it may be that further research will yield little that is new.[99] The right to make halakhic decisions was carefully regulated and controlled in a manner that almost certainly excluded women. Other avenues of leadership may have been open to women, but lawmaking required extensive knowledge and study available only to an elite group of men. The few women like Beruriah who could argue fine points of the law were probably rare exceptions.[100] Yet Rachel Biale may be overstating the case when she says that "women . . . participated in the evolution of the halakhah" only insofar as they encountered problems in daily life that required legal decisions and carried them out once they were made.[101]

Making law directly is not the only way of affecting the legal process. Legislators often formalize already prevailing custom or refrain from passing laws they know will be widely ignored. Maimonides' statement that the daughters of Israel imposed certain restrictions on themselves in relation to menstrual purity (*niddah*), restrictions that now have the force of law, suggests that women may have influenced the legal process by taking on certain extralegal obligations.[102] Were there mechanisms through which women's behavior might have precipitated or delayed halakhic change? What was the relationship between rabbinic legislation and wider Jewish practice? And aside from women's influence on halakhah, what was the influence of halakhah on women? If, for example, it was women who strengthened the laws of *niddah*, did they do so out of religious fervor and commitment to the law or a desire to protect themselves from male sexuality? Could women find ways to shape the law to their own purposes, with what consciousness and in what ways?[103]

These questions point to areas of historical research that are essential to a feminist analysis of halakhah. Yet a feminist analysis cannot rest with the historical evidence but must also raise the further issue of the relationship between halakhah as a category and women's experience. Halakhah was and is a central vehicle of Jewish religious expression. Historically, women would have had to adapt to it, to accept and respond to it in some way. But that does not mean that law is especially congenial to women or that women would have expressed themselves through law given other options. The historical question must thus be separated from the contemporary one: Is there a feminist critique of the law as law? Or to phrase the issue as baldly and badly as possible: Is law a female form?

Put flatly in this way, the question is problematic. It seems to presuppose an innate female nature that may or may not be at odds with legal reasoning. It also implies that law is dispensable, that at some point it sprang into being as a male invention rather than evolving gradually from the existence of basic obligations and customs that characterize all human cultures.[104] Yet the issue of the relation between law and gender needs to be posed in some form, for modern studies of children's play have uncovered differences in the games of boys and girls that raise intriguing questions about women and certain aspects of law. It appears that (at least in some strata of modern western culture) boys, through childhood, are "increasingly fascinated with the legal elaboration of rules and the development of fair procedures for adjudicating conflicts, a fascination that . . . does not hold for girls."[105] When conflicts arise in the course of boys' play, boys create a system of rules to resolve them, often appearing to enjoy the legal debates as much as the games themselves. Conflict is more likely to end girls' play; continuing a game is less important than continuing relationships. Rules for girls are largely pragmatic; they can be discarded when a game is no longer enjoyable for its participants. "Girls are more tolerant in their attitudes toward rules, more willing to make exceptions, and more easily reconciled to innovations."[106]

It is possible to make too much of this slender and culturally specific data. But it does suggest that the socialization of girls to the importance of relationships may make them uncomfortable with clear and elaborate rules. Girls' games *do* have unspoken rules, rules about the significance of relationships. But girls seem to experience the development of secondary rules as conflicting with the specificities of relationship, as subordinating the concreteness of friendship to an abstract system. These studies may add up only to the obvious point that, in a culture in which women are not the lawmakers, women are not socialized to make law. But then women's exclusion from halakhic decision making in traditional Jewish culture might be supported by a socialization process that makes halakhic argument seem basically uninteresting. Would women's spirituality then be less fully halakhic than the spirituality of the male elite? I do not mean by this that halakhah would have been unimportant in women's lives, but that, excluded from the spiritual path of legal study and argument, women might have developed other avenues to God more fully.

This suggestion is highly theoretical and speculative, of course. Though it is tempting to do so, it is also dangerous to read contemporary research back into a different social world. Leaving the historical questions to historical investigation, a safer feminist approach to the centrality of law in contemporary Judaism would begin with feminist experience and the issue of whether it points in non-nomian directions. It could be argued that the emphases on fluidity and relationship in feminist spirituality at least raise questions about halakhah and its role in a feminist Judaism.

Feminist rituals provide an interesting case in point for considering the relationship between feminism and halakhah. Insofar as a developing Jewish feminist spirituality expresses itself in ritual, open structure has been a central value. Many Rosh Hodesh groups, for example, draw their themes from the particular month or use parts of the traditional Rosh Hodesh ritual, but these elements provide only a framework around which to weave the individual concerns and contributions of the members.[107] The primary item on the agenda is the religious needs of the women present, their associations with the topic of the day, and their lives in the month that has passed. In other contexts as well, fluid structure is a significant aspect of feminist ritual. Indeed, sometimes it appears to be largely structural openness that defines a ritual as feminist.[108]

Why fluidity should be so important is unclear.[109] In part, commitment to fluidity may be linked to an implicit critique of hierarchy. In the consciousness-raising groups that marked the beginning of the second wave of feminism, open and nonhierarchical structure was highly valued. No one and no thing was to exercise power over the group, for every woman had something to contribute, and every woman had a right to be heard.[110] In a highly structured ritual, the form itself dominates the group, and that domination may feel inherently unfeminist. Not even the structure of a service should control the participants—certainly not the structure of the traditional male service. But while the necessity for openness is itself an unspoken feminist rule, there is clearly an antinomian side to the value placed on openness. Whether this value is inherent in or necessary to feminism or represents a residue from the encounter group and the 1960s is another question.

Criticism of hierarchy is not the only reason for fluidity in feminist ritual, however. More important is the fact that open rituals both foster relationships among the members of a group and turn relationship into an important theme of ritual. The emphasis on relationship, its psychological and historical significance for women, and its ethical and religious value has been a hallmark of feminist writing.[111] In allowing for the free flow of energy in a group, and in making space for group process to be part of the subject of ritual, feminist rituals nourish a spirituality of relation. The power and excitement of feminist rituals emerge out of the web of relation rituals create, and the sacred is met or experienced through the power of relation. Given the centrality of relationship in feminist spirituality, the most significant tensions between feminism and halakhah would likely be located here.

Whether an emphasis on relationship is inherently non-nomian is an interesting question. While many feminists may no longer be able to participate comfortably in such community, traditional Jewish worship certainly can create community among the participants. In addition, the accepted lack of decorum in many traditional synagogues testifies to the important relational function worship serves. What a feminist service tries to integrate into the ritual, a traditional service accomplishes informally and semi-illicitly. Beyond the ritual context, moreover, it is hardly the purpose of halakhah to impede relation. Indeed, it might be said that all relationships presuppose basic moral rules. The motive behind halakhah in codifying these rules is to remember the relationship to God in every moment of existence, to sanctify every action and interaction with others. The sanctification of everyday experience would affect the quality of human relations and foster relation with the law's ultimate source.

But if halakhah has its religious origins in the passion for relation, it may nonetheless block relation in a variety of ways. For one, the law comes to attain its own life apart from the fabric of relation, and that independent life may become a barrier between people and between human beings and God. A frequently cited midrash has the sages on one side of a halakhic conflict call on the divine power to support their cause. God makes the walls of the academy lean, a brook run backward, and a voice call out from heaven to support the decisions of a particular rabbi. But the sages on the other side of the dispute do not accept these miracles. "It [the law] is not in heaven" they say—and prevail. "For the Torah has already been given from Mount Sinai and we pay no attention to a heavenly voice."[112] Of the many lessons that can be drawn from this fascinating story, one is the autonomy of the legal order. Once the rabbis have elaborated a series of rules for deciding halakhah on the basis of earlier texts and decisions, legal judgment and reasoning can operate quite free of the divine presence, and the resulting independent system may have considerable fascination and charm. Observance of the law can then come to substitute for the original relation, with "God's law" replacing God in a system that is self-enclosed and self-perpetuating.[113]

But it is not just God who is no longer necessary to an autonomous halakhah. The delights of legal argumentation can also lead to a certain distance from the concrete world of people and things.[114] There is a paradoxical sense in which the great and loving detail of halakhah turns it into an abstraction. On the one hand, the beauty of halakhic spirituality is that it is connected to this world in all its particularity. On the other, the halakhist's delight in possible particulars can distract attention from what actually is. When as much or more consideration is lavished on the specifics of a Temple ritual long suspended as on laws still in daily use, the solid world fades before the alternate reality halakhah creates. What is earning a livelihood, or what are runny noses next to the laws of tents and leprosy?[115] Or, in terms of the little girl penetrated before age three, what is her horror and pain next to the question of how her marriage contract should be written?

Another way in which the law may block relation is on the level of individual decision. Every legal system must balance the demands of equality and predictability with the demands of substantive justice. "When there is too great a commitment to upholding the autonomy and integrity of the legal process," justice can be undone.[116] Where the law changes to take into account every particular circumstance, the resulting rules are too variable to be usefully relied on. But insofar as law must generalize, it cannot necessarily respond to the situation of the individual person. It must subordinate the concreteness of relation to the rationality of the legal order. This may be why the little girl on the playground uses rules with some freedom and abandons them easily; they are less important than the details of friendship. It may also be why Martin Buber, the great philosopher of relation, refuses to accept the law as the essence of revelation. "I cannot admit the law transformed by man into the realm of my will, if I am to hold myself ready for the unmediated word of God directed to a specific hour of my life."[117]

The result of these deliberations is ambiguous. Halakhah may block relation, or it may not. The rules it prescribes for ritual may prevent important interaction in a group or provide a structure within which community can happen. Halakhah can replace God as the center of religious life or lead to God as its purpose and meaning. It can be a wall between the individual and the world or a way to apprehend the world more deeply. This ambiguity is deepened when we realize that feminist Jews are ourselves creating new norms to govern our communities. The "law" that Jewish women should be counted in a minyan is as deeply held a religious principle for feminists as its contrary for traditional Jews. The convictions that women should study and read Torah, serve as witnesses, and have equal legal rights in marriage are fundamental to feminism. Are these principles and convictions "halakhah" or are they not? Perhaps what distinguishes feminist Judaism from traditional rabbinic Judaism is not so much the absence of law in the former as a conception of rule-making as a shared communal process.[118]

Certainly, when it comes to the presuppositions that traditionally have undergirded the halakhic system, the feminist critique is much clearer than it is of law itself. The assumption that halakhah is sacred in all its details because it was given by God to Moses on Sinai is challenged by a feminist "hermeneutics of suspicion" that regards the law as a human creation and examines it critically in light of the social order it presupposes and creates. Halakhah may represent a response to profound religious experience, but the law itself is not divine; it is formulated by men in a patriarchal culture. Halakhah is thoroughly androcentric. It envisions and supports a patriarchal order. Those whom the law benefits may see it as God-given, but the outsider, the Other, knows it differently.

The feminist as feminist, then, must insist with the liberal Jew that whatever the religious origins of halakhah, it is also rooted in and serves a human social order. For the feminist who chooses to work with halakhah, this presupposition potentially frees the halakhic process from some of its rigidity and abstractness. Obviously, it entails rejecting the argument that halakhah cannot be altered because it represents the will of God. But beyond this, if halakhah gives structure and content to a human religious and social vision, then it is the responsibility of those who shape the law to ensure it expresses and forwards a vision that is humane. From a feminist perspective, recognition of the human origins of halakhah must find expression in the commitment to forming a new and more inclusive religious and social order. If feminism is hardly alone in asserting the human character of halakhah, the depth of its critique of the law demands a more imaginative and wide-ranging transformation of halakhah than has thus far been undertaken by any group that takes the law seriously.

But if feminists can imagine an attitude toward halakhah that is compatible with radical halakhic change, we must also be suspicious of the claim that only halakhic change is legitimate, that without halakhah there is no Judaism.[119] The historical evidence indicates that halakhah has played very different roles in different Jewish communities. Some Jewish groups never accepted rabbinic authority; other groups accepted halakhah as a stepping-stone to a fuller apprehension of God, but displaced it from the center of religious experience. Those who define the "normative" tradition have the privilege of identifying their understanding of tradition with what the tradition is and can be. They thus both set the parameters of the legal system and determine the importance of that system in Jewish religious life. But since feminism questions any definition of "normative" Judaism that excludes women's experience, it cannot accept the idea that a Judaism that includes women's experience will necessarily fall within certain predetermined boundaries.

At least one clear point emerges from these considerations. Any halakhah that is part of a feminist Judaism would have to look very different from halakhah as it has been. It would be different not just in its specifics but in its fundamentals. It would begin with the assumption of women's equality and humanity and legislate only on that basis. Laws governing the formation and dissolution of relationships, for example, would acknowledge women's full agency, so that the present laws of marriage and divorce would be ruled unjust and unacceptable. It would be different not only in its content but in its practitioners. Women would shape halakhah along with men, codetermining the questions raised and the answers given. The boundaries of the legal system would be both contracted and expanded as certain questions would become unthinkable, others imperative. It would be different also in method, for it would know that law is human and be aware of and humble before its own potential ideological abuse and captivity. It would be open to continual transformation in the light of deeper understandings of justice.

Such a revolution is not theoretically impossible. The very centrality of the halakhic system was a fruit of the revolutionary changes induced by the destruction of the second Temple. The upheavals wrought by emancipation in general and feminism in particular have brought and demand revolutionary responses. Yet given the political unlikelihood that the whole Jewish world will undergo such a transformation, it is not surprising that some feminists reject halakhah entirely, and others quietly promote revolution in their own communities, making real in their lives the Judaism they hope some day to see in the wider Jewish world. Indeed, as an increasing number of women are being ordained as rabbis or otherwise gaining access to halakhic knowledge, and as an increasing number of communities are functioning at least partly on the basis of deeply held egalitarian principles, a halakhic revolution is already in process.

Insofar as this process is just beginning, however, the deeper question of the compatibility of feminism and law must be left open. It is clear that there are certain tensions between the feminist emphasis on fluidity and relationship and the rigidity and abstractness of the traditional halakhic system. Feminist Judaism is guided by certain norms and principles, but it has not yet reached a stage where the issue of codification has arisen. It is not clear whether a transformed halakhah could respond to basic feminist concerns or what the role of halakhah would be in the broader Jewish feminist religious worldview. Nor is there any reason why there should be just one answer to these questions. Some feminists might choose to commit themselves to a halakhic Judaism, working to change present law so that it no longer hobbles women's lives. Others might take halakhah seriously or articulate and codify the guiding norms of a new feminist practice but without making either set of norms the heart of the religious system. Others may make a sharp distinction between feminist principles and halakhah, defining the latter as fundamentally antithetical to feminism.

The place of halakhah in the feminist transformation of Torah stands, then, on the boundary of past and future. The history of what halakhah has done to women and of women's relationship to halakhah is part of the broader reconstruction of Jewish memory. Women's halakhah, however, and women's self-defined relation to halakhah await the present and the future. The issue of law leads us, therefore, from the past and the question of Torah into the reconstruction of community, the reconceptualization of Israel.

3. Israel: Toward a New Concept of Community

The project of creating a Jewish feminist theology begins with memory, for Jewish existence is rooted in Jewish memory. Both the patriarchal character of Judaism and resources for transforming the tradition are grounded in the Jewish past. Feminists cannot hope to understand women's marginalization within Judaism without understanding where we have come from. Nor can we alter Jewish belief and practice without knowing how our history has shaped us for good and for ill.

Memory is not a static deposit, however; it is neither rules nor happenings that confront us unchanging. As members of living communities, Jews continually re-remember; we retell and recast the Jewish past in light of changing communal experience and changing communal values. Memory is formed and reformed from the interaction of every generation with the fluid richness of Torah. The remembered past provides the basis for a particular present, but the nature of the present also fosters or inhibits particular kinds of memory. In the last chapter, I argued that feminists must retrieve more of Torah, recover a fuller Jewish memory as the foundation for a contemporary community in which women are full participants. It is equally the case, however, that the actual shape of Jewish communities affects what can be remembered, what seems important to preserve and retell.

The issue of Torah, then, is tied to the issue of Israel—a term that, for most of this chapter, I will define as the nature of Jewish community and the Jewish people.[1] Torah is Jewish memory as it lives in and forms the present, and Israel is the people that remembers and transforms memory. If, from a feminist perspective, it is essential to recapture and recreate women's Torah, *the nature of Israel must be such that women's Torah can be remembered and lived.* In this theology, the section on Israel comes between Torah and God because the Jewish people is the material context for the creation and perpetuation of Jewish memory—as well as the locus for the experience of the divine.

Insofar as the concepts of Torah and Israel are not fully separable, I have touched already on the nature of a feminist Israel. Feminist Judaism begins with the presupposition that women as well as men define Jewish humanity. It assumes that Jewish women's experience is an integral part of Jewish experience, and that no account of Jewish experience is complete unless it considers fully and seriously the experience of Jewish women. But if this assumption necessitates reworking Torah, what are its implications for understanding the concept of Israel? What would it mean to have a Jewish community that takes women's experience seriously? What have been the sources and costs of women's marginalization within the people of Israel, and what would constitute rectification? These questions are practical and theological at the same time. The issue of Israel is an issue concerning Jewish communal form and practice, the embodied shape and nature of Jewish life in the Diaspora and in Israel as a modern state. One cannot hope to create a feminist Jewish people, however, without considering certain theological questions: the significance and spiritual dimensions of community, the conceptualization of difference in Jewish life, and the key concept of chosenness.

Personhood, Community, and Difference

Communal Personhood

Any understanding of Israel must begin with the recognition that Israel is a community, a people, not a collection of individual selves. The conviction that personhood is shaped, nourished, and sustained in community is a central assumption that

Judaism and feminism share. For the Jew, for the feminist, for the Jewish feminist, the individual is not an isolated unit who attains humanity through independence from others or who must contract for social relations.[2] Rather, to be a person is to find oneself from the beginning in community—or, as is often the case in the modern world, in multiple communities.[3] To develop as a person is to acquire a sense of self in relation to others and to critically appropriate a series of communal heritages.

For feminists, insistence on the communal character of human selfhood is articulated over against the individualism of the dominant strand in Western culture, and represents the intersection of a number of streams of experience and analysis. The consciousness-raising groups of the 1960s that marked the beginning of the second wave of feminism provided important evidence of the communal nature of human life. Examining our experience in the consciousness-raising context, women were able to piece together the processes of socialization and learning that shape the female role. We were able to see that our self-understandings, our life choices, our expectations of ourselves as women were not the product simply of our own growth and development but of powerful social forces that had molded us from birth. Moreover, at the same time we came to see the communal origins of the constraints on our lives, we also experienced community as the source of our liberation. Coming to a clear understanding of gender as socially constructed, we experienced a new opening of self, a sense of freedom to be and become our own persons rather than to live out prescriptive social roles. But this new sense of autonomous selfhood, like the traditional female self, came and could have come only with others. It was only as we sat and spoke together, as many women told of feelings and troubles that each had seen as her own, that "hearing drew forth . . . speech" and we were able to experience and understand the connections between what had been laid out for us and our own choices.[4] We apprehended selfhood not as something brought ready-made to community but as both shaped by community and enlarged by common commitment and struggle.

This direct and powerful experience of the connection between self and community has been supplemented by trenchant analytical critiques of liberal individualism as a basis for feminist theory. In *The Radical Future of Liberal Feminism*, Zillah Eisenstein argues that there is a fundamental contradiction between the liberal view of people as isolated and self-created and feminist insistence on the social nature of women's oppression. Insofar as mainstream American feminism unconsciously adopts the dominant cultural assumption that individuals can freely and independently form their own lives, it cannot explain the oppression of women as a class or the role of social and political institutions in protecting patriarchal power relations. Only a theory that understands "sex-class oppression" and that "recognizes the importance of the individual within the social collectivity" can generate a politics that will liberate women.[5] In a more metaphysical vein, Catherine Keller has argued that the notion of a "separative self," a self that develops detached from and in opposition to others, is a core part of the mythological, psychological, and political bases of patriarchy. In her view, the "relational entrapment" that has been women's lot, when analyzed and appropriated from a feminist perspective, offers an alternative picture of the self that is truer to human experience and contradicts fundamental patriarchal assumptions.[6]

Keller's discussion of relation as women's traditional mode of being brings in a third stream in the feminist affirmation of the communal character of selfhood. Feminist experience of communal personhood and feminist political and philosophical analyses of social selfhood cohere with women's historical experience of embeddedness in and responsibility for relation. As the extensive literature on women and relation attests, women generally have been denied the luxury of believing in the separate individual ego; we have been forced to know ourselves as dependent and depended on by others.[7] While much of the literature of relation is based on white middle-class women's experience, the testimony of minority women only expands and deepens this insistence on connection. For many minority women, the sense of group solidarity in oppression has been a basic reality of existence.[8] In discussing the survival strategies of black women, for example, Delores Williams highlights "relational forms of independence": black women have endured by forming strong bonds with other women and with men, developing broad kin and friendship networks for childcare and housing, and engaging in organized resistance to the conditions of oppression.[9] Under the conditions of patriarchy, women's experience of relation has been distorted by sex, race, and class oppression, and women have been kept from self-determination within the web of connection. But this cannot negate the fact that women's relegation to the sphere of relation has kept women alive to a basic dimension of human experience that feminism affirms even as it seeks to transform the material character of human relations.

The knowledge that human beings are located in community is, of course, not limited to women; shared by many cultures, it is central to both Jewish theology and the Jewish social experience. If to be a woman is to absorb and wrestle with a cultural understanding of femaleness, so to be a Jew is to absorb the history of the Jewish people. Jewish memory is communal memory and centers on community even as it forms and is formed by community. The patriarchal nature of the Bible does not abrogate its thoroughgoing insistence on the social nature of human and divine existence. The statement in Genesis that "it is not good for the earth creature to be alone" (2:18) finds its echo in the divine plural—"let us make humankind in our image" (1:26)—that enters the text only with the creation of the first human beings.[10] The covenantal history that begins with Abraham, Isaac, and Jacob finds its fulfillment only at Sinai, when the whole congregation answers together, "All that the Lord has spoken we will do" (Ex. 19:8). Though the Israelites are designated a people even in Egypt (Ex. 1:9), it is only when they receive life and teachings as a community at Sinai that their prior history becomes important to remember. If you obey my covenant, God tells them, "you shall be to me a kingdom of priests and a holy nation" (Ex. 19:6); at the moment of establishing the covenant, its corporate nature is affirmed.[11] Indeed, according to Martin Buber, the purpose of the decalogue given at Sinai is none other than to establish a community "by means of common regulation." It is not the religious and ethical life of the individual the Ten Commandments address but that of the nation. The commandments deal with community: first, with the God of community, second, with the rhythm of weeks and of generations in the national life, and third, with the space of community, with norms "for mutual relations between its members."[12] From Sinai on, the Jewish relationship to God is mediated through this community. The Jew stands before God not as an individual but as a member of a people.

The theological significance of community in Judaism finds expression in religious, social, and national life. While the observant Jew is expected to pray three times daily whether alone or with others, there is a definite bias on behalf of public prayer. Maintaining a daily minyan is regarded as an important function of the synagogue. Certain key prayers simply cannot be said unless there are ten men (sic) present, and the divine presence is said to rest in a unique way on the congregation. According to Rabbi Johanan, "When God comes to a synagogue and does not find a minyan there, [God] is angry, as it is written, 'Why, when I came, was there no one? When I called was there no one to answer?' (Isa. 50:2)"[13] It seems that once God establishes a covenant with the people as a whole, God is fully present only with and among the community. The individual who prays privately loses an important dimension of worship, and God hardly recognizes the people unless they are together.

Beyond the requirements of prayer, the sociological exigencies of Jewish existence also made for community. In some areas of the Diaspora, anti-Semitic legislation compelled Jews to live in certain districts; but even in areas where ghettos were not mandated by law, the Jews' relation to the larger political order was mediated through the Jewish community. Local communities (*kehillot*) operated semi-autonomously both in relation to each other and the wider Gentile culture, offering their members a range of services that today would be provided by a combination of charitable, religious, and state institutions.[14] In Israel's Museum of the Diaspora, a panorama of Jewish communal institutions in thirteenth- and fourteenth-century Germany includes a rabbinic academy, synagogue, ritual bath, rabbinic court, ritual slaughterer, burial society, soup kitchen, shelter for the destitute, and associations for charity, hospitality, and visiting the sick. Just as the Jew's relationship to God is mediated through membership in the Jewish people, so the Jew's relationship to society was mediated through the *kehillah* which, in addition to providing for individual and communal needs, levied the taxes to be paid to the government and generally managed relations with the non-Jewish world.

Diaspora communities were never to be the ultimate expression of Jewish communality, however. In biblical times, and later in hope and prayer, community was to manifest itself in a national life. From God's first call to Abraham, the existence of the Jewish people was linked to the promise of a land (Gen. 12:1–2; 17:1–8), and the "holy nation" established at Sinai was to embody its relationship with God with a fullness possible only on its own soil. Diaspora communities, for all their richness and diversity, represented a compromise with historical circumstances. Jews scattered from China to India to Europe would have shared the hope of a messianic restoration to Zion where God, people, land, and community would no longer be in tension and the covenant would find expression in every detail of communal life.

Women in the Jewish Community

The similarities between feminist and Jewish understandings of the relation between self and community are substantial and genuine, and I have addressed the theme of community in Judaism without irony. Yet from a feminist perspective, the Jewish emphasis on community is deeply ambiguous and ironic, for it coexists with the subordination of women within Jewish communal life. Affirming community, Judaism affirms a male community in which the place of women is an open and puzzling question. At times, it seems as if women are simply not part of Israel at all; more usually, women's presence in the community is assumed, but assumed as clearly peripheral.

When, for example, God enters into a covenant with Abraham and says to him, "This is my covenant, which you shall keep, between me and you and your descendants after you: Every male among you shall be circumcised" (Gen. 17:10), women can hear this only as establishing our marginality. Even if circumcision is not itself the covenant but only the sign of the covenant, what role can women have in the covenant community when the primary symbol of the covenant pertains only to men? This important passage seems to presuppose a religious community composed of males only, an impression reinforced by other texts. The covenant at Sinai is spoken in male pronouns, for example, and its content assumes male hearers.[15] But the very same sources that can be taken to indicate the exclusion of women from Israel are often contradictory or equivocal. The appearance and disappearance of women in the story of Sinai, the fact that women's presence is assumed even in Moses' injunction to the men to stay away from them, legal treatment of women's sexuality and status where unique biology or some anomaly demand it, make clear that, while women are hardly equal in the Israelite community, they are also not simply absent.

The place of women in the community of Israel is illuminated most fully by Simone de Beauvoir's notion of woman as Other.[16] De Beauvoir points out that women *cannot* simply be excluded from community, for the relationship between men and women is not like other relationships between oppressor and oppressed. Men and women are parts of a totality in which, biologically speaking, both sides are necessary. Without women, it is impossible that any community could continue. Yet as far as normative Jewish texts are concerned, women are perceived largely in terms of the need for biological continuity. Women do not participate in defining the values that make the community distinctive or that warrant its perpetuation. As de Beauvoir says, "Humanity is male and man defines woman not in herself but as relative to him."[17] Thus women *are* part of the covenant community, but precisely in a submerged and nonnormative way.

A recent theological text provides an excellent example of this ambiguous status of women in Jewish society, for it translates biblical modes of thinking about women into clear, contemporary terms. Michael Wyschogrod's *The Body of Faith: Judaism as Corporeal Election* assumes the identity of Jewishness and maleness and yet leaves room for the existence of Jewish women, who represent Israel's unredeemed flesh. In this book, circumcision is the core symbol of a concept of election that takes seriously the embodied, corporeal life of the Jewish people. The exclusionary implications of God's covenant with Abraham are reiterated and elaborated as circumcision becomes the root metaphor for all forms of sacrifice demanded by the divine/human relation. "Israel's symbol of the covenant is circumcision, a searing of the covenant into the flesh of Israel and not only, or perhaps not even primarily, into its spirit." "The Law cuts into all the human modes of exercising the life-force: eating, drinking, appropriating property, etc. All of these are circumcised in Judaism." It is not difficult to gather who constitutes Israel here or who is excluded from this understanding. Still women are not entirely invisible, for they point us to the "thick underbrush," the "greater darkness" of a flesh that is not cut or sacrificed.

Israel is a people of great spirituality, but it is also a people of the flesh, which was well known to the prophets who lamented the seductive tinkle of the ornaments that bedecked the daughters of Israel. . . . The daughters of Israel do not fully understand the function of their beauty, the role in the divine plan played by their charm.

Women are the flesh of the fleshly community, a role that is necessarily unconscious and which therefore must be articulated by men.[18] Thus at the same time women are members of the community, they are members as Other—the Other who easily vanishes behind a male-defined understanding of Israel.

It is not simply narrative and theological sources that reveal the place of women in the Jewish community, however, but also halakhah. Halakhah seeks to regulate communal behavior and concretize communal ideals. The exclusion of women from public religious life and women's disabilities under family law arise out of and delineate a conception of women's communal role. As Moshe Meiselman suggests, the traditional sphere of women is captured by the verse from Psalms (45:14), "The entire glory of the daughter of the king lies on the inside." This passage, which is used by the rabbis to discourse on the appropriately private nature of women's role, is enforced and given structure through halakhic rulings.[19] The exemption of women from public prayer and Torah study and the careful regulation of women's place within the patriarchal family together carve out a sex-linked division of the community. Since in many periods of Jewish history, women helped earn the family livelihood, this division does not correspond exactly to the public/private distinction in our modern sense. It does write into law, however, male control of public religious values and the male definition of women in terms of female biology.

Because women's Otherness in Jewish communal life corresponds to women's silence in Torah, I have already examined many of these ideas from a somewhat different angle. Approaching women's situation in Judaism from the perspective of the concept of Israel, however, clarifies the mechanisms through which silence is accepted as natural. If women's absence from Torah is used to justify the subordination of women in contemporary Judaism, the marginalization of women within the Jewish community confirms and validates a history that ignores women's agency. As long as women's Otherness is an accepted part of Jewish life, the past understanding of women as Other need never be questioned. Thus the unequal role of women in Judaism perpetuates false memories that are accepted as accurate because they are felt to be in continuity with present practice. In other words, *an Israel in which women are Other is the material base for the preservation and reenactment of a partial view of Torah.*

But if focusing on Israel helps illuminate the context in which androcentric memories are preserved, it also, and most poignantly, highlights the spiritual disempowerment sustained by Jewish women. Jewish feminists have often, and with reason, seen the place of women in the Jewish community as a justice issue. The fact that we have been excluded from the public religious forum and socialized to a limited set of family roles has kept women from fully developing as people and has deprived the Jewish community of the energy and talents of half its members. Halakhah has cordoned off from women just those avenues of religious expression the tradition values most highly. Torah study, Torah reading, leadership of the congregation, daily participation in public prayer are important vehicles of religious experience that women either have not been encouraged to develop or have been altogether denied.

Yet once we see the importance of community in the Jewish experience, we must add to all this another dimension of loss that women suffer. Over and above the value of participation in any particular religious activity is the spiritual aspect of community itself. It is not just that community is the space within which one fulfills a range of religious duties and reaps a range of spiritual rewards, but that community is the primary vehicle and place of religious experience. Thus God did not establish the covenant at *Sinai* because it was easier to speak to the people when they were gathered together than to address them individually. God's presence constituted them a community, and it was as a community that they heard the voice of God. If women are submerged in the covenant community at Sinai, then we are peripheral to the central moment of Jewish religious experience. There is no Jewish way to go off into the desert and have an independent relationship to God. Relationship to God is experienced and mediated precisely through the community that in reality and in memory maintains women's marginality.

No panegyric on the virtues of private spirituality can disguise the fact that the nature of religious experience in Judaism is fundamentally communal or that the historical importance of public worship has a spiritual grounding: The divine presence rests in community in a uniquely powerful way. But this means that the exclusion of women from full membership in the Jewish community is *in itself,* apart from exclusion from this or that religious obligation, exclusion of women from a profound and central dimension of Jewish spiritual life. Women's Otherness is not just a matter of social and religious marginality but of spiritual deprivation.

The reality and significance of the spiritual dimension of community is clear to many Jewish feminists, for feminist community too is a place and vehicle for relationship to God. Women discovering in community the power of our individual and collective voices have discovered that this power is connected to a greater one that grounds and sustains it. If, for both Judaism and feminism, community is not in conflict with selfhood but allows and nurtures it, so community itself is rooted in and succored by a more embracing reality that is also the ultimate horizon of the self. The feminist experience of personal empowerment can lead to a sense of participation in an energy and process that finally enfolds the cosmos and that is responded to and enacted by the individual and the community. Richard R. Niebuhr, in his description of rejoicing, captures perfectly the experience of many feminists that discovering our own autonomy also means discovering our relation to a larger project that embraces and transcends humanity.

[Rejoicing] entails consciousness of liberation into the stream of life, a sense of collectedness, a feeling of the union of one's own power with power and energy itself, and finally a sense of effectiveness and of recognition as an agent in a human commonwealth that transcends the present.[20]

In linking together community, connection to divine power, and the sense of personal power and agency, Niebuhr's work clarifies further the extent to which the traditional Jewish framework deprives women spiritually. On the one hand, exclusion of women from public religious life means that women are excluded from a source of communal connection with God that can foster a sense of individual purpose and agency. On the other hand, the suppression of women's agency through the perpetuation of false memory and women's subordination within the community means suppression of the divine energy within the self that is connected to a greater power. Thus the limited roles assigned to women constrict our spirituality, and the constriction of our spirituality fosters acceptance of limited roles and a partial version of our history. The traditional structures of the Jewish community limit women's ability either to add to Torah or to remember the Torah that is ours.

Toward a Redefinition of Israel

At the same time, however, that the suppression of women is a real and significant aspect of Jewish life, it is just one side of Jewish women's situation. It is also the case that control of women's agency and spirituality never has been wholly effective. Though women's roles have been restricted and rendered invisible, women have in fact functioned as actors and have found outlets for their spirituality in licit and illicit places. The identification of normative Jewishness with maleness has had a profound effect on women. Yet it cannot alter the fact that Jews are men and women, and we can know Israel and its history only by looking at the experience of both.

To redefine Israel from a feminist perspective, we must incorporate the reality of women's presence into the understanding and practice of the Jewish people so that women's contributions to Jewish community are not driven underground, thwarted, or distorted, and men's are not given more weight and status than they ought to enjoy. Until that happens, both our concept of

Israel and the dynamics of Jewish life will remain thoroughly misshapen by sexism. The contributions of women to Judaism will continue to be passed over in silence. Women's roles in the community will be limited, our spirituality constricted, our activity forced to find its way around blockages or to define itself over against traditional restrictions. Male activity and spirituality will continue to enjoy a false universality and normativeness that distort our understanding of Jewishness and further disguise and limit women's participation. And the Jewish community as a whole will remain deprived of its full history, and of the energy, interplay, and creative differences of its members.

These dynamics are entrenched and complexly interwoven. Yet, on the theoretical level at least, it appears fairly easy to imagine a way around them. Ostensibly, the goal of Jewish feminism is precisely the equality between men and women that would throw off the limitations placed on women and allow us to take our place beside men as full participants in Jewish life. The subordination of women is the center of the feminist critique of Judaism, and access for women to Jewish institutions and ceremonies is the basic feminist demand. There may be numerous practical impediments to achieving this end, but on a conceptual level, the goal seems clear. How can the equality of women now a fact in many individual Jewish communities become the norm in Jewish life? How can women in any individual congregation organize effectively to gain access to roles from which they have been excluded? Are there ways to reinterpret particular legal impediments to women's participation in and leadership of Jewish ritual? What are the best ways to encourage and facilitate halakhic change? Will the Orthodox community ever allow women a fuller role, and what steps might lead to desired reforms?

But while feminists need to address the concrete obstacles to women's involvement in Jewish life, and Israel needs to change in the world and not only on paper, restructuring the nature of Israel is conceptually less simple than the goal of equal access makes it seem. Equality cannot be the central feminist aim, for equality assumes as given the system in which women are to be equal.[21] Women joining egalitarian minyanim often take for granted the content of weekly worship. Women fighting for equal rights in the public Jewish forum do not necessarily question the sexual division of spheres that undergirds women's marginalization. Women striving for halakhic change generally assume the legitimacy and authority of halakhah. Women as individual Jews seeking entry into a male-defined system do not necessarily look at the ways in which the Otherness of women as a class has shaped the development of Judaism from its origins.

If we are to take seriously, however, the importance of community in human life, we cannot repeat in relation to Judaism the liberal feminist mistake of seeing women as individuals who happen to be discriminated against in the Jewish system. If women fight for equality on liberal terms, then we will gain access to a community that structures its central ideas and institutions around male norms, without changing the character of those ideas or institutions. Women in Judaism—like women in any patriarchal culture—are rendered invisible *as a class;* we are seen as Other *as a class;* we are deprived of agency *as a class.* Until we understand and change the ways in which Judaism as a system supports the subordination of Jewish women as a sub-community within the Jewish people, genuine equality of women and men is impossible.

The real challenge of feminism to Judaism emerges, not when women as individual Jews demand equal participation in the male tradition, but when women demand equality *as Jewish women,* as the class that has up until now been seen as Other. To phrase the feminist challenge to Judaism in an other than liberal way, we might say that the central issue in the feminist redefinition of Israel is the place of difference in community. Judaism can absorb many women rabbis, teachers, and communal leaders; it can ignore or change certain laws and make adjustments around the edges; it can live with the ensuing contradictions and tensions without fundamentally altering its self-understanding. But when women, with our own history and spirituality and attitudes and experiences, demand equality in a community that will allow itself to be changed by our differences, when we ask that our memories become part of Jewish memory and our presence change the present, then we make a demand that is radical and transforming. Then we begin the arduous experiment of trying to create a Jewish community in which difference is neither hierarchalized nor tolerated but truly honored. Then we begin to struggle for the only equality that is genuine.

The Issue of Difference in Community

Since the insistence that women be accepted in Judaism as women may seem neither new nor radical, it is important to define where its challenge lies. It is not the recognition of difference that is in itself difficult. Judaism has always recognized—indeed insisted on—the differences between women and men. But it is of the essence of these differences as traditionally understood that they have been hierarchalized and defined from the perspective of the dominant group. What is new about Jewish feminism is that *women* are claiming the right to define and assess our differences, that we are revaluing and renaming what has been used to oppress us. The fact that this undertaking on the part of Jewish feminists is analogous to struggles both of minority feminists and of Jews in the modern West brings into focus the enormous obstacles to creating communities rich in diversity and accountable to different perspectives. Examining some of the connections between the feminist, Jewish, and Jewish feminist situations may help clarify what is at stake in redefining Israel as a commmunity that honors difference.

The feminist context is in some ways the most instructive for understanding the problem of difference in community because contemporary feminism has had a strong ideological commitment to including all women. The consciousness-raising groups of the 1960s tried to free themselves from the structures of domination in the wider society in order to provide spaces where every woman could be heard. Commitment to the bonds of sisterhood in the face of the pervasive nature of sexism was supposedly rooted in affirmation of all women's experience and each woman's struggle. As minority women increasingly have made clear, however, feminist theory and priorities often have ignored the multiple communities that shape women's lives. Assuming that male/female difference is the oldest and only important social difference, white middle-class feminists many times have constructed accounts of women's experience that falsely universalize a particular cultural and class perspective.[22]

For instance, Betty Friedan's *The Feminine Mystique*, the landmark book of liberal feminism, spoke of "the problem that has no name"—the longing for something beyond house and family—as if all women share the plight of college-educated married white women, and as if women of color and poor white women had not always worked to support themselves and others.[23] Her identification of "woman" with a particular group of women is echoed and reechoed in feminist writing. It is illustrated by the persistence of anti-Semitic stereotypes in feminist literature, the additive analyses of sexism and racism that ignore the reality of many women's lives, and exclusionary phrases such as "women and blacks" that appear and reappear in feminist writing.[24] The message such work communicates to minority women—Jewish women as well as women of color, although in different ways—is that if we want to be part of the "women's" movement, we should bring ourselves as women in the abstract (that is, women of the dominant group), leaving aside the particular women we happen to be.[25]

Commitment to feminism does not, then, automatically entail willingness to relinquish race, class, and religious privilege—or even to acknowledge they exist. In part, the persistence of race and class prejudice within the women's movement can be attributed to a liberal ideology that disguises the real power relations within society; but fear of difference is itself a factor that continues to divide women from each other. Once we acknowledge the diversity and multiplicity of women's loyalties, what guarantee is there that we will find a common ground? Moreover, Audre Lorde suggests that when women have been educated in a society that sees all difference in terms of inferiority and superiority, "the recognition of any difference must be fraught with guilt."[26] Concerned that—as has so often happened in the past—recognizing difference will lead to inequality, feminists repeatedly have adopted the strategy of pretending that differences between women do not exist. But, of course, denying differences does not abolish them; it simply allows traditional forms of domination to continue unacknowledged. Moreover, avoiding differences prevents women from mining the knowledge and power that are rooted in our racial, ethnic, and religious particularity and from using "difference as a springboard for creative change."[27]

If feminism claims to respect difference and yet at the same time denies it, the modern West's offer of civil rights to the Jews was never premised on the acceptance of difference, even as a theoretical possibility. Jewish emancipation—the grant of full citizenship and legal equality—was based on the expectation that "in the absence of persecution and enforced segregation, Jews and Judaism would assimilate to the prevailing social and cultural norms of the environment."[28] The dominant groups in various European nations explicitly claimed the right to define the reality to which Jews would accommodate themselves. Jews were granted free access to the wider culture, but only at the cost of the communal autonomy that had characterized Jewish life for centuries, and that had provided Jews with community, identity, and a set of common beliefs and values. In the words of a liberal deputy to the French national assembly, "One must refuse everything to the Jews as a nation but one must give them everything as individuals."[29] Relinquishing all Jewish particularity, Jews were to become Germans or Britons or French-people of the Jewish religion, a religion that would now stress universal values and give up its peculiar and discriminatory forms. Insofar as Jews insisted on continuing to define their identity in ethnic as well as religious terms, they were regarded as reneging on a clear bargain and as occasioning the discrimination that legal emancipation did not eradicate. As *The Christian Century* asked rhetorically in a 1930s editorial, "Can democracy suffer a hereditary minority to perpetuate itself as a permanent minority, with its own distinctive culture sanctioned by its own distinctive cult form?"[30] The writer is unable to imagine a democracy in which citizens share certain common values, yet also maintain allegiance to traditional subcommunities.

In the early period of emancipation, Jews embraced the benefits of citizenship, accepting—sometimes willingly, sometimes out of necessity—the implicit or explicit conditions that went along.[31] The Assembly of Jewish Notables that gathered in Paris from 1806 to 1807 in response to a decree of Napoleon insisted that as "Frenchmen professing the religion of Moses, . . . they are fully determined to prove worthy of the favors His majesty intends for them, by scrupulously conforming to his paternal intention."[32] Modernizers adopted Jewish liturgy to bourgeois tastes; Reform Judaism rejected the authority of halakhah and denied that Jews were in exile; even Orthodoxy combined strict adherence to the law with outward assimilation to secular life and culture.[33]

Two hundred years later, however, the communal and individual costs of emancipation are very clear: assimilation, fragmentation, loss of self-determination, loss of common identity and purpose. In traditional society, Jews may have been outsiders, but they had an important defense against indifference or hatred; their own communal self-understanding radically contradicted the world outside. In the modern world, Jews have more deeply internalized society's expectations and values, becoming divided from the Jew within the self. Social contempt for Jewish particularity finds its echo in Jewish contempt for Jewish noses, Jewish hair, Jewish assertiveness, Jewish mothers, Jewish history, Jewish religious life. Jews unable to affirm our own Jewishness or even to understand its meaning have little energy or creativity to bring to our Jewish communities.

The long struggle by Jews in the modern era to "prove the religious, intellectual, and social viability of Judaism within an open . . . society" —and the struggle of contemporary minority feminists to address differences within the feminist community—makes *The Christian Century*'s question anything but rhetorical.[34] Why is it unthinkable for minority communities to perpetuate themselves within a democracy—or within a movement? Is communal identity and cohesion really at odds with participation in a wider society? Given that, in the modern world, most individuals belong to more than one community, that communal loyalties diverge and overlap, is it not possible to affirm a common commitment to a national or feminist identity without denying other aspects of the self? Is it not possible that the interaction of distinctive subcommunities could enrich a total community? And given the tremendous costs of self-division, given that our full energy is available to us only when we integrate all parts of who we are, is it not in the interests of the state or the women's movement to allow individuals their communal roots?[35] Is not the dream of many Jews in the modern world—acceptance by the broader culture in and through our particularity and not despite it—a worthy starting point for reconceptualizing community?

And what then of Jewish feminists? Jews among feminists, feminists among Jews, Jewish feminists have experienced the burden of difference in all the various communities to which we belong. The distrust of difference that has characterized feminism in relation to minority women and modern nationalist movements in relation to Jews is equally present in the Jewish community. Indeed, non-Orthodox Judaism places women in the same position in the Jewish community that Jews have found ourselves in in relation to the modern state. The bargain is less obvious because the character of Jewish women's bonds and culture is less obvious, being part of the great silence that shrouds women's experience. But insofar as women have distinctive rituals, a history, literature, modes of connection that grow out of centuries of sex role segregation, these are to be abandoned for the privilege of participating in a dominant male culture that does not recognize anything of value in what will now be lost.[36]

Moreover, since Jewish women, like Jews in modern society, are expected to internalize the values of the dominant group, we are also to forget our own history and forget even that it has been forgotten. Lacking a community of Jewish women to counter the perceptions of a male-defined Jewish culture—or a WASP-defined feminist one—our heritage of power as Jewish women is translated into anxiety lest we be dominating Jewish mothers, lest we be perceived as "taking over," or lest there be a Princess lurking in our souls. The Other's Other, we take in both the images of Jews and specifically Jewish women in the wider society, and also the projections of Jewish men.

Clearly, the liberal notion of equality cannot provide an adequate theoretical basis for transforming Israel on feminist terms. Yet the gains of liberalism must not be repudiated in moving beyond liberalism, any more than the costs of emancipation mean it should be revoked. Historically, liberalism made possible the recognition of Jews and women as human beings, an achievement that is the indispensable prerequisite of our true equality. But once we realize that recognizing others as individuals is fully compatible with fostering the power and self-understanding of dominant groups, it becomes necessary to move to an understanding of community that incorporates the accomplishments of liberalism and at the same time responds to its flaws.[37] Jewish feminists want from the Jewish and feminist communities what women of color want from the feminist community, what self-affirming Jews want from the wider culture: equality in our particularity, acknowledgment of the many communities that shape our lives, acknowledgment of our complex history and experience, and attention to that history and experience in the formulation of cultural or religious norms and values.

Chosenness, Hierarchy, and Difference

It is not sufficient, however, simply to call the Jewish community to an acceptance of diversity. To understand more fully
those aspects of Judaism that thwart Jewish acceptance of difference without gradation, we must examine further those ideas
that have contributed to Judaism's long history of conceptual-
izing difference in terms of hierarchical separations. The suspicion and ranking of difference are not things Jews learned
from other peoples; they have been aspects of Judaism since its
beginnings. Thinking of itself as a "kingdom of priests and a
holy nation," the Jewish people understood its own holiness
partly in contradistinction to the beliefs and behavior of surrounding nations. Serving the Lord meant shunning and de-
stroying foreign gods and morality, thus refusing the "snare"
of a different religious system (Ex. 23:23–33). Paralleling external differentiation were a host of internal separations that set
apart distinct and unequal objects, states, and modes of being.
On a religious level, to be a holy people was both to be different
from one's neighbors and to distinguish between and differently honor pure and impure, Sabbath and week, kosher and non-
kosher, Cohen, Levi, and Israel (grades of priests and ordinary
Jews), and male and female. On a social level, the Otherness of
women was the first and most persistent among many inequalities that have marked Jewish life. Differences in wealth, learning, and observance; differences in cultural background and
customs (between, for example, Jews from Eastern Europe,
Spain, or the Orient); differences in religious affiliation and understanding (for example, between Hasidim and Mitnadim—
opponents of the Hasidim—in Europe) have all provided occasions for certain groups of Jews to define themselves as superior
to different and nonnormative Others. The distinction men/
women was never a unique hierarchy but emerged as part of a
system in which many people and aspects of existence were
defined in terms of superiority and inferiority.[38]

This hierarchical understanding of difference is perhaps the most significant barrier to the feminist reconceptualization of Jewish community. Jewish feminists cannot transform the place of women's difference within the people of Israel without addressing the larger system of separations in which it is embedded. This system can be approached from a number of directions.[39] In the context of the reconceptualization of Israel, however, it is the notion of chosenness that is the chief expression of hierarchical separation and therefore the most important focus for discussion. As a central category for Jewish self-understanding that is emblematic of other gradations, chosenness provides a warrant and a model for ranked differentiations within the community and between Israel and others. If Jewish feminism is to articulate a model of community in which difference is acknowledged without being hierarchalized, it will have to engage the traditional Jewish understanding of difference by rejecting the idea of chosenness without at the same time denying the distinctiveness of Israel as a religious community.

Chosenness is a complex and evolving idea in Judaism that is not always associated with claims to superiority. There is a strand in Jewish thinking that attributes chosenness to special qualities in the Jews and that argues for Jewish hereditary spiritual uniqueness and supremacy; by and large, however, Israel's election is viewed not as a matter of merit or attributes but of responsibilities and duties.[40] When the notion of chosenness first appears in the Bible simultaneously with the establishment of Israel as a covenant community, there is no apparent motive for Israel's special status but God's steadfast love and (itself unexplained) earlier promise to the patriarchs (Deut. 7:7–8). Israel's standing as God's "own possession among all peoples" (Ex. 19:5–6; Deut. 7:6) is linked to acceptance and observance of the covenant; this constitutes its specialness in its own eyes and in the eyes of others (Deut. 4:5–7). When Deutero-Isaiah shifts emphasis from election of Israel as holy community to election of Israel as servant to the world, he still gives no reason for God's selection. This prophet of exile calls Israel "a light to the nations" and interprets its suffering as a sign of chosenness and future redemption (Isa. 49:6; 53); but election is marked by suffering, not by exaltation.[41]

If ascription of supernatural sanctity to Israel is the exception rather than the rule, however, this eliminates only some of the troubling aspects of the notion of chosenness. When election is understood as obligation or taken for granted as the foundation of the halakhic life, the privileged nature of Israel's relationship to God remains even while explicit claims to superiority are absent.[42] After all, the traditional male Jew who each morning blesses God for not making him a woman is said to be giving thanks for the special burden and responsibility of halakhic observance, rather than deliberately vaunting his prerogatives. But however humbly he accepts his legal burden, his prayer nonetheless presupposes that women are exempt from halakhic responsibility, that the other side of his privilege is their exclusion. This same dichotomy applies to the gift of chosenness which is similarly acknowledged in the morning blessings. The Jew is grateful to be a Jew because the burden of Jewishness is a boon and privilege others do not share. As the daily liturgy makes amply clear, the lot of the Jews is singular; their special destiny is God's unique choice, not one path among many:

It is our duty to praise the Master of all, to exalt the Creator of the universe, who has not made us like the nations of the world and has not placed us like the families of the earth; who has not designed our destiny to be like theirs, nor our lot like that of all their multitude.[43]

Whether this destiny is characterized in terms of the *noblesse oblige* of witness and service or straightforward claims to metaphysical superiority, it still constitutes a hierarchical differentiation.

Michael Wyschogrod's theology is helpful in clarifying the import of chosenness (just as it was helpful in understanding women's Otherness), for Wyschogrod tries to give meaning to the idea of chosenness without either overstating or fleeing from its implications. For Wyschogrod, as for the tradition as a whole, election is essentially mysterious, stemming not from any special deserving in the Jews but from God's free choice. In Wyschogrod's novel formulation, God fell in love with Abraham, as unaccountably as any person falls in love, and entered into a covenant with Abraham's seed because there God continues to see the face of his (sic) beloved. But if God loves Abraham with a special love, there are others whom God does not love in the same way. "If God elects one individual or group, there is someone else whom he does not elect and that other is left to suffer his exclusion."[44] Were this not true, God's love would be abstract and not directed; it would not encounter human beings in their individuality. As Wyschogrod sees it, God is not a father who stands in a legal and impartial relationship to his children but a father who—like all fathers—loves some of his children more than others. On the one hand, this means that the other children will be hurt, that they will suffer sibling rivalry, and that they will direct their anger toward the favored child. On the other hand, were God an impartial judge, he would have no favorite but would be a self-sufficient absolute and not a father at all. "The mystery of Israel's election thus turns out to be the guarantee of the fatherhood of God toward all peoples, elect and nonelect, Jew and Gentile."[45]

This formulation of chosenness, because it continues to insist on the favored status of the Jews even while it avoids imputing to them special merit, clarifies the fundamentally hierarchical nature of the concept of election. Whether favor lies in the parent's will or the child's desert, the favored child is still favored. To express the import of election in relation to the issue of difference, chosenness says that the Jewish difference is different from other people's difference; that Jews are different differently from the way in which other groups are different from each other. Jewish difference is not one among many, the uniqueness of a people as all peoples are unique, having their own history and task. Jewish difference is a matter of God's decision, God's mysterious and singular choice bestowing upon the Jews an unparalleled spiritual destiny. This difference is a hierarchical difference, a statement of privilege—even if burdensome and unmerited privilege—in relation to those who are not chosen.

Feminists troubled by this hierarchical understanding of the relation between Jews and others are hardly alone in our concern. Since emancipation, the concept of chosenness has been as much a source of embarrassment to Jews as of sustenance. Its exclusivity has seemed to many Jews to be in conflict with the desire for civic equality; its assumption of a special destiny in tension with the simple humanity of the Jew emancipation assumed. Dissolution of barriers between Jew and Gentile has made the meaning of chosenness harder to specify, and the potentially pernicious effects of Christian use of the notion of chosenness have become clearer and clearer.[46] Thus, in the last two hundred years, the concept of chosenness has been almost endlessly refashioned as Jewish thinkers have tried to find ways to discard and retain it at the same time. Chosenness has been reinterpreted in terms of mission to the nations and universal ethics; the notion of Jewish superiority has been roundly rejected; the boundary between God's choosing and Jewish God-consciousness has been thoroughly confused.[47] Yet with the exception of the Reconstructionists' explicit repudiation of election, few of these reinterpretations have eliminated the stubborn implication of privilege the concept of chosenness entails.

In this situation, feminist criticism of chosenness may seem simply to add one more small voice to what is already a surfeit of inconclusive discussion. Yet if feminists share many of the concerns of other critics, we also have a distinctive perspective to bring to the conversation. Most reinterpretations of election have focused on the relation of Jews to the wider society—seeking to reconcile chosenness with equality and participation in a pluralistic culture.[48] Feminism, however, calls attention to the function of chosenness in relation to Jewish self-conception and the internal dynamics of the community. Feminist objections to the idea of chosenness center not just on its entanglement with external hierarchical differentiations but with internal hierarchies as well.

Chosenness, after all, is not just a statement about Jewish relations with other peoples but a focus for Jewish self-understanding. If Jews are set apart from others through a unique call to God's service, this call must first express itself in Jewish communal life. The holiness that leads to external differentiation is lived out through observing the internal separations that mark a holy community. Since chief among these many separations is the differentiation between male and female, chosenness becomes linked to the subordination of women and other groups in the rhythms of Jewish existence. It is not that one can draw a direct line from the idea of chosenness to the creation of Others within the Jewish community or that the former provides an explicit model for the latter. But both are part of a cluster of important ideas that make graded differentiation a central model for understanding difference, and the two are also linked to each other both historically and psychologically.

It is worthy of note, for example, that in the same period in which Deutero-Isaiah elaborated the notion of chosenness, placing its significance in a world-historic context, there emerged for the first time persistent use of female sexuality as a symbol of evil. In an earlier period, when election was understood primarily in terms of Israel's observance of the commandments, women's sexuality was strictly controlled within the patriarchal family but was not seen as negative in and of itself.[49] This means that as the experience of exile gave rise to a new and more elevated interpretation of chosenness, the status of women diminished. The precise connection between these ideas is difficult to establish, but their historical correlation speaks to the real association between different types of hierarchical thinking.[50] Moreover, the fact that both ideas emerge in relation to the exile suggests that the process of distinguishing between normative and nonnormative Jews may be linked to the notion of chosenness through the dynamics of Jewish suffering.

The concept of chosenness has been an important solace to Jews in the face of anti-Jewish oppression, and it was often articulated more strongly where suffering was more severe. Certain elaborations of the idea of election can be read as direct responses to aggravated anti-Semitism or to Christian claims to the mantle of chosenness.[51] Emphasis on the unique destiny of the Jewish people and on the differences between Jew and Gentile would have provided an important counterbalance to the painful messages of the world and helped make Jewish misery intelligible and bearable. The self-concept that emerged as a compensation for suffering and outward rejection, however, was exaggeratedly elevated. As such, it was necessarily in tension both with the constant realities of life in a hostile culture and with the truth of human imperfection. Though nothing in their lives would have made this realization easy, Jews were not really so different from their neighbors, except that the complex of forces that made for their oppression also kept from them acting out their sense of superiority and/or rage. In this situation, in which an enlarged self-concept was challenged by daily experience, someone had to bear the weight of Otherness reflected in the mirror of the Gentile world, and also the pain and anger, lusts and temptations that Jewish flesh is heir to. Although there were many groups within the Jewish community that, in different periods, carried part of this burden, the Jewish woman was always a safe recipient of Jewish male projection. Marginalized in the wider society as well as Jewish culture, she represented both the Otherness the male Jew rejected for himself and the qualities that could not be acknowledged in a chosen people. A member of the elect, she was nonetheless the underside of that election—in Wyschogrod's terms, the unconscious flesh of a carnally elected community.[52] It is thus no coincidence that a new notion of chosenness and a new image of women entered the world together, for one demanded the other as its psychological complement and completion.

A dynamic in which an over-elevated self-understanding must be balanced by the creation of Others within the elect community points the way to change, however, through its own reversal. If the notion of the Jews as the chosen people seems to require the subordination of women and other groups—whether they be Sephardim or Ashkenazim, poor Jews or others—the withdrawal of projection from all these Others is the correlate of a measured and clear-eyed understanding of the self. The male Jew's acknowledgment of his own simple humanity is integrally related to the recognition of Jewish women as normative Jewish human beings, just as the acceptance of women as human fosters the recognition of all Jews' simple humanity. The rejection of chosenness and the rejection of women's Otherness are interconnected pieces of the wider project of finding ways to conceptualize and live with difference that are not based on projection and graded separations.

If feminists reject the concept of election, however, what remains of the distinctiveness of Israel and its relationship to the choosing God? Modern Jewish thinkers have hesitated to give up the idea of chosenness because they have been afraid that, with it, they would surrender the rationale for Jewish existence. But chosenness is necessary to justify Jewish life only on a view that does not take seriously the communal nature of human existence. If human beings are isolated individuals who must be persuaded to link ourselves with others, then Jewish commitment, like any form of communal engagement, requires argument and warrant. If, however, community is constitutive of personhood, then it needs no supernatural vocation to connect the Jew with Jewish living. Jewishness is a rich and distinctive way of being human, of linking oneself with God and with other people, of finding a pattern within which to live that gives life depth and meaning. That is enough reason to be a Jew.

Without necessarily having any concept of chosenness, without feeling singled out in relation to the law or living lives very different from those of Gentile neighbors, many, even assimilated, modern Jews retain a strong—if sometimes amorphous and ambivalent—sense of Jewish identity. They may experience Jewishness as simply a given, as an identity they are caught in willy-nilly. They may feel Jewish identity as a burden and/or assert it with different degrees of clarity and different meanings. They may give various explanations for the difficulties of shedding a Jewish connection.[53] To me, it comes down to this: Contrary to the premise of emancipation, one cannot be a human being in general. Each of us comes from somewhere and has a history; there are people whose past has formed us. If we are fortunate, there is also a community to which we can belong.[54] In a society that pretends that generic humanity is possible, particularity may come with a sense of guilt and discomfort. Yet it can also be affirmed, studied, lived out, chosen as a fundamental and meaning-giving reality of our existence.

To argue for the self-justifying nature of Jewish life is not to reduce Judaism to a sense of group belonging or to define Israel without reference to God.[55] The Jewish people came into being as a result of and in response to profound religious experiences, and it has been the purpose of its long history to ever more deeply comprehend and live out the relationship to God that drew it from its first hour. As I shall argue in the next chapter, the notion of a supernatural deity who singles out a particular people is part of the dualistic, hierarchical understanding of reality that the feminist must repudiate. But to reject this idea of God is not to reject the God who is met in community and wrestled with in history. Nor is it to deny that loyalty to God has been at the center of Jewish identity and an important part of what makes that identity distinctive.

Indeed, the purpose of a feminist critique of chosenness and redefinition of Israel is not to truncate Jewish spirituality but to liberate it from its connection with hierarchical dualisms. So long as the Jewish people holds onto a self-understanding that perpetuates graded distinctions within the community, Jewish spirituality will be defined by and limited to a small proportion of Jews. Women, the unlearned, *mamzerim* (bastards—that is, those born of forbidden unions) and others will be excluded from the relationship with God that comes through full participation in community. The history of their experience and understanding of God will be excluded from Jewish memory. The secret Torah of many of the souls who stood at Sinai will be lost to Jewish life. Only a Jewish community that permits and desires its members to be present in their particularity and totality can know in its fullness the relationship to God that it claims as its center.

What must replace chosenness, then, as the model for Jewish self-understanding is the far less dramatic "distinctness." The Jewish community and the subcommunities within it, like all human communities, are distinct and distinctive. Jewish experience has been variously shaped by gender, by place of dispersion, by language, by history, by interaction with other cultures. Just as the total Jewish experience is always located within a wider world, so the experiences of Jewish subgroups have taken place in some relation to a larger Jewish life and self-understanding. The term distinctness suggests, however, that the relation between these various communities—Jewish to non-Jewish, Jewish to Jewish—should be understood not in terms of hierarchical differentiation but in terms of part and whole.

The use of a part/whole model for understanding difference has a number of implications. First, it points to the greater unity to which different groups belong, making it possible to acknowledge the uniqueness of each group as part of a wider association of self-differentiated communities.[56] Jewish women, Sephardim, Ashkenazim, Paradesim, Malabarim (groups of Jews in Cochin, India) are part of the larger Jewish community as Jews are part of a larger heterogeneous culture. The parts are distinct. They have their own history and experience, and depending on their character, their own institutions, religion, practices, and beliefs. It is the content of this distinctness that creates an internal sense of group identity and community and also that allows the group to distinguish itself from others. Without this distinctiveness—were such a "without" even imaginable—we would lack the richness and diversity, the color and the passion, the insights and the wisdom that make up human history and culture. But while distinction is necessary, inevitable, a cause for celebration, the boundaries of distinction need not be rigidly guarded by graded separations. Boundaries can also be places where people can touch.[57] Awareness of the wider communities to which any community belongs fosters an appreciation of distinctness that need not be rooted in hierarchy or in projection onto others of rejected aspects of the self.

Second, if the different groups and subgroups that make up a community or nation are parts of a greater whole, there is no whole without all the pieces. Though Jewish history frequently has been abstracted from its varied surroundings and studied as an independent subject—and though the histories of other peoples often make scant reference to the Jews—Jewish history is part of the history of the peoples and cultures among whom the Jews have lived. Thus, for example, unless European history includes the experience of Jews, it is not truly "European" history but the poorer and less complex history of dominant Christian cultures. Similarly, unless Jewish history and community include the history and experience of women, Jews in India, Jews in the Arab world, it is not truly "Jewish" history or "Jewish" community but male Eurocentric Jewish history and community. This exclusion is destructive not only to the groups ignored but also to the rich tapestry of Jewish life that grows in distinctness and beauty with the distinctness and beauty of its various portions. The creation of Jewish communities in which differences are valued as necessary parts of a greater whole is the institutional and experiential foundation for the recovery of the fullness of Torah.

Third, what is true of communities is also true of selves. Where the boundaries between communities are marked by hierarchical separations, normative humanity is defined without reference to groups that are less valued. Thus Europeanness is defined without reference to Jews, Jewishness without reference to Jewish women, Jewish homosexuals, converts to Judaism, or any of those defined as Other. But the further effect of this separative understanding of community is that individuals within subordinate groups repress those aspects of themselves that are despised in the culture. Jews do not bring the special contributions of Jewishness to bear on wider social issues. Jewish women, as we gain equal access to Jewish communal life, deny our own experience for normative male practice and discourse. Those whose differences might have enriched and challenged the greater communal life learn to forget or keep hidden pieces of themselves.

We are brought back to the spiritual injury that such forgetting entails, and to the potential for liberation in a different model of community. To be wholly present in our lives in all our power is to touch the greater power of being that is the final unity within which all particulars dwell. To deny our complex particularity, as individuals or communities, is to diminish our connection to the God known in and through the experience of empowered selfhood. The community or self that spends its energy repressing parts of its totality truncates its creative power and cuts itself off from its full possibilities.[58] A Jewish community that defines itself by walling itself off from others without and within marshals strength at its boundaries to the detriment of the center. It nourishes selves that must deny parts of themselves and thus cannot bring their uniqueness to the enrichment of a common life. To create Jewish communities that value particularity is to create places where Jews in their complex wholeness can bring their full power to the upbuilding of Jewish community and the other communities in which Jews dwell. It is not in the chosenness that cuts off but in the distinctiveness that opens itself to difference that we find the God of Israel and of each and every people.

The State of Israel

The challenge of creating Jewish communities that nurture particularity without hierarchy takes on an important added dimension when Israel is considered not simply as a (landless) people but also as a state. While my theology is that of a US

Jew, writing out of and for a particular Diaspora situation, I cannot think about the transformation of Jewish community without taking into account the place in the world where Jews have deliberately and self-consciously sought to create a Jewish society. The human difficulties in dealing with difference, the social implications of traditional attitudes toward difference, the continuities between the modern Jewish construction of difference and historical Jewish treatment of Others all emerge with special vividness in the context of the state of Israel. It is therefore important to look at the crucial issues of community and diversity with which feminism is concerned in relation to the national community that Jews have created.

The Zionist movement emerged in the nineteenth century partly as a response to the intractability of Jewish difference. Some of its early theoreticians, responding to the failure of emancipation in the East and the persistence of anti-Semitism in the West, argued that assimilation was impossible and that only a Jewish homeland could resolve the question of the place of Jews in the world. Zionism drew on the sense of connection with and longing for the land of Israel that Jews had maintained through centuries of exile, but it also radically transformed that longing from a religious dream into a modern political movement. Its messianism was the progressive faith of the nineteenth century, and its goal was the creation of a modern liberal state that would take its place among the family of nations, removing the irritant of Jewishness from the other countries of the world.[59]

Creating a Jewish community in Palestine was not simply the solution to continuing anti-Semitism, however, but also an opportunity to establish a whole and vigorous modern Jewish life. Many possibilities that had been denied or distorted by exile—creating a Jewish peasantry, connecting to a soil, developing a national language and culture, shaping a Judaism that could grapple with the full range of issues life presents—were potentially realizable in a Jewish home. Thus Zionism reached behind two thousand years of Jewish wandering to the biblical vision of an integrated communal/economic/family/spiritual life. Moreover, as Zionists imagined it, this vision was to be achieved not on antiquarian terms but in full confrontation with modernity. If Zionism was to ensure the spiritual and cultural survival of the Jewish people, it could do so only by going through the modern Jewish experience, not by denying it.

The vision of an abundant and self-determined Jewish life both in continuity and contention with tradition has much to commend it to the feminist imagination. It is rooted in awareness of the importance of community, and the desire for a community that can nurture its members. Growing out of the experience of emancipation and continued anti-Semitism, it knows the issue of difference and the importance of particularity. In providing an opportunity to bring renewed life to traditional Jewish values while taking seriously the lessons of the modern world, a Jewish homeland challenges Jews to create a culturally rich and diverse society on the basis of a new understanding of difference. The fundamental feminist question concerning the state of Israel is whether it has found fresh ways to accommodate particularity or has perpetuated the same hierarchical construction of difference that has hitherto shaped Jewish communal existence.

While the early Zionists imagined an egalitarian community in Palestine formed by Jews from many lands of dispersion, numerous factors in the development of Israel have conspired against the realization of their vision. The complexities and conflicts of Zionist ideology and history, and the story of the many forces at work in shaping the state are well beyond the scope of this volume.[60] But what is important from a feminist perspective is that the enduring inequalities of the Jewish community have found new and complex embodiment in the laws and structures of a nation state struggling to secure its existence and survival.

With reference to women, for example, the establishment of a Jewish homeland provided an unparalleled opportunity to "start afresh," building a community and nation in which women would define and shape Jewish history side by side with men. Since most early Zionists had little sympathy with the strictures on women's roles delineated by religious teaching, their understanding of Jewish community seemed to promise a new beginning for women who wanted to live full Jewish lives and at the same time free themselves from traditional Jewish restrictions. Yet while the *myth* surrounding Jewish Israeli women is that their aspirations for liberation were realized, in fact sexual equality never was taken seriously in Israel as an important social goal.[61] The image of pioneer women draining swamps, changing the face of the land, fighting enemies alongside male comrades, projects as *reality* the *hopes* of the first Zionist women settlers. These women envisioned a society in which differences would be treated equally, in which they could bring their full physical and intellectual capabilities to all aspects of common life.[62] The Labor Zionist movement with which they identified, however, subordinated women's emancipation to the overriding project of establishing a Jewish home. Just as was the case with many liberal Jewish institutions in the Diaspora, sexual equality was taken for granted in principle and ignored in the concrete. Women found that many male settlers simply could not comprehend or take seriously women's desire to build the land side by side with men. Even in the communes that were forerunners of the kibbutz, women were assigned limited, primarily domestic, roles and were considered to work for the men rather than being full members of the collectives.[63] Indeed, on the kibbutzim themselves, while there were women who fought for and won the right to do men's work, no one ever suggested that men ought to be in the kitchen and nursery; the sexual division of labor went unquestioned.[64]

With the establishment of the state of Israel in 1948, important new factors came into play that served to consolidate and intensify sexual inequality. The role of Orthodox parties in the formation and governance of the state guaranteed that, even for the non-Orthodox majority, important areas of women's lives would be shaped by Orthodox patriarchalism. Israel has a declaration of independence granting "equal social and political rights for all citizens, irrespective of religion, race, or sex"—but this declaration functions only as a statement of general principles that does not have the force of law. Lacking a constitution, Israel ensures the rights of its citizens through statutes that are open to ongoing modification. In 1951, Israel passed a Women's Equal Rights Law, but within the law itself severely limited its application by exempting marriage and divorce. When in 1953 the Orthodox establishment was granted complete control of these areas, equal rights for Jewish women was effectively annulled.[65] While secularist compromises with Orthodox parties have had a profound effect on many areas of Israeli life, in the case of women, they have functioned to give institutional and legal sanction to some of the most disabling aspects of halakhah.

Another factor that has profoundly shaped women's lives is Israel's ongoing concern for survival and the consequent emergence of its citizens' army as a major institution in the Israeli state. While in this case also myth would have it that Israel is one of the few countries in the world to include women in the military on equal terms, here too myth obscures a very different reality. Of the 50 percent of women who serve at all in this major socializing institution, the majority do the same kind of office work they perform in the civilian market. Rather than serving alongside men, women replace them in clerical, switchboard, and social services so that men are freed for combat. Women's jobs in the army accord with a traditional understanding of female roles. The name of the women's corp—Chen, meaning charm—indicates the expectation that women are to humanize the military, strengthening the morale of male soldiers and making the army a "home away from home." Sexual relationships, formally ignored, are informally encouraged, and women are to provide amenities and forms of support that men are accustomed to in a patriarchal family.[66]

This supposed humanizing and softening effect of women on the armed services signals the presence of a "cult of true womanhood" at work in Israel.[67] In a situation of continuing profound insecurity, women and the home come to be constructed as antidotes to, and havens from, the harsh realities of Israeli life. As the exemption of married and pregnant women from national service indicates, the role of women in the country's defense is less important than their role in the home. Or rather: the crucial role of women in Israel's survival is the role of mother. Living constantly in the fear of war and concerned that a growing Palestinian population will threaten the Jewish character of the Israeli state, many in Israel see procreation as women's most important contribution to the Israeli future.[68] Thus the vision of equality in difference that was shared by at least some of Israel's founders has given way to traditional forms of women's subordination, now shaped and colored by the exigencies of an embattled nation-state.

The subordination of women is not the only hierarchical differentiation in Diaspora Jewish life that has found expression in Israel. The relationship between Ashkenazim (Jews of Eastern European origin) and Mizrachim (Jews from Africa, Asia, and the Middle East) is also hierarchically ordered, with the "first" Israel (Ashkenazim) setting itself up as normative and expecting the "second" Israel to adapt to Ashkenazi standards. Like the subordination of women, this hierarchy is also a product of the Diaspora, with the politics of statehood giving new form to older class and ethnic divisions. In the Diaspora, Jews of different cultural and national backgrounds each regarded others as Other! There were hierarchies within the Eastern European Jewish community and also between that community and outsiders. Jews from Lithuania looked down on Jews from Galitzia and also the religiously different Sephardim (Jews of Spanish or Portuguese descent). Sephardim in turn saw themselves as superior to Jews of Eastern European origin. In addition, each community had its own class structure, based on inequalities in wealth and learning. In Israel, traditional ethnic and cultural differences came to coincide with class differences in a way that realigned and solidified the divisions of the Diaspora community.

Zionist belief in the fundamental unity of the Jewish people was put to the test quite soon after 1948 by the influx of great numbers of Oriental immigrants from many Arab lands. Viewed with consternation and contempt by the Ashkenazi founders of the state, these "primitive" people from "backward countries" were expected to modernize and westernize, acculturating to Israeli society by taking on European customs and values.[69] Since this process was not to be reciprocal—Ashkenazi Israelis were not to learn from or be influenced by the culture of Middle Eastern Jews—Ashkenazim effectively identified their own interests with the interests of the state. The resulting glaring social and economic discrimination against Oriental Jews and their exclusion from Israeli leadership have been important items on the Israeli national agenda for many years.[70] Although the relationship between Ashkenazim and Mizrahim has shifted and been complicated by the Oriental community's important role in the election of Likud (in 1977), this shift has not fundamentally altered the discomfiting role of ethnic pluralism in the Jewish state. In a situation in which many activist Oriental Jews have themselves been ambivalent about whether they are claiming equality within an Ashkenazi state or demanding recognition of a separate Oriental Jewish identity, Israel has been no more effective in mining the creative possibilities inherent in differences among Jews than have Jews in the Diaspora.[71]

It is the Palestinians, however, rather than the Mizrahi Jews, who pose the most fundamental test of Israel's capacity to deal with difference, and whose situation highlights the connection between the creation of hierarchies within the Jewish community and between that community and others. Palestinian Israelis (Palestinians living within the pre-1967 borders) constitute a segregated and peripheral underclass whose grievances, unlike those of the Mizrahim, seldom capture the attention of the wider society. Formally granted equal rights by the same Declaration of Human Rights that gave equality to women, Palestinians are in fact excluded from the central symbols and institutions of the Jewish state. Both the ordinary operation of

Israel's major institutions, and specific government programs and policies have fostered the isolation and internal fragmentation of the Arab community and its economic dependence on the Jewish majority.[72] While the operation of these dynamics is complex, massive, and subtle, the barring of Moslem Arabs (the vast majority of the Arab population) from military service can serve as a symbol of the Palestinian population's isolation and lack of access to important resources. The question of Palestinian army service is a difficult one, tied up with broader questions of Jewish Israeli security and self-definition. Yet since the army is a key institution in building a sense of Israeli identity, transmitting a wide range of skills, and providing entrée to jobs and public assistance programs, the exclusion of Palestinians from the army means they are "cut off from the major dynamic processes of social integration and mobility which exist in Israel."[73]

The contradictions of a democracy in which 17 percent of all citizens are suspected as a third column and subjected to discrimination are vastly intensified by Israel's direct military rule of over a million and a half Palestinians on the West Bank and in Gaza. In the Occupied Territories, there is no pretense of democracy. Palestinians have no control over the government that determines the conditions of their existence, no right of appeal against the judgments of military courts, no secure rights to the land on which they live.[74] While these conditions are supposedly temporary, pending a permanent peace settlement, the Palestinian uprising has dramatized the untenability of such rule and the profound effects of twenty years of it on Jewish Israeli attitudes and values. Those Jews who favor annexing the Occupied Territories do not imagine offering Palestinians equal rights within a "Greater Israel." An increasingly vocal and militant religious right claims divine sanction for Israeli expansion, expansion that leaves no room for non-Jewish citizens within a Jewish state. As some religious nationalists understand it, equality of rights is at best an alien—that is,

European—democratic principle; and at worst it is a violation of the biblical commandment to exterminate Amalek. Thus twenty years of military rule have created a situation in which Israeli government policy is to treat occupied Palestinians as intruders in their own land, and in which some Jews are actually advocating expelling or killing Palestinians in the name of chosenness.[75]

While the conflicts and inequalities between Jews and Palestinians and Eastern European and Oriental Jews have their own distinct origins and manifestations, they are also interstructured with the inequalities between women and men. As a few examples can make clear, the fact that many Israeli women are Palestinians or Oriental Jews means that the relations between men and women are shaped partly by these other rifts; and, conversely, the subordination of women means that anti-Arab or Mizrahi discrimination falls differently on women than on men. Thus, when Palestinian society was radically disrupted by the creation of Israel in 1948, one reaction of Palestinian men was to maintain cultural stability by increasing their traditional control over Palestinian women. As this control has relaxed and Palestinian women's independence has increased over the last twenty years, Israeli politicians have sought to control Palestinian women's political activism by appealing to the traditional Arab value system in relation to women.[76] Or, if we look at the role of (Jewish) women in the Israeli army, it is striking that of the approximately 25 percent of women exempted from service for lack of basic qualifications (insufficient level of literacy, inability to tolerate discipline), almost all are Oriental. Just as most Palestinians are excluded from the important integrative and social functions the army performs, so are large numbers of Oriental Jewish women.[77] Or, as Israeli occupation of the West Bank and Gaza has brought the number of Palestinians under Jewish Israeli control to 30 percent of the population, the pressure on Jewish women to bear large numbers of children has increased greatly. The Jewish Israeli woman must serve as a breeder not only to supply future soldiers to the army but also to do her part in the "demographic war" for a continued Jewish majority in the state.[78]

As we look at this picture of interstructured hierarchical differentiations in Israeli society, a striking analogy emerges. The embattled Israeli Jew ignoring the inequities of Israeli society bears a disquieting resemblance to the oppressed ghetto Jew ignoring the internal inequalities in the Jewish community.[79] In the ghetto situation, God was believed both to vindicate Jewish suffering and to define and justify the subordination of women within Judaism. The rage engendered by male powerlessness was projected onto women who become the doubled Other in a community of Others. Israeli Jews wish to see themselves as new and free people, but in fact are as surrounded by enemies as the Jews of the Diaspora. In this situation, they claim a struggle in which they have "no choice" as warrant for oppressive policies toward Palestinians and for diversion of financial and moral resources from the resolution of internal social conflicts to the military budget. As in the Diaspora situation, struggle with the enemy outside also fosters the oppression of women, whose formal equality is in fact sacrificed to the needs of a beleaguered state.

It seems that the Jewish experience of oppression has led not to the just exercise of power by Jews in power, but to the Jewish repetition of strategies of domination. The many forms of oppression to which Jews have been subject, from denial of fundamental rights and outright expropriation of resources, to lack of respect for Jewish culture, to discrimination in housing and employment, are recapitulated within and between various groups in Israel. Not only has the Jewish historical experience not served as a lesson and warning, past oppression has even been used as a justification for the right to oppress others. Past Jewish suffering is presumed to confer a moral purity that covers over and excuses moral weakness and rage.[80]

If this cycle in which oppressed becomes oppressor is psychologically comprehensible and historically familiar, it is, nevertheless, not inevitable. While the Israeli government often has set aside internal debate about the nature of Israel in the name of building and protecting the state, Israel's citizens have shown a persistent and remarkable willingness to discuss and reassess the purpose of Israel's existence and to question the values that have informed its actions.[81] Books and articles examining and criticizing various aspects of the State are widely read and vigorously debated, and numerous organizations have been formed to deal with the inequalities of Israeli society. Thus alongside discrimination against women and Mizrahim, there exist battered women's shelters, the Israeli feminist movement, numerous self-help organizations for Mizrahim, and groups working to facilitate Mizrahi and Ashkenazi cultural integration.[82] Alongside the multi-faceted discrimination against Israel's Arab citizens and governmental unwillingness to consider the existence of a Palestinian state, there exist literally dozens of organizations working for peace and Arab-Jewish reconciliation, trying to create a future in which Jews and Palestinians can peacefully and respectfully coexist.[83] Moreover, just as the various forms of discrimination in Israel are interstructured, so efforts toward ending discrimination seek to form coalitions across various structural lines. In the major cities of Israel, Jewish and Palestinian "Women in Black" hold weekly vigils to protest the occupation of the West Bank and Gaza. Women in Black is just one of many groups formed by women trying to create a new political situation by dealing directly with the conflicts between them and the pain and complexity of their lives.[84]

These groups and organizations working toward a new vision of community shift the boundaries of community, creating out of the multiple allegiances and identities that define the modern experience communities committed to a common purpose, able to address the issues that unite and divide them. Rather than leaving Ashkenazim and Mizrahim, Jews and Palestinians confronting each other across an abyss, projects for justice, peace, and dialogue forge—however temporarily—a shared Israeli, or woman's, or Middle-Eastern identity that, without denying differences, places them in a new context. Projects like these enact the conviction that difference need not be expressed in dominance or strife. If people work to make it so, shared oppression and resistance to oppression can be a bridge to mutual understanding and joint action. There may be no guarantee that the oppressed will not become oppressors, but it is nonetheless possible to forge links between oppression and the commitment to justice by careful and conscious insistence on remembering and using one's experience precisely for that purpose.

While the impulse toward self-questioning characteristic of many Israelis has sometimes been connected to the notion of chosenness, it is more appropriately linked to particular values central to Jewish memory and to the historical experience of oppression. The recent history of the religious right in Israel would seem to suggest that belief in chosenness can go hand in hand with the worst idolatry of the state and the willingness to justify any sort of abuse of the non-Jewish Other.[85] Over against this willingness lies the pain of oppression experienced in one's own flesh and the injunction of memory: "You shall not wrong or oppress a stranger, for you were strangers in the land of Egypt" (Ex. 22:20, altered). The multiform wrongs that the Jews have experienced, the commitment to remembering these wrongs as part of the struggle against them, the continuing quest for integrity and self-definition as a community fuels questions about what kind of society the state is fighting to protect and whether there are forms of self-defense that undermine what supposedly is being defended.

If the state of Israel is to find modes of self-preservation compatible with and productive of a just society, it must learn from the whole Jewish experience what makes a society just. Surely, a just society is one in which the rights of minorities are not simply promised but guaranteed in law and in practice, in which the resources of the society are available to and shared by all its members, in which citizens are free from religious coercion, even if it be the coercion of their own tradition. It is a society that recognizes not simply the individual citizens who dwell within it but also the diverse communities, that acknowledges the different needs and traditions of these communities and expects that all will contribute to shaping the character of the nation as a whole. Such internal justice is not possible, moreover, unless a society recognizes the rights of its neighbors and has done its utmost to live in peace with them. The economic, social, and moral costs of military occupation make it incompatible with equity within one's own boundaries. The rightful claim of Palestinians to a land of their own renders occupation profoundly unjust.

I have seemingly wandered far from this chapter's initial focus—creating a Jewish community in which women are present and equal as women. Yet since different forms of hierarchy and oppression intersect with and reinforce one another, none finally will be abolished until all have fallen. A Jewish feminist vision must apply the model of community in which difference is nurtured and respected to all communities and all differences with which Jewish feminists are involved. A commitment to restructuring difference harbors risk and change, whether the context is Israel, Diaspora Jewish communities, or the feminist movement. The recognition of diverse constituencies as parts of larger communities involves an obligation to redefine communal life as the sum of all pieces. When one part has been accustomed to speaking for the whole—male Ashkenazi Jewish Israelis for Israelis, elite male Jews for Jews, middle-class white feminists for women—this redefinition may mean dislodging long-fixed patterns of dominance with difficult and dramatic results.

Such transformations are never easy, but they promise much, and not simply to those whose experience is obscured or denied by the reigning order. An Israel that honored diversity might transform itself from a fortress state into a country enjoying the energy and resources of a remarkably rich and varied multicultural citizenry. Diaspora communities respecting particularity might find themselves with both a broadened and enlivened Jewish memory and present spiritual resources of unexpected depth. A women's movement that grappled with difference might discover strategies for empowerment and change rooted in the particular histories of its members but accessible to the movement as a whole. If difference is threatening, it also holds power. The struggle to find new models for relating to difference is a struggle to bring the manifold riches of a complex human heritage to the careful nurturing of communal and individual life.

4. God: Reimaging the Unimaginable

From the recovery of women's Torah and the reconstruction of Jewish community, we move to the subject of God. The location of this topic as the last of the three central concepts of Judaism requires some explanation. Ontologically, and in traditional Jewish thought, God is first. Torah is God's gift, incomprehensible without God; Israel is God's chosen, formed and sustained through the choosing. Jewish thinking traditionally begins with God because God is the beginning, the sine qua non of Jewish existence and experience.

My postponement of the subject of God to this point in the book is not meant to deny the centrality of God in Jewish thought and experience or to demote God for some feminist motive. Rather, I have placed God third in the triad Torah/Israel/God because of the intended parameters and focus of my discussion. It is not my purpose to produce a full-scale philosophical reconceptualization of God, nor any account of God's nature that could anchor an understanding of Torah and Israel in some noncircular way. I am interested instead in exploring and transforming the metaphors for God that have formed the Jewish imagination and shaped Jewish self-understanding and behavior. These metaphors are not reducible to Torah or Israel, but neither do they exist without them. Torah provides us with our images and conception of God, and Israel is the locus for the experiences of God that find expression in the images of Torah. The representation of God as male, for example, is comprehensible only in the context of an androcentric Torah that is elaborated and rendered plausible by a male-defined community. While this does not mean that the Jewish concept of God is simply the projection of a male-dominated society, it does mean that the experience of God is sustained and interpreted in the categories of a patriarchal culture. It makes most sense to analyze the Jewish picture of God from a feminist perspective, then, after having explored the context in which it develops.

If the Jewish understanding of God emerges from Torah and Israel, it is also the case that the concepts Torah, Israel, and God are mutually reinforcing. Since a central part of the Jewish picture of God is that God is the giver of Torah and covenant partner of Israel, images of God ground the notions of Torah and Israel in a distinctly circular fashion. The image of God as male that arises out of a community in which women are Other in turn supports an androcentric understanding of Torah and Israel. Conversely, as new feminist metaphors for God begin to emerge out of a Jewish community already in the process of change, these metaphors support further change in a feminist direction. Thus, while my discussion of God will build on the foundations of Torah and Israel, it will have to look at the interrelation of what are finally mutually supportive concepts and images.

As I see it, the goal of a Jewish feminist approach to God-language is to incorporate women's Godwrestling into the fullness of Torah by finding images that can communicate and evoke the experience of the presence of God in a diverse, egalitarian, and empowered community of Israel. The experience of God in community is both the measure of the adequacy of traditional language and the norm in terms of which new images must be fashioned and evaluated. It is in light of this norm that images of God as male and as dominating Other have been judged limited and oppressive. And it is in faithfulness to this norm that a range of new metaphors for God have been elaborated, tried on, and discarded or preserved. A consideration of Jewish images of God from a feminist perspective takes us from criticism of established God-language to efforts to open up the metaphors we use, to attempts to reorient the Jewish conception of deity.

Traditional Images of God

The Image of God as Male

A feminist critique of Jewish God-language begins with the unyielding maleness of the dominant Jewish picture of God. If the Jewish understanding of God is in many ways a complex and contradictory weave of biblical and philosophical categories, the maleness of God is a consistent theme in all elements in the fabric. God's maleness is so deeply and firmly established as part of the Jewish conception of God that it is almost difficult to document: It is simply part of the lenses through which God is seen. Maleness is not a distinct attribute, separable from God's anger or mercy or justice. Rather, it is expressed through the total picture of God in Jewish texts and liturgy. God in the Jewish tradition is spoken of in male pronouns, and more importantly, in terms of male characteristics and images. In the Bible, God is a man of war (Ex. 15:3), a shepherd (Ps. 23:1), king (for example, 1 Sam. 12:12; Ps. 10:16), and father (for example, Jer. 3:19; 31:9). The rabbis called him "father of mercy," "father in heaven," "king of all kings," and simply "he."[1] Every blessing evokes God as lord and king of the universe, and throughout the liturgy, he is father God and God of our fathers, lord of hosts, and king of the earth.

These are not the only epithets applied to God, but neutral and even female images do little to counter this dominant picture. Attributes and actions that are themselves gender-neutral are read through the filter of male language, so that the God who performs these actions is still imagined in male terms. There is nothing intrinsically male, for example, about the action of liberation or about the most mysterious of all names for God: *Ehyeh-Asher-Ehyeh* (I am who I am, or I will be who I will be, Ex. 3:14). But when the Exodus narrative is read in the context of the Song at the Sea that celebrates the Lord of war triumphing over his enemies (Ex. 15), and when, in a male-dominated society, it is assumed that power is the prerogative of maleness, God comes to be seen as male throughout. The hand that leads Israel out of Egypt is a male hand, whether or not it is called so explicitly.[2]

Female images that might balance the prevailing male meta-phors exist in Judaism, but—except in the marginalized mysti-cal tradition (to be considered below)—they must be ferreted out as a tiny minority strand. Isaiah, for example, is one of several biblical writers who uses images of God as mother (42:14; 66:13), and feminist scholars have been at pains to point out that God appears in the Bible as wet-nurse and midwife, and provider of water and food.[3] But while these attributes are an important reminder that God is not literally male, and they provide resources for the construction of alternative imagery, they are not picked up in the liturgy and are vastly oversha-dowed by masculine terminology. Like the mystical notion of the *Shekhinah* as God's female presence, they have had virtually no impact on the dominant image of God.

If anything moderates God's maleness or allows for its obfus-cation, it is not so much the existence of female images as the influence of Jewish philosophy. The vivid personality of God found in the Bible and in many midrashim is roundly dis-claimed by the Jewish philosophical tradition, which tries to free its idea of God from any anthropomorphisms.[4] The com-posite nature of the conception of God that results from the interweaving of midrash and philosophy allows Jews simulta-neously to imagine God as male and to declare "him" incorpo-real and therefore ungendered. As one prominent scholar puts it, "The truth is that the God of Israel, though described chiefly by masculine nouns and verbs, is a relatively genderless male deity. . . ."[5] The obvious self-contradiction in such a statement is underscored by feminist experiments with liturgical change that substitute female pronouns and imagery for the standard male ones. The disgust and passionate resistance aroused by such efforts reveals clearly that Jews hold a deeply gendered understanding of God—one that is only masked and kept in place by appeals to God's incorporeality.

While establishing the ubiquity of male images of God is not the same as proving their harmfulness, from a feminist perspective these images are highly problematic.[6] Obvious and innocuous as male God-language has come to seem, metaphors matter—on both an individual and social level. Though long usage may inure us to the implications of our imagery, religious symbols are neither arbitrary nor inert. They are significant and powerful communications through which a religious community expresses a sense of itself and its universe. Religious symbols give resonance and authority to a community's self-understanding and serve to support and sustain its conception of the world. The male images Jews use in speaking to and about God emerge out of and maintain a religious system in which men are normative Jews and women are perceived as Other. Drawing on the experience of only some who stood at Sinai, they validate a community that is hierarchically structured.

One sort of evidence for the political function of male God-language is provided by the circumstances of its emergence. This language was not the natural and spontaneous mode of prayer of a patriarchal society; it had a history, taking hold gradually with the rise and consolidation of patriarchal religious and social institutions in ancient Israel. The Bible provides extensive evidence of a long struggle in Israel over how God/the gods should be envisioned and who should serve in their cult.[7] In the polytheistic ancient Near East, gender was not a significant category either in assigning the characteristics of the gods or in deciding who should serve them. In Israel, on the other hand, the rise of the one male God was correlated with a deep concern for gender as a central determinant of appropriate behavior in both cult and society, and with the exclusion of women from public religious life.[8] Although detailed relationships between changes in God-language and social patterns in Israel remain to be traced, Israel's choice of male language is consistent with the gradual marginalization of women within the religious realm and serves as a partial ideological justification for their subordination.[9]

The ways in which male God-language continues to legitimate male authority are difficult to demonstrate, for this language has become so familiar, it is simply taken for granted. Since we "know" that male language is generic, and we subject God-language to many layers of translation, it is difficult to imagine that the literal level of images has any effect. As Mary Daly argued years ago, however, the symbol of the father God—or the godfather as she calls him—is rendered plausible by patriarchy and, in turn, authorizes male-dominated social structures by making women's oppression appear right and fitting. "If God in 'his' heaven is a father ruling 'his' people, then it is in the nature of things and according to divine plan and the order of the universe that society be male dominated."[10]

A social scientific understanding of the nature of religious symbolism can help elucidate more fully the how and why of this connection, for it shows that a central purpose of symbols is to depict and authenticate the worldview of which they are part. Religious symbols express both the sensibility and moral character of a people and the way in which it understands and structures the world. In Clifford Geertz's language, our sense of God or the "really real" colors our "sense of the reasonable, the practical, the humane and the moral." Religious symbols do not simply tell us about God; they are not simply *models of* a community's sense of ultimate reality. They also shape the world in which we live, functioning as *models for* human behavior and the social order. The Sabbath, for example, as a model of God's action in creating the world, is also a model for the Jewish community which, like God, rests on the seventh day. The double reference of symbols—up and down—enforces a community's sense of the factuality and appropriateness of those symbols.[11] If God rested and enjoined rest on the seventh day, how can we fail to rest also, and how can our rest not bring us closer to God?

When this analysis is applied to male images for God, it is clear that such images also function as models of and models for. They both claim to tell us about the divine nature, and they justify a human community that reserves power and authority to men. Occasional explicit appeals to such language to support male dominance help illuminate a powerful circular argument which is always implicit in its use.[12] When God is pictured as male in a community that understands "man" to have been created in God's image, it only makes sense that maleness functions as the norm of Jewish humanity. When maleness becomes normative, women are necessarily Other, excluded from Torah and subordinated in the community of Israel. And when women are Other, it seems only fitting and appropriate to speak of God in language drawn from the male norm.

While the function of the male image of God in an androcentric religious system is the chief focus of the feminist critique, there is another problem with this image that is separable from and yet buttresses its role in supporting patriarchy. When particular symbols for God become deeply established and familiar, they lose their transparency as symbols and come to be seen as descriptions of God that provide unique access to the nature of divine reality. Though this can happen with any much-used symbol, the image of God as male seems especially to function in this unconscious way. God's maleness has been so completely taken for granted that it is even exempted from the philosophical injunction against ascribing positive attributes to God. Maimonides, for example, considers it illegitimate ever to characterize God in positive terms, for this might imply that God is similar to other existing things. Yet throughout his discussion of negative and positive attributes, Maimonides continually refers to God as He and Him without ever taking note of the fact that maleness is a positive trait or applying to this attribute his doctrine of negation.[13] In recent times, the anger and fear awakened by feminist attempts to alter male God-language similarly bespeak a profound, often previously unarticulated, attachment to this image, and a dread of losing along with it the very nature of God.

When a metaphor is assumed and defended on this level, it has ceased to be an image and become an idol. The metaphor is no longer simply a way of pointing to God but is identified with God, so that any change in the image seems to defame or disparage God "himself." The claim that only male language may be used for God—whether defended explicitly or disguised behind a liberal "what difference does it make, anyway?"—attributes ultimacy to particular male symbols. It then becomes maleness that is worshiped instead of God. While Jews are used to thinking of idols as pillars and stones, verbal idols can be every bit as powerful as sculpted ones—indeed more powerful for being less visible.[14] What will dislodge male idols, however, is not hammers or fire but structural changes in the patriarchal system and the concurrent creation of new metaphors that lead the imagination down untrod paths.

The Image of God as Dominating Other

It is not simply male metaphors for God that need to be broken, however, but also the larger picture of who God is. Were feminist objections to Jewish God-language confined to the issue of gender, the manipulation of pronouns and creation of female imagery would fairly easily resolve the difficulties described. In fact, though, experiments with changing liturgical language by adding female metaphors only call attention to larger problems in the underlying conception of the God who is male. Thus, while feminist criticisms of traditional language begin with gender, they come to focus on the deeper issue of images of God's power as dominance. Such images are connected to God's maleness insofar as they mirror male social roles, but the use of gender neutral or even female language does not itself guarantee that images of dominance have been addressed.[15]

The issue of divine power is complex, for Jewish images of God's power are more diverse than gender imagery for God. Metaphors of power as dominance predominate in the tradition, but not with the ubiquity of God as male. The central affirmation that God is the God of the covenant immediately places God's power in the context of a relationship with rights and obligations on both sides. If sometimes Jewish acceptance of the covenant is itself depicted as the result of divine threats and domination, other times it is seen as a free choice. God lifts up Sinai over the heads of Israel to force the people to accept his law, but he also peddles his Torah from nation to nation.[16] God comes down on Sinai with thunder and fire (Ex. 19:18–19) but is afterward heard in "a still small voice" (1 Kings 19:12). God gives the laws and judges Israel by them, but God must also abide by the same norms and values.[17] In confronting the catastrophes that have time and again befallen the Jewish people, certain rabbis dared to depict God as powerless, accompanying his people into exile and weeping over the destruction of the Temple.[18]

Despite this diversity of images of divine authority, however, certain images have been more central than others, acting as lenses through which counterimages have been appropriated and interpreted. Of the various sources for a Jewish conception of God's power, none has been more important than liturgy, for it is above all in the repetition of prayer that a portrait of God is formed. Selecting particular images as fundamental, downplaying others, the liturgy has come to have a formative role in shaping the Jewish picture of deity. Since metaphors of God's power as dominance are central to the liturgy, these metaphors have profoundly affected the Jewish imagination, building and solidifying a particular understanding of God. The God of Jewish liturgy is a king robed in majesty, a merciful but probing father, and master of the world. His sovereign Otherness is elaborated extensively: his dominion over creation, his control of history past and future, his revenge against his enemies, his power over the human soul. The purpose of prayer is to establish a relationship between the Jew and God, but this relationship is never balanced: The intimacy of the "you" addressed to a listening other is overshadowed by the image of the lord and king of the universe who is absolute ruler on a cosmic plane.[19] Next to this God, human beings are as nothing, "men of renown as though they never existed, the wise as if they were without knowledge."[20] The prayerbook as a paean to God's glory and daily wonders, as a plea for his forgiveness and mercy, presents an image of God's power as "power over" others, a power that is partly defined through the contrast with human weakness and dependency.[21]

This understanding of divine power as domination, crystalized and promulgated by the liturgy, is also amply attested by other sources, so that it can be specified and elaborated in broader terms. God's power as dominance means, first of all, that the relation between God and human beings is profoundly assymetrical.[22] God's maleness connotes power, and God's power is an extension of his maleness, but God is not powerful in the same sense as ordinary men. His power is supreme, absolute, infinite, completely Other than human authority. God created the world through his word and continues to rule over it, so that all that happens in the universe is the result of his sovereign will and action.[23] To him, "The nations are but a drop in a bucket" (Isa. 40:15); he brings their counsels to nothing (Ps. 33:10). His glory is like a devouring fire (Ex. 24:16), his presence more than mortals can bear (Ex. 19:12–13; 2 Sam 6:6–7). God sees and rules the earth from his dwelling place in heaven (for example, Ps. 14:2), and he does what he pleases, consulting no other will (Ps. 115:3; 135:6). In the Bible, this wholly Other God is also the God of the covenant, a God who walks on earth and whose word is near. When, however, the biblical picture of a powerful, awe-inspiring deity is combined with the "omni" attributes of the Jewish philosophical tradition—omniscience, omnipotence, omnipresence—the result is a picture of a personal God who is unutterably distant, majestic, and exalted.[24]

Second, this utterly Other God is a being outside and over against the world who controls the world "in a way that inhibits human growth and responsibility."[25] Unlike the wise parent who encourages children to develop autonomy and self-reliance, God insists that humans obey him, that they concede their limits and God's overwhelming superiority. As with authoritarian parents, God enforces obedience through a combination of bribes and punishments, a mixture of "domination and benevolence," both of which discourage independent activity.[26] God's interactions with Israel are marked by an alternation of threats and promises designed to secure Israel's compliance. If Israel obeys God's commandments, the people will be rewarded with peace and prosperity; God will be with them, and all shall be well. The cost of disobedience, however, is famine, war, and exile, the latter meted out by other nations guided by God's hand. All the earth is his to be piloted toward his purposes, purposes humans can forward or rebel against but never escape.

The notion of God as dominating Other finds quintessential expression in the image of the holy warrior who punishes the wicked with destruction and death. The God who hears the groaning of his people in Egypt is a fighter more powerful than all the armies of Pharaoh, a God whose arm can destroy the Egyptians, drowning them in the sea (Ex. 15). When Israel enters the promised land, God is present in his ark at the head of its marching armies, giving military victory over city after city (Joshua). Hardening the hearts of the local people, God ensures that they "should receive no mercy" but be "utterly destroyed" (Josh. 11:20). Fire, tumult, slaughter, mass death are the retribution of the wicked, retribution that can be turned against Israel itself (Amos 2,3). Since God's passion for justice is enforced partly by acts of war, an Israel that "trample[s] the heads of the poor" will find itself trampled by a force no bowman can escape (Amos 2:7,15). Prophetic calls for social justice are juxtaposed with threats of divine punishment, interlacing images of righteousness with metaphors of violent destruction.[27]

Unlike images of God as male, which may on the surface appear innocuous, images of God as dominating Other more often evoke a troubled response. In depicting God's power as

domination, the tradition draws on symbols of political authority that are not only foreign to citizens in a democracy but also
morally repugnant. Metaphors of sovereignty, lordship, king-
ship, and judicial and military power evoke images of arbitrary
and autocratic rule that have been rejected in the human political sphere at the same time they live on in religious language.[28]
If the image of God as male provides religious support for male
dominance in society, the image of God as supreme Other
would seem to legitimate dominance of any kind. God as ruler
and king of the universe is the pinnacle of a vast hierarchy that
extends from God "himself" to angels/men/women/children/an-
imals and finally the earth. As hierarchical ruler, God is a model
for the many schemes of dominance that human beings create
for themselves. As holy king, he chooses the nation Israel as
his holy people. As holy warrior, he sanctions the destruction
of peoples perceived as Other. As holy lawgiver, he enacts the
subordination of women in the Jewish community. This God
authorizes the subjection of women, but also, and more specifically, the rape of females taken as spoils of war (Num. 31:17–
18, 32–35) and the extermination of Amalek (Deut. 25:19).[29]

Such images of God's dominance give rise to the terrible irony
that the symbols Jews have used to talk about God as ultimate
good have helped generate and justify the evils from which we
hope God will save us.[30] The image of God as dominating Other
functions as a fundamental and authorizing symbol in a whole
system of hierarchical dualisms that includes, but is by no
means limited to, the hierarchical relationship between Israel
and other peoples discussed in the last chapter. As traditionally
depicted, God incorporates the "higher" qualities in a host of
cleavages that correspond to various forms of human domination: He is male rather than female, regal rather than simple
and poor, Jewish rather than pagan, spirit rather than flesh.
Seen from the side of religious language, such symbols under-
gird a worldview in which it seems "practical, humane, and
moral" for people who identify with the higher side of these
dualisms to oppress those they associate with the lower. Seen

from a societal perspective, this image of God is the theological projection of a human community bent on denying its own place among a multitude of peoples, all connected to and dependent on the earth.

This conception of God as Other provides a larger framework than the maleness of God for thinking about the interconnections between the Jewish picture of God and the hierarchical, androcentric understanding of Israel. The parallels between Jewish perception of non-Jewish others and Jewish perception of women take on new meaning as aspects of a system in which God represents the superior side of a range of hierarchical differentiations. The image of God as exalted one, compared to whom everything else is of lesser reality and value, both fosters and mirrors the tendency to conceptualize all difference in terms of graded separations. If the God who dwells beyond the earth chooses to ally himself with particular people and particular values, then these take on importance that is also understood in terms of superior and inferior, higher and lower.

Yet while the portrait of God as dominating Other seems to fit well with the traditional understanding of the chosenness of Israel, it also threatens to undermine the relationship between God and Israel. For the Jewish tradition affirms that the God who is Other is nonetheless at the same time the covenant partner of Israel—a partner who enters into an alliance that involves commitments on both sides. The language of domination, however, is in tension with the language of covenant, because it denies the reality of human power and responsibility that the covenant presupposes. God as all-powerful lord and king foresees and controls the outcome of historical and cosmic processes. As the liturgy continually reminds us, he is everything, we are nothing; he is eternal, we are dust. But this juxtaposition of divine might and human frailty is neither appropriate nor conducive to the human accountability and effort that the covenant demands. On the one hand, the notion of divine omnipotence encourages human passivity. On the other, images of human weakness and nothingness foster a self-abnegation that can paralyze the capacity to act. It is not by contemplating our own worthlessness that human beings are encouraged to take responsibility for ourselves and the world. Human accountability stems from our real, if limited, power, and it is out of a realistic sense of that power that we can act most effectively. Thus, while images of God as dominating Other sanction oppression, they also fail to acknowledge or evoke from us the energy and empowerment required to struggle against oppression.

On the Nature of God-Language

These problems with traditional images of God generate a need for new language that can better express the meaning of God for a pluralistic and responsible community. But the move to new images, as well as feminist criticisms of traditional God-language, presuppose an understanding of what images of God are about that needs to be made explicit before we can turn to construction. Criticism of received images of God is not, of course, criticism of God. It is criticism of ways of speaking about a reality that, in its full reality, is finally unknowable. Taking seriously the established Jewish suspicion of anthropomorphisms—without for that reason ceasing to use them—feminists insist that our language about God is constructive and metaphorical. Everything we say about God represents our human efforts to create, recapture, and evoke experiences of God sustained within linguistic and cultural frameworks that already color our experience and interpretation. All our images have an "as if" or "as it were" in front of them that reminds us they are to be taken neither literally nor as final, but as part of an ongoing quest for language that can provide a framework for meaningful living and give expression to our experience.[31]

In seeking metaphors to use for God, Jewish feminists never start from zero, but draw on the Jewish concepts and symbols that have come down to us. But these symbols themselves are also human attempts to speak of the experience of God who stands at the center of Jewish life. They emerge out of the Godwrestling of our ancestors and represent their efforts to name and comprehend the God they knew as with them on a long and various journey. These traditional symbols are privileged insofar as they are a formative part of Jewish memory and so shape the ways in which contemporary Jews imagine and experience our relationship with God. They are not privileged, however, in giving us access to the "true" reality of God or a knowledge of God of which we ourselves are incapable. They are arrived at through the same methods of listening, struggling, and constructing meaning in historical context that we go through in trying to make sense of our religious experiences. Traditional symbols for God thus provide resources to be taken seriously in reconstructing Jewish God-language, but they are not binding. Rather, they provide models of a *process*, which we ourselves continue in seeking images of God that will be adequate for our own time.

Obviously, Jews today respond to traditional God-language in a context very different from that in which it was forged. Coupled with the enormous social and political changes in which the Jewish community has participated, feminist consciousness itself alters the cultural framework and understanding of reality within which God is experienced and named. Metaphors for God that might once have been compelling despite—or because of—their political resonance, not only have lost their immediacy and power but have become morally suspect and disturbing. Especially those images of God drawn from political and family life have changed in their associations and meanings with changes in and new perspectives on the family and political order. Once images become socially, politically, or morally inadequate, however, they are also religiously inadequate. Instead of pointing to and evoking the reality of God, they block the possibility of religious experience. When this happens, it becomes incumbent on those who feel the inadequacy of traditional language both to articulate its deficiencies and to name the aspects of divine reality that have been neglected or deemphasized by traditional Jewish sources.

While continual renewal of God-language is incumbent on all Jews, the fact that traditional images of God are male-defined makes the task of contemporary reconstruction all the more urgent and compelling for women. Jewish feminists seek to open up the range and character of our symbols for God both so that their metaphorical nature becomes experientially clear, and so that they evoke the experience of coming to selfhood in community so central to Judaism and feminism. While we can only speculate as to the hidden Torah of women that has been lost to us—the buried experiences of God that peek out from the interstices of male texts or struggle to define themselves within the constraints of patriarchal forms—we can as women find the images of God that speak to us in the present and in doing so rethink and transform the tradition. In this way, we both bring women's experience to the naming of God and continue the long process of Jewish Godwrestling that demands of each generation that it search for and speak its own symbols, standing again at Sinai with the consciousness of today.

Jewish Feminist God-Language and Feminist Spirituality

Jewish Feminist God-Language

When Jewish feminists first recognized the problems with traditional God-language, we responded to the hegemony of the omnipresent "he" by using female pronouns and images to refer to God. In what was probably the first article to deal theoretically with the issue of female God-language in a Jewish context, Rita Gross argued that, "If we do not mean that God is male when we use masculine pronouns and imagery," there should be no objection "to using female imagery and pronouns as well."[32] Exclusively masculine imagery for God, she contended, tells us nothing about the deity, but it does say a great deal about an androcentric Judaism that regards female images as degrading precisely to the extent that it has degraded and marginalized women. Impersonal, neuter language for God is not a solution, Gross reasoned, for it prevents us from speaking to God, and at the same time permits us to hide our sexism behind abstractions. Jews, she said, must begin to address God as "She." "God-She" is not an addition to Jewish God-language, but applies to every aspect of God within the tradition.

Everything that has ever been said or that we still want to say of *ha-kadosh baruch hu* [the holy one, blessed be he] can also be said of *ha-k'dosha baruch he* [sic] [the holy one, blessed be she] and, conversely, 'God-She' is appropriately used in every context in which any reference to God occurs."[33]

In the same period that Gross offered a theoretical argument for female language, Naomi Janowitz and Maggie Wenig were independently giving liturgical life to her assertions by producing a new feminist version of the Sabbath prayerbook. While some of their prayers simply recast the English translation of the liturgy in female pronouns, others experimented more boldly with new metaphors, reimaging God in feminine form. The God that emerged from *Siddur Nashim* was partly the traditional deity in feminine garb and partly a more thoroughly transformed divinity. Addressed as the "blessed and glorified, exalted and honored, magnified and praised . . . Holy One, blessed is She," she was also a Mother birthing the world and protecting it with her womb:

Blessed is She who spoke and the world came to be. . . .
Blessed is She who in the beginning, gave birth. . . .
Blessed is She whose womb covers the earth.
Blessed is She whose womb protects all creatures.[34]

Some of Janowitz and Wenig's liturgy has weathered well the more-than-a-decade since it was written, but ten years have also clarified the incompleteness of its explorations. The very accumulation of female pronouns in certain prayers is a glorious celebration of women's power that is rare in the culture and rarer still in a religious context. But while female imagery is important for many reasons, of itself it does not address the nature of God as dominating Other. Although changing pronouns and some imagery modifies and softens the traditional picture of God, it does not fundamentally alter the conception of a great potentate fighting for his/her people and ruling over the world. The God of Janowitz and Wenig is still a deity strong of arm, a savior of Israel who rescues her children from slavery and drowns Egyptians in the sea. Gross and Janowitz and Wenig are wrong in assuming that any attribute applied to "God-He" is equally well applied to "God-She." If the image of God-He as dominating Other is part of a whole system of dualisms that includes the subordination of female to male, then introducing God-She into this system poses a fundamental contradiction that threatens to disrupt the system and throw it into question. Female pronouns and imagery inserted into otherwise traditional forms can only *initiate* a process of examination and discussion that needs to end in a more radical transformation of religious language.

The same ambiguous or initiatory status that belongs to experimental use of female pronouns and imagery belongs also to the Shekhinah, the female aspect of God in the mystical tradition. It is not surprising that, in seeking female images for God, Jewish feminists turned early on to the one developed image Judaism has to offer—the image of the Shekhinah as the indwelling presence of God. While in the Talmud and midrash the Shekhinah represented the manifest presence of God without any suggestion that this presence was female, in Kabbalism the Shekhinah became a feminine element in God alongside the masculine "Holy One, Blessed be He." The marriage between God and his bride Israel reflected in biblical sources was transferred to the inner life of God as a sacred union within the Godhead itself. The Shekhinah-bride was described in a host of images—princess, daughter, queen, mother, matron, moon, sea, faith, wisdom, community of Israel, mother Rachel—many, though not all of them, female in fact or association.[35]

While the image of the Shekhinah was an important constituent of Kabbalism that gained widespread popularity, it was never incorporated into the liturgy as an accepted counterweight to the masculinity of God. Feminists have tried to use it precisely in this way, however, invoking the Shekhinah in a variety of liturgical contexts. Lynn Gottlieb, for example, replaces the traditional *Bor'khu et Adonai* (Blessed are you God [masculine]) with *Brukha Yah Shekhinah* (Blessed are you Shekhinah), a formula that has been used at many feminist gatherings. She also addresses God as Shekhinah in more fluid ways, naming variously the "the feminine presence/ She-Who-Dwells-Within."

> Shechinah
> calling us
> from exile
> inside us exiled
> calling us
> home
> home[36]

Other feminists have also played with images of the Shekhinah, swearing, in the moving words of Rachel Adler, "I'll never again/ Pray against my own flesh."[37]

There are obvious advantages to having a feminine element in God that is a firmly established aspect of tradition. Yet when the tradition is a male one—both with regard to Judaism in general and Kabbalism in particular—female images are apt to come with certain limitations. Two of the virtues of the image of Shekhinah from a feminist perspective are that it is an image of divine immanence and an image of God in nonhierarchical relation. It thus deliberately offsets the picture of God as dominating Other and at the same time fits in well with the general emphasis on mutual relation in feminist spirituality. The Shekhinah, as opposed to the totally unknowable *Kadosh Barukh Hu* (holy one, blessed be he), is precisely that aspect of God with which we can be in relation, and it is experienced in joint study, community gatherings, lovemaking, and other moments of common and intimate human connection.[38]

These positive aspects of the image are tied to its shortcomings, however, for this immanent, relational element in God has never been on an equal footing with the ineffable, masculine Godhead.[39] Just as in the Bible, Israel is the bride of God, so the Shekhinah is the subordinate bride and consort within God. It is the feminine as the male understands that secondary aspect within himself, not as it is seen or experienced by women. And just as the bride Israel can also be whore and adulterous, so the Shekhinah is the ambiguous male projection of what woman can be—nursemaid, mother, bride, wife, but also wanton seductress, devouring monster, and bringer of death.[40] Like the use of female pronouns, then, the image of Shekhinah counterbalances the male nature of God and raises important questions without representing a full solution to the problem of traditional God-language. The Shekhinah is a usable image for feminists only if it is partly wrenched free from its original context, so that the tradition becomes a starting point for an imaginative process that moves beyond and transforms it.

As step three, then, in seeking alternative ways of imaging God, feminists have begun to look for new symbols that resonate with tradition but also come out of and express women's experiences. While the image of Shekhinah begins to combine female metaphor with an understanding of God's power as immanent in the world, it leaves intact the traditional image of *Ha-Kadosh Borukh Hu* (the holy one, blessed be he) in a way other feminist experiments seek to avoid. Attempting to link the reimagining of God to a new vision of community, feminists repeatedly choose metaphors that picture divine power not as something above and over us but in and around. God's power is not a power that dominates us, but one that elicits our power, meeting us in the shifting and changing forms of our lives. This open-ended quest for new imagery is in its early stages, with experiments taking place in quiet corners, passed on by word of mouth, and circulating privately. Lynn Gottlieb and Marcia

Falk, as two Jewish feminists whose very different work on God-language is at least in part publicly available, can represent some of the range of feminist efforts to find new ways of speaking to and about God.

Lynn Gottlieb's new namings of God are performance pieces, written/spoken in a dramatic, incantatory style, and drawing together the imaginal resources of a number of religious traditions. Her "A Psalm," for example, moves behind the biblical Psalms to their ancient Near Eastern precursors, drawing on the Babylonian Hymn to Ishtar to sing in praise of God. Images from the original hymn are combined with many names for God from the Jewish tradition, yielding a litany of names and images that evoke the infinite, changing, and flowing depths of God's nature.

> PRAISE HER
> MOST AWESOME OF THE MIGHTY
> REVERE HER
> SHE IS A WOMAN OF THE PEOPLE
>
>   *   *   *   *
>
> TEHOMOT · ELAT
> ACHOTI CALAH
> YAH TZVAOT · EL SHADDAI
> EM HAMRACHAMIM
> SHABBAT CHAI OLAMIM
> PRAISE HER WHEN YOU COME UPON HER NAME
> SINGING INSIDE YOU
> SHE IS THE BREATH OF ALL LIVING
> PRAISE HER. . . .[41]

Frequently using a series of traditional names for God to break the idolatry of a single image, Gottlieb is very concerned about female metaphors, sometimes elaborating the feminine resonances or associations of particular appellations. What characterizes her God-language above all, however, is not just its femaleness but its sense of fluidity, movement, and multiplicity, its daring interweaving of women's experiences with Jewish, Native American, and Goddess imagery that leaves the reader/

hearer with an expanded sense of what is possible in speaking of/to God.

Marcia Falk, on the other hand, tries to perpetrate a quieter revolution by focusing on the blessing form that plays such an important role in Jewish life. To her mind, the traditional blessing formula—*Barukh atah adonay eloheynu melekh ha-olam* (Blessed are you, lord our God, king of the world)—is sexist, hierarchical, and idolatrous in its fixedness, requiring dislodging through a series of new metaphors. In choosing new images for her blessings, she tries "to confront the full extent of our liturgical idolatry," uprooting not simply the male image of God but anthropocentrism generally. Falk thus takes her metaphors from all aspects of creation, trying to connect the origin of blessing with the aspect of reality being blessed. Her blessing over bread, for example, praises the source or wellspring of life that "brings forth bread from the earth." The image of wellspring or source is nonhierarchical, suggesting an immanent presence that rises from the earth rather than a God who is ruler or lord over it. At the same time, the fact that the word for source is feminine in Hebrew produces a subtle shift in the language of the blessing, displacing the ubiquitous masculine. Moreover, she begins the blessing "Let us bless the source of life," referring the act of blessing to the community of human beings that blesses at the same time the community acknowledges its connection to a deeper, underground reality. Other blessings are the subject of different sorts of experiments—allowing divinity to appear in unexpected places, connecting prayer to issues of social justice, grappling with the ranked differentiations that characterize many areas of Jewish thinking.[42]

> Let us acknowledge the source of life
> for the earth and for nourishment.
> May we conserve the earth
> that it may sustain us
> and let us seek sustenance
> for all who inhabit the world.
> *   *   *   *

Let us distinguish
parts within the whole
and bless their differences.
Like Sabbath and the six days of creation
may our lives be made whole
through relation.[43]

Writing new blessings becomes an expression of commitment to a tradition in the process of becoming, a tradition continually needing to be recreated even as it remembers the past.

The Emerging God of Feminist Spirituality

As Jewish feminists seek to name God out of our own experiences, transforming traditional conceptions of God in a deep and far-reaching way, our efforts become part of a wider movement to rename and reconceptualize God that is taking place among women of different faiths all over the country. Jewish feminist attempts to reimage God, insofar as they reflect an engagement with women's experience, flow into the broader stream of writing and ritualizing that is the women's spirituality movement. To be sure, there are significant differences and disagreements between feminists of differing religious commitments. But there is also a commonality of experience and insight that shapes feminist God-language in diverse contexts and that makes the arguments and images of non-Jewish women an important challenge to and resource for Jewish feminists.

For example, the flowing, moving, changing God of Lynn Gottlieb's incantations is linked to the dynamic "becoming" deity that, from early on, has appeared in much feminist discussion, liturgy, and writing. In 1972, a gathering of—mainly Christian—women met for a week at Grailville in Loveland, Ohio, to explore theology together. In one of the small working groups that was a daily part of the conference, the women realized that traditional names for God no longer adequately reflected their experience. They began to call out words that meant God to them, putting their designations on a large newsprint board. One of the fascinating aspects of the resulting list

was its large number of "ing" words—changing, creating, enabling, nurturing, pushing, calling into question, suffering,
touching, breaking through. The God of their experience was
not an immutable being "out there," but a process of which
they were part. Feeling themselves newly empowered through
participation in feminist community, they knew God as the dynamic source and context of that empowerment—a power to be
named through rhythm and movement as much as through
words.[44]

Interestingly, Mary Daly's *Beyond God the Father* had not yet
been published at the time of the Grailville gathering, for the
conference anticipated her naming of God as a dynamic verb.
Grounding her theology in the experience of women turning
away from the "pseudo-reality" of patriarchy, Daly argued that
God is not a Being, in fact, not a noun at all. Rather God is Being, the most active of verbs, the reality in which "we participate—live, move, and have our being." Women newly learning
to say "I am" to themselves and each other experience their
own unfolding as related to the "endless unfolding of God."[45]
This sense of connection to a source of personal/communal/
cosmic power is the experiential base for a host of conceptions
of a becoming deity that have emerged since Daly's book.
Whether described in the philosophical categories of process
thought or enacted in the chants and swirling forms of feminist
ritual, God is always moving in and through the shifting web
of life, enabling and necessitating continual growth and
change.[46]

Another aspect of feminist spirituality related to the conception of a changing God is avowal of the holiness of all that is.
If God is not a great king who rules the world, but the power
that sustains and moves it, then God is present in the whole of
reality—all the processes of development and transformation,
growth and decay that make up cosmic existence. Thus Marcia
Falk's attempt to dislodge the anthropocentrism of traditional
Jewish language by drawing metaphors for God from the whole
of creation is very much part of a wider feminist inclination to

turn to nature as a source of religious imagery and to insist on the value of the nonhuman world. For both certain recent literature by women and the women's spirituality movement, human beings are not the acme and end of creation but participants in a broad and complex web of life all of which is sacred.[47]

While the sense of spiritual connection to nature could be illustrated from many feminist authors, nowhere is it expressed more clearly and prototypically than in Alice Walker's *The Color Purple*. In this novel, as if in exemplification of feminist theological arguments, women's discovery of the sacred in the natural world is linked to the process of self-empowerment through relation and the rejection of the dominating white, male God. For the first two-thirds of Walker's novel, Celie, the poor, black, molested, and raped heroine, writes letters to God—the only one who hears or cares about her. As, through her relationship with her lover Shug, however, Celie reconnects with her beloved sister Nettie and comes to a sense of her own dignity and worth as a human being, she becomes furious at the God who is as "trifling . . . and lowdown" as all the other men she knows. True, Shug tells her, the white, male God found in church is just part of the structures of domination that keep black people in their place. But "you have to git man off your eyeball," Shug says, "before you can see anything a'tall."

She say, My first step from the old white man was trees. Then air. Then birds. Then other people. But one day when I was sitting quiet and feeling like a motherless child, which I was, it come to me: that feeling of being part of everything, not separate at all. I knew that if I cut a tree my arm would bleed. . . .

Later in the novel, Celie herself has the experience that—in Shug's words—"God is everything . . . that is or ever was or ever will be." Sitting and smoking pot with family around the table, she hears an insistent humming coming from the world outside the window. "I think I know what it is, I say. They say, What? I say, everything. Yeah, they say. That make a lots of sense."[48] Terse as this conversation is, it would be difficult to find a more powerful affirmation that God is found within the world and not over and above it.

Images of a God in process and metaphors taken from the natural world cross religious lines. For some feminists, however, this dynamic, immanent deity has a face and name: She is the Goddess. Drawing on widespread traditions of Goddess worship but also freely modifying them, feminist followers of the Goddess find in her both a rich and life-affirming alternative to the (upstart) male God and the point of intersection for all the themes of new naming feminist spirituality involves. The Goddess is, of course, God-She, but in a clearer and more powerful way. Not simply a feminine reworking of the masculine deity but an ancient power in her own right, she gathers to her all the qualities and prerogatives of the goddesses of many names. She is Asherah, Ishtar, Isis, Afrekete, Oyo, Ezuli, Mary, and Shekhinah. She is lover, creator, warrior, grantor of fertility, lawgiver, maiden, mother, and crone. All the images predicated of God-She are found in her in their original female form.

For some followers of the Goddess, this plurality of names and images signifies the plural nature of reality; for others, the many names of the one source of being. In either case, qualities of the Goddess are not to be reified or overinterpreted. They are important as images that make us aware of aspects of reality that might otherwise have escaped attention; yet as images, they can be taken off and put on.[49] "We know the Goddess is not the moon," says witch and priestess Starhawk, "but we still thrill to its light glinting through the branches. We know the Goddess is not a woman, but we respond with love as if She were."[50] Taking symbols seriously but not literally, followers of the Goddess pull together the various themes in feminist spirituality, combining the centrality of female imagery with the evocation of a changing, moving deity and the sense of the sacred as present in and experienced through the natural world.

Issues in Jewish Resistance to Feminist Spirituality

These connections between Jewish feminism and broader trends in feminist spirituality raise a number of troubling questions, for such parallels are exactly what critics of Jewish feminism most fear. Not simply explicit mention of the Goddess, but suspicion she may be lurking somewhere behind any attempt to alter traditional God-language raises charges of "paganism" that are considered themselves sufficient to condemn all feminist work. Direct acknowledgment that there are similarities between Jewish feminist and Goddess spirituality certainly threatens, then, to place Jewish feminism beyond the pale—even when Jewish feminists do not invoke ancient goddesses and have no interest in doing so. In trying to formulate a Jewish feminist conception of God, it is important to sort out the issues that lie behind the "pagan" label and to try to determine when, if ever, they are legitimate and when they reflect either religious prejudice or continuing attachment to patriarchal aspects of Judaism that might better be transformed.

In historical terms, cries of paganism hark back to biblical times, recalling the intense, prolonged physical and spiritual battle between two different modes of religious expression and understanding. As I remarked in discussing the concept of chosenness, Israel, from its beginnings, understood its own distinctiveness partly by defining itself over against the customs and beliefs of surrounding peoples. What made Israel "a kingdom of priests and a holy nation" was both obedience to the law and—what was in some ways the same thing—separation from the practices and worship of the Canaanites. Throughout the Bible, the Canaanite cult is repeatedly characterized in terms of idolatry and licentiousness. Canaanites did not simply worship false gods—idols of wood and stone that could neither see nor hear and could do nothing for the worshiper—they "whored" and "played the harlot" after them. To keep pure from such practices, Israel not only had to abjure worship of other gods, but also to follow the stringent sexual regulations laid out in the law to differentiate it from its neighbors. In practicing sexual restraint, moreover, Israel had its God as a model. Unlike the neighboring deities, whose sexual exploits were detailed in myth, Israel's God had no sexual partner; in biblical Judaism, there is no sacred marriage within the deity.

This struggle between two different religious perspectives was not simply a struggle between Israel and Canaan, however, but also a struggle within Israel. The Bible makes amply clear that there were many in Israel who long continued to worship other gods and goddesses alongside Yahweh. Indeed, the prophetic writings can be read as an account of a prolonged battle between the minority in Israel who advocated exclusive worship of Yahweh and the majority who worshiped Yahweh . . . and others. Metaphors of whoredom and adultery are applied by the prophets first of all to Israel, because it is Israel who continually abandons and betrays Yahweh to whom she is supposedly married. But while the Bible condemns the worship of all deities other than Yahweh, Ba'al is singled out as the rival of Yahweh far more often than any specific goddess. Though the reason for this may be that Ba'al was most appealing to Israelites, it is also possible that Goddess worship was less threatening to the male Yahweh than was the worship of competing male gods. Certainly, the presence of an Asherah in the Temple for much of its existence suggests that Israelites were hardly indifferent to goddesses. Rather, it seems that, despite prophetic invective and theology, for a good span of Israelite history, Yahweh was popularly regarded as having a consort.[51]

Whatever the reality of Israelite practices, however, it is through the eyes of the victorious prophets that Jews see the struggle against "idolatry," and it is above all this fact that fuels emotions around the issue of paganism. The prophetic caricature of Canaanite religion as the literal and sensuous worship of sticks and stones has become so much a part of Jewish self-understanding that we no longer stop to think about whether it corresponds to anything we know about ancient worship, or the religious use of images in contemporary living traditions. It is forgotten that what the prophets attack is another religious system—not the later Jewish one to be sure, but one that sustained people for millennia, and that many Israelites apparently found nourishing and meaningful. Paganism plays essentially the same role in the Tanakh that the Pharisees play in the New Testament: Each is set up as the despised Other over against which the superior new religion defines itself.[52] The parallels between Christian treatment of Judaism and Jewish treatment of paganism should themselves alert Jews to the danger of unthinking contempt for another tradition and the need to examine the historical reality that underlies prophetic invective. Where it is basically this contempt that feeds condemnations of Jewish feminism as pagan, such condemnations need not be taken seriously.[53]

The substantive issues raised by Jewish fears about paganism are difficult to disentangle from this prejudicial welter of feelings. Anxieties about polytheism, sensuousness, female imagery, and goddesses tend to get lumped together both with each other and the general opprobrium the term paganism arouses. The following passage from an essay by Cynthia Ozick provides a good example of the intellectual muddle the specter of paganism evokes. Discussing the feminist suggestion that Judaism needs female God-language and that for "King of the Universe" we might substitute "Queen of the Universe," Ozick says:

The answer stuns with its crudity. It is preposterous. What? Millennia after the cleansing purity of Abraham's vision of the One Creator, a return to Astarte, Hera, Juno, Venus, and all their proliferating sisterhood? Sex goddesses, fertility goddesses, mother goddesses? The sacrifices brought to these were often enough human. This is the vision intended to "restore dignity" to Jewish women? A resurrection of every ancient idolatry the Jewish idea came into the world to drive out, so as to begin again with a purifying clarity? The answer slanders and sullies monotheism.[54]

Ozick jumps here from the idea of female metaphors for God to the worship of ancient goddesses, from goddesses to sexual-

ity and fertility, from sexuality and fertility to charges of human
sacrifice and idolatry, and from here to worry about monotheism. If we sift out the hysterical and historically false implication that Goddess worship usually involved human sacrifice (a
charge frequently leveled by competing religious traditions at
their rivals), and set aside the vague but threatening images
meant to be aroused by "every ancient idolatry," there seem to
be three issues raised by this passage: the relationship between
female imagery for God and Goddess worship, the meaning of
monotheism, and the relationship between female imagery and
nature and sexuality. Since these same issues emerge in many
criticisms of Jewish feminism, they require some clarification
and response.

First of all, the equation of female God-language with Goddess worship either presupposes that the God of Judaism is so
irrevocably male that any broadening of anthropomorphic language must refer to a different deity, or it simply makes no
sense at all. The overwhelming majority of Jewish feminists
who have experimented with religious language in no way see
themselves as imaging or worshiping a Goddess; they are
trying to enrich the range of metaphors Jews use in talking
about God. Since efforts at new language are experimental, and
not everyone who feels the inadequacy of old images has the
skill to create alternatives, some new images may be awkward
and even faintly ridiculous. "Queen of the Universe" may be
such an infelicitous image, for it lacks the familiarity of king
and at the same time is equally wanting in contemporary cultural resonance. But the use of this image does not stem from
any intention to set up a queen alongside a king; it is simply
an unsuccessful attempt to speak of the one God in a new way.
Rationally, it seems contradictory to argue that the Jewish God
transcends sexuality, that anthropomorphism is not to be taken
literally, and at the same time insist that new metaphors slander
and sully monotheism.

The second issue, then, that is raised by fears of paganism is
the meaning of monotheism itself. Some years ago, there was

an extended debate in academic religion circles about whether monotheism or polytheism is more inclusive. Does polytheism embrace monotheism as one of its possibilities, or does the One include the Many?[55] The debate was not very fruitful because it rested on divergent conceptions of monotheism, the same divergence that surfaces in discussions of Jewish feminism. On one understanding—probably the more popular—monotheism is the worship of one finite God imaged as infinite, as if the chief deity in the ancient pantheon were elevated to *the* deity, the only deity, the king of all the earth. On the second understanding, the one God incorporates the qualities and characteristics of, so to speak, the whole pantheon, with nothing remaining outside.[56] Monotheism in this second sense may be thought of in terms of the same part/whole analogy that I used to characterize differences within community. Just as the subgroups within a community are all parts of a larger unity, so any individual image of God is a part of the divine totality that in its totality embraces the diversity of an infinite community. Only when our metaphors for God are sufficiently inclusive that they reflect the multiplicity both of a pluralistic Israel and of a cosmic community will God truly be one—which is to say, all in all.

When monotheism is not understood in this inclusive sense, but is identified with the worship of a single image or picture of God, what passes for monotheism is really monolatry. God's oneness, instead of being all-embracing, excludes central aspects of reality. The Jewish tradition has been well aware of the dangers of such exclusion, at least in relation to certain areas of existence. Thus it has held God responsible for evil, for example, rather than allowing evil to be seen as an independent power. When Isaiah says, "I form light and create darkness, I make weal and create woe, I the Lord do all these things" (45:7), he is speaking out of the inclusive understanding of monotheism as embracing the totality of experience. This same insight concerning God's inclusiveness has not been applied to the issue of gender, however. But it is no less true of gender than of the problem of evil that a God who cannot include all experience is a God over against an Other. Such a god is an idol made in "man's" image, not the creator, source of maleness and femaleness, relativizer of all gods and goddesses who nonetheless includes them as part of God's self.

The use of female imagery, then, so far from "sullying" monotheism, becomes a test of whether Jews are able to sustain a genuinely monotheistic framework. Is our God sufficiently God that we are able to incorporate the feminine and women's experience into our understanding of divinity? It is true that multiple images of God involve certain hazards, but the Jewish tradition has faced these hazards before and has developed ways to deal with them. A wonderful passage in *Pesikta Rabbati*, discussing the many guises in which God has appeared to the children of Israel, responds to the "whoreson" who insists that the guises are different gods. Say to him, it says, "I am the One of the sea and I am the One of Sinai."[57] Extending this reply, feminists need to assert that the full range of images for God we have tested and will test are also different guises of the same One. Indeed, the capacity to see the One in and through the changing forms of the many, to glimpse the whole in and through its infinite images, is finally what monotheism is truly about.

The practice of Jewish feminists who invoke the names of goddesses as part of their worship can be understood in the context of this inclusive monotheism. Aside from the fact that these names may have been called on by our foremothers and thus can connect us in community to them, using the names of goddesses in liturgy is one way of capturing and conveying multiple images of female power—images that have resonance and weight in the midst of a culture that provides almost no positive models of female strength or authority. While the decision to use such names necessarily places those who make it on the boundary of the tradition, its purpose often is not to destroy but to express that inclusive monotheism that is not yet real when God incorporates the characteristics of the male deities of Canaan but excludes the qualities of the goddesses. Only when reciting the names of goddesses is meant to name ultimate reality as plural do feminists surrender the vision of a unity that embraces diversity—a vision I would want to affirm as central to a Jewish feminist understanding of God and community.

There is another aspect of the "purity" of monotheism that is at stake in the dispute over female images, and that is the association of the feminine with sexuality and nature. This is the third issue Ozick raises, for she jumps from the "Queen of the Universe" to sex, fertility, and mother goddesses. On one level, this jump constitutes just one more distortion of historical Goddess worship. Goddesses, while often mothers who ensured fertility of humans and the earth, also regulated and presided over many cultural functions, representing social order and wisdom as well as natural regeneration. But this common enough misrepresentation also signals a deeper problem—the persistent religious and cultural connection of women with body and the earth, qualities that in turn are seen as related to paganism.[58] If male/female, culture/nature, spirit/flesh, restraint/sensual indulgence are all dichotomized, and in each case women symbolize the inferior "pagan" side of the dichotomy, then female God-language is bound to arouse deep feelings of discomfort and even revulsion. It threatens to reconsecrate aspects of existence that were once considered holy but were desacralized by Judaism as part of its long battle against paganism.[59]

From a feminist perspective, however, this threat of reconsecration and the association of women with body and earth from which it arises are arguments in favor of female language rather than motives to reject it. Female language, precisely because it disturbs and offends, throws into question long-established patterns of dualistic thinking. On the one hand, feminists must protest the identification of femaleness with sexuality—as if men were not equally sensual and sexual beings rooted in the natural world. On the other hand, insofar as women continue to be linked with sexuality and nature, the use of female imagery for divinity can help to counter and dispute the disparagement of sexuality and the earth that are unfortunate corollaries of the battle against paganism. The ability to affirm our bodies and their home in the natural world is an important aim of the feminist transformation of tradition. The reexamination of Jewish attitudes toward sexuality and nature—a process catalyzed partly by the use of female imagery—will not "paganize" Judaism so much as restore to it values disparaged and lost in the process of defining itself over against another religion.

Gathering the Strands: Toward a Jewish Feminist Understanding of God

Where does all this leave us in terms of a Jewish feminist understanding of God? It should be clear from all I have said that one aspect of such an understanding would have to be advocacy and appreciation of a plurality of images for God, a plurality that includes some traditional metaphors but that also goes well beyond them in embracing the experience of those who have hitherto been excluded from the process of naming the sacred. Just as the feminist rethinking of Torah involves broadening Jewish memory, and the reconceptualization of Israel involves acknowledging and respecting the diversity of Jewish community, so the feminist reimaging of God entails reclaiming and shaping sufficient metaphors for God that the diversity of Jewish community is reflected in its naming of divinity and the commitment to communal diversity is grounded in an inclusive monotheism. If identifying God with a particular set of metaphors both limits God and supports a community in which some people have more value than others, using a broad and changing variety of metaphors brings home on the nonrational level on which images function that God has many guises, no one of which is final. When we feel free to try on and play with a range of images for God, then our speaking and praying becomes explicitly a "naming toward God,"[60] and all Jews are challenged to reach into the depths of our experience to speak out the names we find there.

The affirmation of multiple images for God is thus an essential aspect of Jewish feminist spirituality; yet it is not its center. Any particular community, even when it knows its symbols for God are tentative and open, is still likely to express itself through a set of images that reflect its own central experiences, experiences that become normative for sifting and creating imagery. We have seen that at the center of the women's spirituality movement, for example, is a sense of connection to the natural world that controls the metaphors adopted for the sacred. In dethroning the white male God who is in the "white folks' white bible," Shug begins with "trees. Then air. Then birds." Only "then other people."[61] Goddess spirituality is rooted in the intuition that "the earth is holy," and that the Goddess is found in the elements that surround us: earth, ocean, stars, air, sky, moon, flowers, trees.[62] In this spirituality, people are part of the natural world, persons among others without holding a privileged position within the natural order.

This use of natural imagery for God is enormously important in a culture that has trampled on and violated the natural world and that threatens the whole biosphere with ecological and nuclear destruction. The affirmation that the earth is holy and that all parts of creation have intrinsic value provides a powerful corrective to the view that human beings are the measure of all things. Yet to my mind, the rediscovery of human connection with nature and the search for adequate metaphors to express it is just one aspect of a Jewish feminist spirituality. The other aspect—and one feminists have been less successful in translating into imagery—is the presence of God in empowered, egalitarian community. The emphasis on community that Judaism and feminism share means that the God who sustains the world is experienced not only in relation to nature, but also in the coming together of human beings who see their communal purpose as transparent to a larger purpose in which it is grounded.

As I argued in discussing the spiritual dimension of community in the last chapter, community "can be the primary vehicle and place of religious experience," and "the divine presence rests in community in a uniquely powerful way."[63]

The centrality of human community to the Jewish religious experience is clear. Jews first found God in the midst of community, and, finding God, were constituted a community. But I would also maintain that insofar as women's experience of the holiness of nature has been named in a feminist context, in the feminist case too, it is the experience of community that has allowed the articulation and development of a nature spirituality. Feminism created a communal context in which women could identify and claim experiences that they might otherwise never have brought to full consciousness or might have regarded as purely personal. What Carol P. Christ has called "communal mysticism"—a form of mysticism in which "the great powers to which women awaken are experienced through social groups or movements"—would thus accompany and support the "nature mysticism" that is the more prominent theme in feminist spirituality.[64] My point is not to insist that the one form of spirituality is more fundamental or valid than the other; different emphases often reflect basic individual differences in religious experience. But I would argue that the relatively neglected human communal dimension of feminist spirituality requires far more attention—and that it is precisely in this dimension that Judaism and feminism converge.

From a critical perspective, of course, the centrality of human community in Jewish religious history may be taken simply as a sign of Jewish anthropocentrism. Yet even if we highlight those aspects of Judaism that recognize the intrinsic worth of nonhuman creation and seek to move the tradition further in this direction, I believe there are still aspects of human community that make it a particularly powerful locus for religious experience. Not only is human community the place and prerequisite of our coming to personhood, but also our relationships with other human beings involve the possibility of a reciprocity and mutuality of intention and commitment that is not available in other sorts of connection. Martin Buber, the philosopher of relation, remarks in his classic work *I and Thou* that there are three arenas of human life in which genuine relationships can arise: life with nature, life with other human beings, and life with "spiritual beings," by which he means ideas and cultural creations. Yet along with Buber's—often criticized—insistence that there can be dialogue with nature, he says that it is only in relation to the second sphere that true mutuality is possible. Relationships between human beings need not hover at the "threshold of mutuality" but can express themselves in language, so that acknowledgement of the other as a person can be both given and received.[65]

This capacity for mutuality in human relations is the foundation for the moral life that also finds expression in human community. Human responsibility for the well-being of the world never can be fulfilled simply through personal action. Human beings come to accountability in the midst of communities that interpret and set out where obligations lie, and community is the context for fulfilling our obligations. Moreover, in coming together with others in mutual commitment to ideas or causes, we ever and again form new communities through which to renew and carry on our purposes. It is as we join with others, in a way that only human beings can, in shared engagement to a common vision, that we find ourselves in the presence of another presence that is the final source of our hopes and intentions, and that undergirds and sustains them. Whether the substance of our cause be our lives as women, the fate of the earth, the pursuit of justice in human community, or some more narrowly religious purpose, it is through the struggle with others to act responsibly in history that we come to know our own actions as encompassed and empowered by a wider universe of action and thus come to know God in a profound and significant way.[66]

The feminist experience of finding in community both a new sense of personal empowerment and mission and connection with its sustaining source may not be so different from the early Israelite experience of discovering in community both a dawning national identity and a covenant with the God who gave it. In both cases, community is the location and vehicle for the experience of God and for the continuing enactment of its meaning. Nevertheless, neither Jews nor feminists have found a vocabulary for speaking about God that adequately reflects the presence of God in the midst of a responsive and responsible community. Feminist spirituality has developed a fuller range of natural imagery than imagery taken from feminist community. And the predominant Jewish language for speaking about God, while it supposedly elaborates the experience of covenant, in fact draws from community those images of dominance that dominate the liturgy. Images of God as lord and king evoke one who is over against community as its ruler and head, not one who is with it as partner, nourisher, and goad. The Jewish mystical tradition provides important alternative conceptions of God that emphasize human community and responsibility, but without translating these conceptions into a range of new images for *Ha-Kadosh Borukh Hu* (the holy one, blessed be he).[67] Jewish feminism, in seeking to draw together into a vision of empowered egalitarian community the Jewish and feminist affirmations of community, needs an understanding of God that emerges out of and is faithful to the place where its God is found.

Insofar as God is experienced in community, changes in communal structure and in the shape and forms of worship can of themselves contribute to a new understanding of God even in the absence of changes in metaphor. Women's religious leadership in many Jewish communities testifies to the presence of God within women. Feminist or havurah-style prayer, which favors small groups whose members face each other during worship and depends on the participation of all present, evokes a sense of God immanent in community. Communities that open themselves to the richness of Jewish diversity gain access to the spiritual resources present in that diversity. One need not explicitly name God for God to be found—a truth Marcia Falk tries to express in her blessings by varying their syntax so that God appears in unexpected or hidden places.[68] Indeed, the experience of God conveyed by the structure of a group can contradict or overpower the messages of a traditional liturgy.

Yet given the power of images and of the traditional liturgy in shaping conceptions of God for the Jewish community as a whole, feminists also cannot avoid the task of suggesting images that express the presence of God in a diverse and egalitarian community. In doing so, we will have to put new emphasis on traditional metaphors forgotten or slighted and bring to birth new metaphors that reflect the experiences of members of the community who heretofore have been subordinated or silenced. Birth is the appropriate image for this process, for naming new metaphors involves not simply invention, but the capacity to listen to what is already happening and to articulate communal experiences as they begin to emerge. It may be that truly satisfying communal images of God await the creation of new communities, for communal structures and communal metaphors are mutually related. One cannot create images in a vacuum; they arise out of new experiences and need time and nurturance to ripen and flower. Feminist images of God name the experience of people on the way, in the process of becoming—as, indeed, do *all* images of God, though this is often forgotten.

Recognizing, then, that the becoming of new images is in its early stages, I would suggest that there are (at least) two kinds of Jewish feminist God-naming that need to be taken together to produce a picture of God that reflects the experience of egalitarian community. The first kind of God-language is anthropomorphic language. Modern Jewish thinkers who have emphasized the importance of a lived relationship with God have tended to speak about God in philosophical language, avoiding anthropomorphisms that might objectify God and thus undermine the immediacy of relation.[69] Similarly, some feminists have sought to solve the problem of traditional male metaphors by using nonimagistic, or at least nonpersonal language. Some women have preferred to fill in names like "God" or "the Eternal" with new experiences, rather than create new images that would reify certain aspects of experience. Others have avoided personal imagery because it necessarily reinforces traditional anthropocentrism and because it implies that God is separable from the world.[70]

But while it is certainly true that anthropomorphic images can be dangerous, supporting patterns of dominance or substituting for the experiences they claim to communicate, such images also appeal to places in our nature that cannot be reached by abstract philosophical discourse or direct designations like "God" and "the Eternal." Even nonpersonal images, though they are important to feminist God-language, are not themselves sufficient, I would argue, to evoke the God of community. Nonanthropomorphic language threatens to leave intact old anthropomorphic images that can continue to coexist with and subvert neutral language. For the English speaker, it is quite possible to avoid pronouns for God and to refer to God as the Eternal or source of life and still picture that eternal source as male. Only deliberately disruptive—that is, female—metaphors can break the imaginative hold of male metaphors that have been used for millennia. For the Hebrew speaker, who has available nonpersonal female images, it is still difficult to convey the presence of God in community while excluding those images that come most directly from the web of interpersonal relations that constitute community. We are roused to remember the God of community and to value and create certain kinds of communities precisely by those images that most vividly evoke our real experiences of community. Just as feminists are struggling to find communal structures that do not involve hierarchy, so we need to find ways of speaking about God's presence in community that do not invoke metaphors of domination. Failing to use the images that emerge from our real-life struggles, we banish as a source of religious expression central aspects of our lives.[71]

To my mind, then, feminists cannot avoid the use of anthropomorphic imagery. Indeed, incorporating the appreciation of diversity that should characterize all feminist God-language, this kind of imagery would include a wide range of metaphors, from purposely disquieting female images, to female and nongendered images that express intimacy, partnership, and mutuality between humans and God. It may be important, for example, to use for a time images like Queen of the Universe and Woman of War in order to jar worshipers, precipitate discussion, and raise questions about the meaning and effects of the imagery we use. What is the source of our attachment to male imagery? Is the image of a monarch—male or female—one we want to affirm? Do women need to claim the warrior within ourselves, and are there images of warrior that are not images of violent destruction?[72] While metaphors of queen and warrior are problematic and will not constitute the lasting contribution of feminism to Jewish God-language, they have an important bridge role to play in presenting images of female religious power to a community that has denied women this attribute.[73] Other, perhaps more enduring, images will try to combine female metaphors with a changed conception of God or use nongendered language drawn from human community. Sallie McFague, in her book *Models of God*, devotes extensive discussion to images of God as lover and friend.[74] These images, along with companion and cocreator, might well be taken up by Jewish feminists and developed conceptually and liturgically.

Images of God as lover and friend are present in the Jewish tradition, but they are greatly overshadowed by father and king and rarely appear in the liturgy. In midrashic parallels to the passage in *Pesikta Rabbati* that describes God's different guises, God as a young warrior at the Red Sea is identified with the lover of the Song of Songs who, at the moment of liberation, comes to Israel as her beautiful bridegroom. Although the image of God as lover-bridegroom later disappears, it and father-judge are the central rabbinic metaphors for the love of God.[75] In McFague's rendering, the image of God as lover validates the erotic element in spirituality and affirms the value of that which is loved. Unlike images of king, judge, and (one side of) father, which promise enduring love *despite* a community's sins, the notion of God as lover proclaims that God loves Israel *because of* who Israel is. The idea that we are loved for what is most valuable in us, that God sees our worth even when we cannot, is far more conducive to human empowerment and accountability than the idea that we are loved despite our worthlessness.[76] In traditional Jewish usage, of course, God as valuing lover is the comely young man wooing (the subordinate) Israel as his bride. Feminist use of the image of God as lover would need to break through this patriarchal model of love relations, envisioning the lover as both female and male. Israel is not "she"; *it* is a community of women and men, all of whom can be lovers and loved of God. The astonishingly mutual imagery of the Songs of Songs presents both male and female lovers as pursuer and pursued. There is no reason why, with this book as a model, only the male should be identified with God—except, of course, for the androcentric context of the history of its interpretation.

The image of God as friend also appears in rabbinic discussion and finds its way into the Yom Kippur liturgy in the multiple metaphors of *Ki Anu Amekhah*.[77] A striking contrast with symbols of God as Other, this image of free and reciprocal connection is a profound metaphor for the covenantal relation. As McFague sees it, the image of God as friend points to a common vision or commitment that brings friends together and that both unites them and turns them to the world. While friendship often implies an exclusive element, it is also possible for people of different backgrounds and abilities to join in friendship around a common undertaking. Friendship is a human possibility, moreover, irrespective of gender and across gender lines.

Indeed, McFague suggests, since all of life is relational, friendship is possible even across ontological boundaries: We can be friends of the earth and friends of God.[78]

Closely related to the image of friend is the image of companion. While both images are ambiguous, and they are often used interchangeably, they can also represent different aspects of the experience of relation. If friendship entails a unique bond between two people that distinguishes their relationship from more casual connections, a companion is simply one who travels on the same way. The image of companion thus lacks the passion and specialness of friendship, but it provides the same sense of equality with a more communal metaphor. One can imagine many companions linked together by some shared task, laboring side by side for the achievement of their ends. Such companionship may be brief or can last throughout a lifetime, lightening shared work with the pleasure of human connection. Metaphors of God as friend and companion capture in different ways the closeness of God's relationship to Israel and the sense of striving toward a common goal. They suggest that God and Israel are mutually related and accountable as they join in the shared project of sanctifying and repairing the world.

Another, somewhat more awkward, image that suggests the shared responsibility of God and Israel has both feminist and Jewish roots. At the Grailville conference at which the participants used many "ing" words for God, they also suggested the term "cocreator" as evoking important aspects of their week together.[79] The prefix "co," which might in fact be used with a range of images, conjures the sense of personal empowerment and mutual responsibility that emerges out of speaking and acting in community with others. The feeling of possibility that comes with seeing the limits placed on women and envisioning a life beyond them fosters a sense of significant participation in the larger project of world-creation, a project that God and human beings share. To name the self and name the world in new ways is to enter with God into the act of creation. Insofar as human beings are cocreators with God, God is also a cocreator. Creation is not a discrete event completed by God in six days but a process that continues in dialogue with human beings who can carry forward or destroy the world that God has brought to be. This image of God as cocreator strongly accords with the sense of the Jewish mystical tradition that human beings are responsible for fulfilling the work of creation, uniting the separated aspects of divinity through the power of the deed.

These images of God—lover, friend, companion, cocreator— are more appropriate metaphors for the God of the covenant than traditional images of lord and king. Defining God's power not as domination but empowerment, they evoke a God who is with us instead of over us, a partner in dialogue who ever and again summons us to responsible action. Rather than reminding human beings of our frailty and nothingness, they call us to accountability as partners in a solemn compact that makes demands on us to which we can respond. It is not as we are subjugated, as we feel our worthlessness and culpability, that we can act most responsibly and effectively, but as we know our own value, mirrored in the constancy of God as friend and lover who calls us to enter into the task of creation. Responding responsibly,[80] we do so not because otherwise we are guilty, but because—as the Kabbalistic tradition reminds us—what we do or leave undone as cocreators makes a difference in the world.

Imagining God as friend and cocreator begins to name aspects of the deity lost in metaphors of domination, but it still provides only one stratum of a feminist understanding of God. Human beings become cocreators with God only after we come into being as part of a much larger web of existence—a web we now have the power to destroy but which we did not conceive or create. Moreover, the images I have suggested are still primarily dyadic; and while they can be applied to community, they do not in the first instance take us beyond the interpersonal plane. Anthropomorphic images must thus be supplemented by a second kind of language that can evoke the creative and sustaining power of God present throughout the world and in ever-widening circles of relation. This stratum of language will encompass an even wider range of images than the first—from natural and impersonal metaphors to conceptual terms that express God's relation to all being and becoming.

Images of God as fountain, source, wellspring, or ground of life and being remind us that God loves and befriends us as one who brings forth all being and sustains it in existence.[81] As cocreators with God for the brief span of our lives, we are responsible not just to the community of our fellow persons with whom we especially share the sense of God's presence, but to the larger community of creation that God also loves and befriends. Metaphors of ground and source continue the reconceptualization of God's power, shifting our sense of direction from a God in the high heavens who creates through the magical word to the very ground beneath our feet that nourishes and sustains us. As a tree draws up sustenance from the soil, so we are rooted in the source of our being that bears and maintains us even as it enables us to respond to it freely. Images of God as rock, tree of life, light, darkness, and myriad other metaphors drawn from nature, teach us the intrinsic value of this wider web of being in which we dwell. The God who is the ground of being is present and imaged forth in all beings, so that every aspect of creation shows us another face of God.

More conceptual images for God also have a role in feminist discourse. The traditional image of God as place (*makom*) evokes both the presence of the world in God and the extraordinary presence of God in particular places. As Rabbi Jose b. Halafta said, "We do not know whether God is the place of His world, or the world is His place."[82] Lacking personal communal images to refer to God, we can use this richly ambiguous term to point to community as a special place of God's self-manifestation. Community is a place we find ourselves in God; God dwells in this place. Also relevant here is the image of Shekhinah, which like the term God itself, cuts across the layers of anthropomorphic and nonpersonal language. Addressed in myriad personal guises, the Shekhinah is also the presence of God in the place called the world and the one who rests in a unique way in the midst of community.

There are, of course, many other metaphors that can be and have been evoked as part of the feminist naming of God. The images I mention here are just some of those that might convey the presence of God in a diverse, egalitarian community, replacing images of domination with a different understanding of the divine/human relation. Moreover, insofar as these images reflect the experience of a distinct community, they comprise only one of many communal namings of the experience and nature of the sacred. The connection between these different namings remains an important question, particularly as it pertains to the continuing place of traditional images of God in a feminist Judaism.

Certainly, the particular metaphors that emerge out of feminist experience are not meant to replace all other metaphors for God. Feminist metaphors call attention to important neglected aspects of the experience of God in community, and in doing so relativize and modify traditional metaphors by placing them in a different and larger context. Many traditional images of God can be altered in connotation or meaning by being seen in conjunction with feminist metaphors and with the changing social context out of which these metaphors arise. The image of God as father, for example, in a transformed social and metaphoric nexus, is potentially simply a parental image, shedding its implications of patriarchal domination and control. The image of God as judge confronts us when we fail to live up to our own ideals of diversity and mutuality, thus remaining an important counterpart to friend and source of being. But while feminist metaphors are nonexclusive, the experience of God in diverse, egalitarian community is also normative from a feminist perspective and as such functions as a criterion for selecting and rejecting images of divinity. Traditional images like lord and king, for example, evoke by definition relations of domination. Since it is difficult to imagine how such images could be transformed by context, they need to be seen as injurious reflections and supports of a hierarchical social system, and excised from our religious vocabularies.[83]

The rejection of all metaphors of domination raises, finally, a question frequently asked of feminists: What becomes of the Otherness or "Godness" of God when the primary feminist metaphors for God are warm and intimate ones? If God is friend and lover—albeit also ground and source of being—does this not somehow make God less God, less utterly more than us in every way? This question can be answered only by distinguishing among very different meanings of the concept of Otherness. The sense of Otherness I have been criticizing throughout this chapter is the notion of God as a dominating sovereign manipulating the world from outside it and above. I have argued that metaphors that depict God as Other in this sense mirror and sustain destructive social relations that ought never to be sanctified by any religious usage. But rejecting such metaphors does not entail abandoning God's "moreness"; it simply challenges us to imagine that moreness in nonhierarchical terms. Just as a community is more than the sum of its members, for example, without necessarily controlling or dominating them, so God as the ultimate horizon of community and source of unity is more than all things—also without needing to control or dominate them. A second meaning of Otherness found frequently in this book refers to peoples or aspects of reality seen as different from and less than some dominant group, the nonnormative Other in a hierarchical system. Feminist God-language does not simply reject this sense of Otherness, but seeks actively to address and undermine it through finding divinity in what has hitherto been despised. In imaging God as female, as darkness, as nature, and as a myriad of other metaphors taken from realms devalued and spurned, we reexamine and value the many forms of Otherness, claiming their multiform particularity as significant and sacred.

The third meaning of Otherness points to God as mystery and adversary—the presence of God experienced not as friend but as devouring fire, and the relationship of God to the terrible aspects of human existence. Feminists, although we continually confront human evil in the form of patriarchy and other destructive structures of hierarchical relation, have not yet fully addressed the theological question of evil as a feminist issue.[84] This side of God, which we cannot neglect without introducing a fundamental dualism into our conception of the world, can be expressed through images of waning and death, pain and struggle, all of which are aspects of a complex and changing reality. God as source can also be experienced as abyss; God as friend can also appear as enemy.[85] But while we must speak about God as other in this sense, it is unnecessary to do so using images of hierarchical domination. The hierarchies in our world are human creations. The God who brings to birth and destroys, gives forth and takes away, judges my limitations and calls me to struggle, is terrifying not for God's distance, but precisely for God's nearness. That which is awesome, painful, or evil appalls or bewilders me not because it is far away, but because it is all around and as near as my own heart. This otherness is not incompatible with the intimacy of feminist metaphors, but is found alongside and within them as their difficult counterparts and companions.

We are left, then, with a picture of God as a God of many faces—as many as the 600,000 souls that stood at Sinai and the complexities and conflicts of Jewish and human existence. At the center of this picture stands the Jewish/feminist experience of a God encountered in the midst of community—a God revealed as the community and those within it discover their destiny and understand that destiny as part of a larger universe of action and response.[86] This God is male/female lover, friend, companion, cocreator, the one who, seeing what is best in us, lures us to be the most we can become. This God is ground and source of all life, creating, holding, sustaining the great web of existence and, as part of it, the human companions who labor to make the world a home for the divine presence. This God is the God of Israel, the God the nascent community experienced and acknowledged behind the wonderful events at the Red Sea. This is the God the people stood before at Sinai, coming to their identity as a people, responding with the myriad laws, institutions, and customs that have given form and substance to their communal life. This is the God to whom they found themselves tied in a covenant, reciprocally binding through good times and bad: friend, holy terror, persistent goad.

Jewish feminists, in seeking to name this God of our experience, search for images of God that convey God's power and presence in community, at the same time trying to undo that community's hierarchical distortions. Selecting metaphors for God that acknowledge the differences within a covenantal community, we are also aware of the many covenants and greater differences that lie beyond our particular naming. As feminists, as Jews, we come to respond to and speak of God in certain characteristic ways. So every community in its uniqueness imagines the power that surrounds and sustains it. The naming of God and Israel that would turn God into Israel's God and Israel into "his" chosen people is part of the dualistic, hierarchical misnaming of God and reality that emerges out of and supports a patriarchal worldview. In speaking of the moving, changing ground and source, our companion and our lover, we name toward the God known in community that cherishes diversity within and without, even as that diversity has its warrant in the God of myriad names.

5. Toward a New Theology of Sexuality

Rethinking the categories Torah, Israel, and God provides the basic theological foundations for a feminist Judaism. There is a fourth category, however, which—while not foundational to Judaism in the same way—from a feminist perspective, equally requires reconceptualization. This is the category of sexuality. Jewish attitudes toward sexuality figure so significantly in the construction of women's position within Judaism that, on the one hand, much of the ground we have traveled is newly illuminated from the perspective this topic affords, and, on the other hand, it is simply not possible to create a feminist Judaism without transforming attitudes toward sexuality.

When Michael Wyschogrod depicts women as Israel's unredeemed flesh, or critics of female God-language link female images with fertility and sexuality, they are drawing on a long and deeply rooted history connecting women with sexuality in Judaism.[1] Women have been associated with sexuality in Jewish law and legend (Torah), and this association has been the chief manifestation of women's Otherness both in Torah and in the community of Israel. Women have been separated from the (male) community in public prayer because of their supposed danger as sources of sexual temptation. Identification of women with sexuality, goddesses, and paganism contributed to the emergence of male God-language historically and is strongly linked to contemporary opposition to female images. Yet, while attitudes toward sexuality intersect with each of the three major categories of Jewish thought, they do not fit neatly under any one of them, and so I have considered these attitudes only indirectly. My discussion of Torah, Israel, and God now complete, it becomes essential to turn to sexuality as a subject in its own right, looking at the ways in which traditional understandings of sexuality have undergirded women's Otherness in each of these other areas.

In separating out sexuality as a special topic for consideration at this point, I mean to define the term in a particular and limited way. Sexuality as *gender* has been a central subject of this book. The neglect of women's experience, the normative status of maleness, the potential contribution of women's experience to the transformation of Judaism have been major ongoing issues. Now I intend to look at sexuality in its other significant sense: as the complex of attitudes and constructions around sexual orientation and desire, lovemaking and marriage, and as the social definition of licit and illicit sex.

When sexuality is defined in these terms, a series of questions emerges that can provide an agenda for feminist discussion of Judaism and sexuality. What is the relationship between Jewish understandings of women's sexuality and the persistent perception of women as Other? What is the connection between understandings of women's sexuality and the broader construction of sexuality within which women's sexuality finds its place? What is a feminist understanding of female sexuality, and what would it mean to transform Jewish attitudes toward sexuality in the context of a feminist Judaism? Examining these issues can make clear that women and sexuality have been a potent combination for Jewish practice and thought, a combination that intertwines with the themes of Torah, Israel, and God.

Female Sexuality and Women as Other

I have already suggested in my introductory critique of Judaism as a patriarchal tradition that the definition of women as Other in Judaism is closely bound up with perceptions of women's sexuality.[2] Beginning in biblical times and continuing through the rabbinic era, laws concerning the regulation and control of women's sexuality were central vehicles through which women's Otherness was expressed and enforced. The biblical period saw the consolidation of the patriarchal family as the fundamental and normative unit of society, and women's sexuality was directed to serve the interests of this unit—interests identified with those of its male head. Women's sexuality, both as procreativity and source of licit intercourse, was seen as their main contribution to the family, and that sexuality "was regarded as the exclusive property of [a woman's] husband, both in respect to its pleasure and its fruit."[3] Biblical law concerns itself in great detail with the delineation and enforcement of male rights to women's sexuality, protecting against the violation of these rights with severe penalties. I have summarized some of this legislation briefly in the context of my initial critique of Judaism, but it requires closer examination in the context of this discussion of sexuality.

The laws concerning virginity and adultery provide the fundamental safeguards to male rights to a particular woman's sexuality. Ideals of virginity and marital fidelity are expressed in the Bible only indirectly through concern with their infringement, but such infringement is dealt with in the strongest possible terms. If a man married a woman and then accused her of not being a virgin, her father had to bring the "evidence of her virginity" (that is, the bloody sheets) before the elders of the town. If the accusation proved false, the husband paid his wife's father a fine and lost the right to divorce her. If the charges were true, the wife was stoned to death on her father's doorstep (Deut. 22:13–21). The girl who thus committed "fornication" while in her father's house violated both his rights and those of her future husband, defying her father's authority and robbing her husband of his exclusive claim to her sexuality.

The laws against adultery, equally severe, are similarly formulated to protect male interests. Adultery as a capital crime in Israel was defined as sex with a married woman (Lev. 20:10). Unlike male sex with an unattached woman, which simply resulted in marriage, and unlike prostitution, which was tolerated though discouraged, adultery was punishable by death for both parties. The man who had sex with another man's wife stole from her husband his rights and his honor, while the wife violated her primary responsibility to her husband, giving away what belonged only to him.[4] So serious a crime was adultery that the man who even suspected his wife could subject her to the ordeal of the "waters of bitterness" (Num. 5:11–31), a complex and humiliating ritual that was supposed to "prove" her guilt or innocence. If the wife was found innocent, her husband suffered no penalty for his unwarranted jealousy. There was no parallel ritual for the husband of a suspicious wife, for his infidelity was a crime only if it violated another man's prerogatives.

Laws such as these establish the boundaries of communal norms, defining expected behavior by punishing its violation. The importance of control of women's sexuality within the patriarchal family also emerges, though, in legislation and biblical narratives dealing with normal family matters. The law of levirate marriage, for example, required a childless widow—unless released—to marry her deceased husband's brother (Deut. 25:5–10), thus regulating women's remarriage for the sake of the continuity of the dead husband's line. This law fit easily into a system in which entry into and dissolution of marriage were generally under male control, ensuring a stable family within which a man could beget male heirs. Women were "given" and "taken" in marriage (Gen. 11:29; 29:28), a giving they might sometimes object to (Gen. 24:58) but could not actively choose. The law in Deuteronomy pertaining to divorce (24:1–4) similarly placed initiative in the hands of the husband, allowing him to write his wife a bill of divorce and send her from the house. While biblical law sought to provide a durable context for the procreation of children, narrative accounts amplify and clarify the importance of (male) offspring as a woman's contribution to marriage. "Give me children, or I shall die," cries Rachel to Jacob (Gen. 30:1), an entreaty echoed by many another barren biblical wife. Three of the matriarchs offer their husbands concubines to bear in their stead, either to save the women from childlessness or to increase the offspring in the marriage (Gen. 16:1–3; 30:3–9). And although women appear in many roles in biblical stories, it is a very rare woman who is not identified as the mother of a son.

While biblical narratives provide small hints of women's experience within the framework of families regulated by patriarchal law, biblical treatment of sexuality is for the most part utterly lacking in women's perspectives. Not only is the Bible uninterested in the reactions of a raped girl married to her attacker (Deut. 22:28–29) or the feelings of a wife accused of adultery by an unfaithful husband, it does not acknowledge the existence of such points of view. If women's Otherness consists in being named as objects in a male-constructed version of reality, then texts on sexuality provide the core for the projection of woman as Other.

This is not to say that women's sexuality is the "cause" of their Otherness. In theory, it is equally possible that women's capacity to bear children would be an avenue to social prestige and control, so that the devaluation of women's sexuality itself requires explanation. It does seem, however, that the desire to control female sexuality is the chief source of male anxiety about women and thus also the source of the central vocabulary and symbolism for the construction of women's Otherness.[5]

The anxiety about female sexuality that hovers about family legislation is also manifest in biblical taboos surrounding menstruation and childbirth, both of which were disqualifiers for participation in the sacred. A woman with a normal menstrual period was unclean for seven days, during which time she was barred from approaching the divine presence in the Sanctuary or the Temple.[6] Childbirth excluded her from the sanctuary for thirty-three days in the case of a male child, sixty-six days in the case of a female (Lev. 12). While the menstrual taboos are part of a host of regulations concerning the bodily discharges of women and men, the effects on religious practice of a week's uncleanness were necessarily far more significant than those of the day of uncleanness associated with seminal emission. Although it is wrong to impose modern notions of dirtiness or moral failure on the biblical conception of impurity, it can only further signal women's Otherness that the periodic bleeding associated with the normal functioning of their sexuality left women unable to participate in sacrificial ritual for a significant proportion of their adult lives. The strong taboo against sex with a menstruant, mentioned elsewhere in Leviticus (18:19), further underscores the character of menstruation as source of defilement.

The biblical construction of women's sexuality as a locus of both Otherness and social control is not simply maintained in rabbinic sources but vastly expanded. Five of the seven tractates in the Mishnaic order of Women are devoted to laws surrounding the formation and dissolution of the marital bond—that is, to points of transition at which a woman leaves the home of one man to take up residence with another. A woman's departing her father's house to marry or returning to her father's house upon divorce or widowhood entails a transfer of person and property that is potentially disorderly and disruptive. The function of the law is to sanctify these critical moments and thus render them orderly and normal.[7] But while the explicit content of Mishnaic law on women concerns betrothal, marriage contracts, divorce, and death, the underlying danger it addresses is that posed by women's sexuality. Jacob Neusner argues in his extensive work on the Mishnah's system of Women that though the subject of sexuality is scarcely mentioned, "it always is just beneath the surface." The Mishnah assumes that girls will marry at puberty, and that long before, their potential sexuality is problematic. All women's sexual deeds have public consequences, economic results, in the transfer of property from one man to another.

The goal and purpose of Mishnah's division of Women is to bring under control, and force into stasis, all the wild and unruly potentialities of female sexuality, with their dreadful threat of uncontrolled shifts in personal status and possession alike.

A situation so dangerous to the "stable, sacred society of Israel" required serious and extensive reflection and regulation, regulation that would hold the anomalousness of women in stasis by assigning them to some man's domain.[8]

Much rabbinic legislation concerning marriage and divorce simply extended and elaborated laws already laid down in the Bible. In these areas, rabbinic anxiety about control of women's sexuality differs from the biblical in volume but not in kind. There was another area of regulation of women's sexuality, however, that is wholly new to postbiblical literature. This concerns intricate laws of female modesty, careful management of women's public conduct, and the elaborate control of social relations between the sexes.

While the prophet Isaiah castigated "daughters of Zion" who walked "with roving eyes,/ And with mincing gait,/ Making a tinkling with their feet" (3:16), there is no attempt in the Bible to control women's adornment, movements, or general public bearing. The case is quite otherwise with rabbinic sources. Numerous aggadic sayings implying the danger to men of women's sexual attractiveness find concrete expression in legal material seeking to regulate women's public self-presentation. Laws of modesty, for example, required that women keep their bodies covered. A husband could charge his wife with misconduct if she bared her hip, leg, shoulder, arm, or chest in public. Display of hair by women was considered an act of immodesty—so much so that a man was not to recite the *She'ma* in the presence of a woman whose hair was showing. At the same time that rules of modesty circumscribed women's dress, other laws protected against private flirtation and immorality between the sexes. Mutual engagement in entertainment or merriment was considered an invitation to immoral conduct, as was indulgence in small talk or repartée. Indeed, it was considered improper for a nonfamily member to greet a woman, even through her husband. Laws of chaperonage firmly forbid any private meeting between a man and woman, whatever the purpose and whoever gave consent.[9] While this legislation naturally affected men as well as women, its aggadic rationale was always to protect men from the temptations posed by women.[10]

It is not surprising, given the fear of women's sexuality reflected in these sources, that rabbinic attitudes toward women's sexual functions took on an increasingly negative cast. In Leviticus, the laws surrounding the menstruant (*niddah*) pertain primarily to ritual impurity. After the destruction of the Temple, other sorts of impurity legislation fell into disuse, and the laws of *niddah* were transferred to the realm of family life and sexual taboo. Already in the late books of Ezra and Ezekiel, *niddah* had become a metaphor for moral impurity and debasement.[11] This hostility toward female sexuality grew and was elaborated in the rabbinic and medieval periods, as terms like *bet hatorfa* (place of rot) were used to designate the uterus and prophetic passages filled with sexual disgust became the basis for legal exegesis.[12] As other sorts of impurity became increasingly irrelevant, the laws of *niddah* were developed and strengthened. From an original seven days, the period of forbidden intercourse was increased to the actual period of flow plus seven days, with detailed rules guiding women in self-examination. Other laws restricted the nonsexual interaction of husband and wife during this period so that certain ordinary signs of intimacy were suspended. Superstition and custom further served to amplify the uncleanness of the *niddah*. In many communities, women—apparently sometimes on their own initiative—refrained from entering the synagogue during menstruation, did not recite God's name, and did not touch or even look at the Torah scrolls.[13] A menstruant passing between two men was said to slay one of them at the beginning of her period, and at the end, to cause strife between them. "The glance of a menstruous woman poisons the air. . . . She is like a viper who kills with her glance. How much more harm will she bring to a man who sleeps with her?"[14] Whether women's enlargements of the restrictions surrounding *niddah* represented internalization of such attitudes or the attempt to use them to their own ends, the available sources allow us no more than a guess.

Jewish Attitudes Toward Sexuality

Rules of modesty and perceptions of the *niddah* lead us from consideration of female sexuality to examination of Jewish attitudes toward sexuality more generally. The concern to safeguard the relations between the sexes that characterizes the laws of modesty, and the palpable disgust that marks certain exchanges about *niddah*, are necessarily entangled in broader beliefs and feelings about the nature of sexuality. The relation between Jewish attitudes toward female sexuality and sexuality per se is an extremely complex subject, one on which the evidence is often confusing and conflicting. As one commentator on the issue suggests, every attitude toward sexuality from the freest to the most inhibited is found somewhere in Jewish writing.[15] In trying to capture the Jewish stance or stances toward sexuality and relate them to attitudes toward women, it is necessary to find a path through contradiction and ambivalence, avoiding elevating one side of ambivalence as truer or more fundamental than the other.[16]

Some of the contradictions in Jewish attitudes toward sexuality can be accounted for by historical changes and developments. Early biblical literature, for example, while it is concerned to harness women's sexuality to the needs of the patriarchal family, shows little general anxiety about heterosexual sex. Sexuality was accepted as a natural part of human life; the relations between the sexes were relatively easy and open; except for practices associated with or projected onto paganism, there is little preachment about or denunciation of specific sexual behaviors. The postexilic period, by way of contrast, was far more repressive. Social and political upheavals generated a new pessimism about the world that expressed itself in growing concern about human weakness and sinfulness. As easily corruptible creatures subject to the lure of sexual temptation, human beings had to be on guard against even seemingly innocent contacts between women and men. In this atmosphere, women's sexuality also came to be seen with a new negativity; women were perceived as temptresses, beguiling and ensnaring men.[17]

Since the rabbinic period incorporated both of these conflicting attitudes toward sexuality, however, the contradictions in Jewish understandings of sexuality cannot be explained simply by reference to historical development. Rather, these contradictions are held together in the mainstream expression of Jewish attitudes toward sex. The heart of the Jewish ambivalence toward sexuality is roughly this: The sexual impulse is given by God and thus is a normal and healthy part of human life. Sexual relations are appropriate only within the framework of heterosexual marriage, but within marriage, they are good, indeed, are commanded (a *mitzvah*). Yet sexuality—even within marriage—also requires careful, sometimes rigorous control, in order that it not transgress the boundaries of marriage or the laws of *niddah* within it.

This oscillation between affirmation of sexuality and anxiety about control expresses itself in a number of ways, in part through the very naming of the sexual impulse. The rabbis called this impulse the *yetzer hara*—the evil impulse, and yet at the same time acknowledged its necessity to the creation and sustenance of the world. According to one rabbinic midrash, the rabbis of the Second Temple period caught hold of the *yetzer hara* and imprisoned "him" for thirty days. During that period, not a single egg was found in all of Palestine. Finally, they just blinded him in one eye and released him, fearing that if they killed him the world would be destroyed. "Were it not for the evil impulse," said Rabbi Nahman b. Samuel, "man would not build a house, or take a wife, or beget a child, or engage in business."[18] Such midrashic expressions of ambivalence find concrete manifestation in the moral realm in the tension between legal statutes that are relatively permissive (always within the boundaries of marriage) and ethical standards that tend to be much more restrictive, even ascetic.[19]

An excellent illustration of this latter tension is provided by the laws of *onah*, which regulate a man's sexual obligations to his wife. These laws are based on the assumption that women, like men, feel sexual desire, but women are more passive and hidden in the expression of their sexuality and less free to initiate sexual activity. This being the case, it is a husband's responsibility to approach his wife, both at regular times prescribed by law, and when he suspects she might wish it—for example, when he is about to go off on a journey. The frequency of *onah* is adjusted to a man's profession: camel drivers are obligated to perform *onah* once a month, laborers twice a week, scholars once a week. A man may not change his trade to one that would reduce the frequency of *onah* without his wife's permission, and a woman's prenuptial agreement to forego these rights is not considered binding. The *mitzvah* of *onah*, moreover, pertains not just to the number of times a man has sex with his wife, but also to the quality of their relations. A man is expected to rejoice with his wife. He should therefore never force himself on her or initiate sex when they are angry with each other, but should speak words of tenderness to her and seek to give her pleasure.[20]

Within the framework of a male-defined system, the laws of *onah* represent a remarkable concern with and accommodation to female sexuality as well as appreciation of sexuality generally. The laws are formulated from the perspective of women's gratification (of course, as men perceived it), and they represent an understanding of marital sex as more than procreational. Having children is one primary purpose of marital relations, and men (again, the laws of sexuality are addressed to men) are required to be fruitful and multiply—that is, have at least two children. But *onah* is an independent value, a commandment alongside procreation that applies if a woman is pregnant, barren, or past childbearing age.

These "sex-positive" values associated with *onah* in its legal aspects, however, are sometimes modified or compromised by accompanying ethical discussion. Both the Talmud and post-Talmudic thought reflect some conflict about whether the times prescribed by *onah* are a minimum or a maximum. While some authorities see *onah* as the rabbis' guess as to the minimum a woman would want, others feel *onah* should be taken as indicating the outer limits of sexual relations. Similar debate applies to the quality of *onah*. Some authorities are willing to permit any erotic play or sexual position that a couple finds enjoyable, but others are highly suspicious of foreplay and also of postures for intercourse other than the standard "missionary position." Although the lenient attitude is enshrined in halakhah, many rabbis and commentators adjured Jews to follow a stricter standard than the law permitted. The tension or even contradiction between a permissive halakhah and restrictive or ascetic ethic is clearly expressed in the work of Maimonides, who acknowledged the latitude of the law but counseled the pious to limit sexual relations and to direct themselves to contemplation.[21] The issue at stake in this debate on *onah* is not the legitimacy of female pleasure, but the boundaries of reasonable male sexual expression. Male desire is presupposed as an ever-present reality that must be controlled by the legal system. Whether this control is best achieved through abstinence or through moderate enjoyment of what is permitted is a matter for ongoing discussion among rabbinic and medieval authorities.[22]

The tensions and ambivalence surrounding marital sexuality are further deepened by the fact that marital relations are ruled not simply by *onah* but by the laws concerning *niddah*. Restriction of sexual intercourse to the period when the woman is "clean"—that is, has waited for seven days after menstruation and then gone to the ritual bath—means that for up to fifteen days or more every month, sex is simply forbidden. The laws of *onah* apply, then, to only about half of a couple's married life, while the rest of the time sex is equally illicit within marriage as outside it. Legal safeguards against arousal must thus be built into the framework of marriage to ensure that even here there is no violation of the boundaries of the permitted. The resulting rhythm of marital sexuality is closely regulated by prohibitions and prescriptions, a fact that indicates the extent to which rabbinic treatment of sexuality put a premium on control.[23]

If even the marriage relation is subject to sexual immorality, outside its boundaries lies a whole realm of licentiousness and transgression that has to be carefully guarded against with well-defined restraints. In this realm especially, what the law does not specify, ethical standards demand and elaborate, supplementing legislation with a clear moral code. Thus, for example, while there is no explicit prohibition of premarital sex in Jewish law, the whole tenor of ethical discussion limits sexual expression to the marriage relationship. In the Talmud, sexual relations between the unmarried were assimilated to harlotry, and the later codes prescribed public flogging for such improper behavior.[24] Incest, adultery, and male homosexuality, listed in the Bible as sexual transgressions (Lev.18; 20:10), remained serious sins in Talmudic and post-Talmudic literature. Adultery is addressed most extensively by the halakhah, presumably because it was the most common violation. Rabbinic legislation on adultery closely follows the inequalities of biblical law, ruling that a woman who commits adultery must be divorced by her husband and is forbidden to marry her lover. Though ethical expectations were stricter than the law, married men, on the other hand, were legally free to have other sexual relations, provided the woman involved was single. Incest and homosexuality, although major offenses, were regarded as rare in Israel and therefore received less halakhic attention.[25] The rabbis built a fence around the biblical laws of incest, forbidding certain secondary relationships that might seem to violate incest prohibitions. Male homosexuality was condemned as *to'evah* (an abomination) by the tradition, but Talmudic references to it are few and far between and indicate no knowledge of homosexual orientation in the modern sense. Lesbianism, because it involves no intercourse and no "wasting of seed," was a less serious offense, a rebellious and condemnable act that brought no legal penalty.[26]

In the case of all these behaviors, however, whatever the degree of prohibition, prevention was considered a better course than punishment, and so all were surrounded by social and legal restraints. Numerous restrictions controlling social mingling of the sexes were buttressed by the constant watchful eye of the community, a watchfulness more potent than the law in conveying expectations of moral behavior.[27] Though Jewish attitudes toward sexuality are often contrasted favorably with Christian asceticism, one might argue that the energy the church fathers devoted to worrying about sexuality, the rabbis devoted to worrying about illicit sexuality—and with similar implications. While the desire to extirpate the sexual instinct is certainly not the same as the desire to channel and control it, both lead to a consuming focus on the difficulty of containing male sexuality, the lure of female sexuality, and strategies for circumventing sexuality's attraction and power.[28]

Thus every area of illegal sexuality had its corresponding regulations for prevention and control. Restrictions on social mingling connect more general attitudes toward sexuality with the rules of modesty for women discussed above. Laws of female modesty and rules of chaperonage limited the free interaction of the sexes that could lead to fornication or adultery, and the same was true of the increasing segregation of men and women that, from the end of the third century, marked many festive and religious occasions. Beyond such restrictions, men were discouraged from engaging in any action that might conceivably start a train of thought considered unwholesome. A man was not to hold his penis while urinating, unless his wife was in town and clean so there would be no need for lustful ruminations. To walk behind a woman was considered dangerous, for it might lead to erotic meditations about the female form. To pass a coin to a woman with the intention of looking at her, to glance at her little finger, even to gaze at her garments in a closet was considered an invitation to carnal sin. Regulations applying to close relatives were only somewhat less restrictive than those involving acquaintances, so that even within the family the tradition was on guard. A father might kiss his daughter and a mother her son, but otherwise hugging or kissing a woman within the incestuous degrees of kinship was considered inappropriate. The need for safeguards against homosexual liaisons was somewhat more disputed. While the Mishnah records that Rabbi Judah forbade two unmarried men to sleep under the same blanket, in general the sages felt that the rarity of homosexuality among Jews made such preventive legislation unnecessary.[29] In the *Shulkhan Arukh*, Rabbi Joseph Caro cautioned against unchaperoned association between males, but his ruling was suspended a hundred years later, again because it was considered superfluous. Concerning lesbians, Maimonides adjured a man to supervise his wife to ensure she had no contact with women known to be such.[30]

While laws and customs of modesty and avoidance circumscribed the lives of both women and men, these laws are nonetheless strikingly asymmetrical in their rationale, content, and phrasing. We have come to expect that in a male-defined system, the law will be addressed to men and formulated from their perspective. But sexual legislation does not simply omit women's viewpoint; it attributes the turbulent character of male sexuality largely to the provocation and stimulation of women. Although the rules of *onah* presuppose that women's sexuality is restrained and silent so that a husband has the obligation to discern and respond to it, the laws concerning almost every other aspect of sexuality see women's sexuality as an ever-present danger that must be contained within the family and guarded against at all times. Louis Epstein, toward the beginning of his *Sex Laws and Customs in Judaism*, remarks that the rabbis ridiculed the fear of the "dangerous woman" that had occupied authorities in Second Temple times.[31] But as he develops rabbinic attitudes toward sexuality in the rest of his book, this ridicule seems increasingly hollow. When the overwhelming majority of rabbinic laws on modesty pertain largely or solely to women, when a woman's voice or little finger are defined as occasioning lewdness, when "it is better to walk behind a lion than behind a woman," it is difficult to conclude anything other than that women are a source of moral danger and an incitement to depravity and lust.[32]

Attitudes toward sexuality and toward women's sexuality come together, then, in that the overriding concern with control that marks the negative side of Jewish ambivalence about sexuality is rooted at once in what is perceived to be the urgent character of male sexuality and the peril to it posed by woman. It cannot be said that all of male sexuality is projected onto women, for many of the stratagems of avoidance fall on men and enforce their responsibility for self-control. But women are the ubiquitous temptations, the sources and symbols of illicit desire, the ones whose sexuality threatens even their husbands/ possessors with the temptation to illegal action. To speak of control is necessarily to speak of women—of the need to cover women (but not men), to avoid women (but not men), and to contain women in proper (patriarchal) families where their threat is minimized if it cannot be overcome. To speak of sexuality is to speak of women occasionally as fellow people— themselves desirous but subject to social restraint—but mainly as objects, as Others, as dangers to male moderation, as hazards to the balance and regulation that mark the sacred order.

Sexuality and the Sacred

When we look at sexuality within the context of the family and social relations between the sexes, it is clear that sexuality is a locus both for sanctification and disorder. Properly channeled and contained within the patriarchal family, sexuality is a good gift of God, the foundation for a stable and thriving social order. Marital sexuality is the subject of two important mitzvot: *p'ru ur'vu*— procreation—"be fruitful and multiply," and *onah*, the laws specifying a man's conjugal duties to his wife. Indulged in for the proper reasons and with proper moderation, sex is a legitimate avenue of pleasure for both partners in a marriage. At the same time, however, the sexual impulse is named the evil inclination and is seen as continually threatening to break out of its divinely sanctioned boundaries, bringing sin and chaos. The family itself poses the dangers of incest and sex with a menstruant. In the wider world lurk the perils of fornication, adultery, and homosexuality. Especially the man with his insistent sexual impulses must be ever on guard against the temptations of female sexuality and his own evil urge.

This same ambivalence or contradiction that pertains to sexuality in the social order also holds for sexuality in the symbolic and "religious" orders.[33] Sexuality is a symbol of and vehicle for divine unification, and also a potential distraction and disturbance—even desecration—of the divine/human relation and symbolism for the divine. As is the case with sexuality in the social realm, these contradictory attitudes divide to some extent along historical and sectarian lines but also are found within particular periods and movements, forming an intricate and many-layered pattern of conflict. The relation between the sexuality of God and other sexual attitudes is an excellent illustration of the complexities of this pattern.

In my discussion of Jewish objections to paganism in the last chapter, I alluded to the connection between biblical abhorrence of pagan sexual practices and the unique "singleness" of Israel's God.[34] While God is sexual in the sense that "he" is gendered, in biblical and rabbinic thought God is free from sexuality in the narrower sense under consideration here. In contrast to the gods and goddesses of pagan mythologies, God has no sexual partner; we hear of no sexual exploits or feelings within the deity; the whole issue of sexuality pertains to humans as God's creatures, but finds no obvious echo in the depiction of God. While this nonsexuality of God is not part of a full-fledged philosophical dualism linking God as spirit to the human spirit trapped in flesh, the relation between God's nonsexuality and antipagan polemics, and the rabbinic association of sanctification with moderation and control suggest a connection between knowledge of and intimacy with God and the harnessing of flesh to spirit.[35] To express this connection negatively, sexual behavior perceived as immoral is a serious religious offense, and adultery and fornication are important metaphors for human reprobation and alienation from the God who is ever faithful to Israel. To express it positively, adherence to a rigorous sexual ethic is part of the path to holiness, a holiness that has its model in a God who is himself beyond sexual relations.

The implicit interconnections between the image of God as nonsexual and a rigorous Jewish sexual ethic become much clearer when this image of God is threatened by female metaphors. Resistance to female images for God stems not only from the fact that they alter the gender of God but also from their threatening God with sexuality.[36] Having examined the crucial place of women in the Jewish understanding of sexuality, we are now in a better position to see why this should be the case. From a certain male perspective, women, whatever they may be in themselves, represent and elicit sexual desire and temptation. The use of female metaphors for God evokes an extensive and firmly established set of associations between women and sexuality that persists with different emphases throughout the history of the Jewish tradition. Applying female metaphors to God means that God becomes subject to these same associations. The implication of these associations is such, moreover, that those who worry about female images are deeply anxious about their moral effects. Mortimer Ostow, in an article opposing the ordination of women as rabbis, argues that the rabbi represents God. In the case of a woman rabbi, this representation poses a severe problem, he claims, because since woman "unconsciously represents temptation, gratification and sensuality," the appearance of a woman on the *bimah* "unconsciously suggests a regression to indulgence and gratification as a dominant value."[37] The association of women with sexuality, and female sexuality with God, connects God to an ethic of sexual intemperance, potentially wreaking havoc with an ethic of control. Cynthia Ozick takes this reasoning a step further, moving by stages from the introduction of female imagery to the threat of child sacrifice.[38] Such arguments clarify the psychological/symbolic connections between the conception of God as nonsexual male and the importance of control in the Jewish understanding of sexuality. Any changes in this conception threaten to disturb the whole system of control that is held together by a complex web of symbolic associations.

In mainstream Jewish thinking, then, God's nonsexuality is an important pillar in the symbolic and moral order such that changes in the image of God threaten the sacred order by undermining the symbolic restraints on self-discipline and control. In Jewish mysticism, however, the case is quite otherwise, so that Kabbalah provides a quite different—indeed a contradictory—picture of the relation between sexuality and the sacred order. The *Zohar* and Lurianic Kabbalah use extensive sexual imagery to describe the inner life of God, particularly in discussing the relation between the ninth and tenth *sefirot* (emanations). The ninth *sefirah*, *Yesod* (foundation), through which all the higher *sefirot* flow into the feminine Shekhinah, is portrayed in clearly phallic terms and interpreted as the male procreative force dynamically active in the universe. Its sacred marriage with the Shekhinah, queen and celestial bride, is central to the whole process through which the *sefirot* unfold. The separation of the masculine and feminine principles within God is a cosmic calamity that forms part of the drama of creation. The reunion of God and his Shekhinah, the uninterrupted joining of the divine masculine and feminine, is the very meaning of redemption.[39]

It is not surprising, given the importance of sexuality in the Kabbalistic understanding of divinity, that the mystical tradition is the source of some of the more positive strands in Jewish attitudes toward marital sexuality. For the Kabbalist, human sexual intercourse, performed with the right intention and within its proper limits, is an imitation of processes within the divine and a symbolic realization of the reunion of God and the Shekhinah. In *Iggeret Ha-Kodesh*, a popular thirteenth-century mystical text, the author argues that sexual intercourse is called "knowing" because it is an act of great holiness. A husband and wife who conduct themselves properly mirror through their human actions the divine creation of the world. The author teaches husbands how to approach their wives, adjuring men to speak pleasing words that urge their wives to passion. A man should never quarrel with or beat his wife over sex; nor should he take her by force or when she is sleeping. Rather, he should ensure that desire is mutual, checking his own ardor to match hers, so that in their harmony they may enact a divine process.[40]

Contrary to the fears of the mainstream tradition, this view of sexuality, while it added a new dimension to the appreciation and sanctification of sex, by no means altered halakhic sexual boundaries. Whatever the biblical and rabbinic association of God's asexuality with sexual control, Kabbalistic use of female and sexual language for divinity did not lead to the creation of a new sexual morality. It is true that the Sabbatian movement, an outgrowth of Kabbalism, was associated with antinomian acts both on the part of the false messiah Sabbatai Zevi and of his more radical followers, and that these acts often involved transgression of sexual laws.[41] If this antinomianism was connected to the Sabbatian view of God, however, the connection seems not to have affected the rest of Jewish mysticism, which remained thoroughly committed to traditional sexual values. Sex was a significant mystical rite, but within the careful constraints of heterosexual marriage. Misuse of the sexual impulse was a matter of severe anxiety to the Kabbalist, for it was believed to strengthen the forces of evil. For those who aspired to mystic contemplation, sexual transgressions brought in their train stringent practices of self-mortification to disentangle holiness from impurity.[42] Nor can it be said that the presence of a female element in God freed Kabbalah from suspicion of female sexuality. On the contrary, Jewish mysticism associated the feminine with the demonic, and in Kabbalistic mythology, Lilith and her host of female demons provoke men to improperly waste their seed.[43]

If Kabbalah, despite its symbolic unorthodoxy, remained firmly wedded to the value of sexual control, the holiness of marital intercourse is not just a mystical invention. The Talmud prefers the Sabbath as the day on which scholars are to perform the mitzvah of *onah*, and this preference is preserved by the later codes despite their often ascetic bias. Rashi explains the association of sex and the Sabbath on the grounds that the Sabbath is a "time of pleasure, rest, and physical wellbeing." But certainly the choice of Sabbath sex also assumes that marital intercourse will benefit from and contribute to the holiness of the day, a conviction in sharp contrast with certain Christian admonitions to abstain from sex on any holy occasion.[44] Thus while mysticism built on and elaborated the notion of sex as a source of sanctification, it grounded its speculations in earlier mainstream sources.

To give one more turn, however, to an already conflicted picture of the relation between sexuality and the sacred, we might shift from images of God and marital sexuality to the separation of the sexes in the synagogue. This highly contentious issue, which has split many a US congregation, brings us right back to the desire to disassociate God and sexuality with which I began this section. The substantive rationale for traditional insistence on the *mechitzah*—partition separating men and women in the house of worship—is that the *mechitzah* protects the sanctity of worship from the intrusion of sexuality. If the exposed handbreadth of a woman's body, her voice, her uncovered hair, are indecent, then women's presence among men at prayer constitutes a veritable invitation to immorality.[45] Insofar as God's asexuality is symbolically linked to a restrictive sexual ethic, this ethic certainly must operate in the synagogue where the asexual God is worshiped. While the *mechitzah* is just another aspect of the familiar concern with control, expressed from a male perspective and projected onto women, the argument over separation of the sexes in the synagogue also indicates that it is easier for mainstream Judaism to sanctify sexuality than to sexualize the sacred. One may raise sexuality to God by engaging in marital intercourse at the proper time and with the proper intention. But one cannot intensify or raise prayer to God through allowing sexual feelings in a house of worship. Although liberal Judaism, in introducing mixed seating, seemingly ignores this traditional truth, it enforces a new strict decorum in the synagogue that in its own way works against any sexual feeling. Whether through a physical wall or balcony or through decorous worship that comes from a head without a body, public prayer is based on a separation of sexuality and the sacred that coheres with certain elements in the tradition while it stands in tension with others.

Reclaiming the Body and Sexuality in Feminist Thought

This conflicting and conflicted set of attitudes toward sexuality constitutes an extremely problematic heritage for modern Jews, particularly Jewish women. It has been noted frequently that for liberal Jews who take their Judaism seriously, there is no area in which modern practice and traditional values are further apart than the area of sexuality.[46] The insistence that legitimate sexual expression be limited to marriage, and indeed, only certain periods in a marriage, and the insistence on boundaries and control as central aspects of an approach to sexuality, are thoroughly out of tune with both the modern temper and the lived decisions of most contemporary Jews. Troublesome as inherited sexual values are for Jews of both sexes, however, they are especially troubling for women; for these values are a central pillar upholding Judaism as a patriarchal system, and the stigma and burden of sexuality fall differently on women than on men. Men's sexual impulses are powerful—"evil"—inclinations in need of firm control. Women's very bodily functions are devalued and made the center of a complex of taboos: their gait, their voices, their natural beauty are all regarded as snares and temptations and subjected to elaborate precautions. Men define their own sexuality ambivalently—but they define it. And men also define the sexuality of women which they would circumscribe to fit the shape of their own fears, and desire for possession. Women must carve out a sense of sexual self in the context of a system that—here most centrally—projects them as Other, denying their right to autonomous self-understanding or action.

Given the generally ambivalent and problematic treatment of sexuality in Judaism, however, it is precisely the key location of women as the central locus of ambivalence that makes women's voices and experience enormously important to the overall transformation of Jewish attitudes toward sexuality. If control of women's sexuality is the cornerstone of patriarchal control of women, then women's naming and reclaiming our own sexuality poses a major threat to that control and to the understanding of sexuality correlated with it. Such naming and reclaiming, moreover, has been a crucial piece of the contemporary feminist project. Partly in response to the Jewish understanding of sexuality, more fully in response to the explicit dualism of Christianity and the attitudes of a culture shaped by both traditions, feminists have begun to explore and revalue women's sexuality and body experience from a woman-centered perspective. These explorations have potentially profound implications for Judaism, certainly for its understanding of women, but also for its understanding of sexuality and the relation between sexuality and the sacred.

Feminist writing on the body and sexuality has been so rich and voluminous that it is quite impossible to characterize it briefly. It has encompassed everything from compilation of basic information, to analysis of central institutions shaping women's sexual attitudes and lives, to exploration of the sensations and meanings of a woman-defined sexuality.[47] It has delineated important male ideas about sexuality and their impact on women and also described women's experience of and reflections on our own sexual lives. If there is any key insight that unifies this very diverse writing, it is the insistence that sexuality, like gender, is socially constructed. While sexuality has a biological base, its interpretation and meanings are neither genetically inscribed nor divinely ordained, but rather change through time and space, shaped by the many ideas and institutions that make up human culture.

Adopting a social constructionist model of sexuality has enabled feminists to trace the relationship between particular social and economic configurations and specific attitudes toward sex, and also to illuminate broader patterns of thinking about sexuality that continue to have an impact on contemporary culture. This model allows us to examine the social context of rabbinic anxieties about women, to try to understand the sources of concerns that today appear peculiar or puzzling. What is the cause of rabbinic apprehension about the effects of looking at a woman's finger, for example, or contemplating her clothes in a closet? Is it explained by a social situation in which the sexes led largely separate lives? Did covering the female body mystify and eroticize it? Was the preoccupation with female exposure itself an invitation to desire? How did men *learn*, in other words, both to react sexually to any sign of a woman's body and to reject that reaction as morally wrong?

Feminist work on the history of Christianity has focused on the impact of hierarchical dualisms on the understanding of women's sexuality, and in doing so has highlighted an important determinant of contemporary attitudes toward women. Rosemary Ruether's pioneering work on dualism has set out the connections between male/female and mind/body dualisms in Christian theology, showing how a dichotomized and objectified understanding of female sexuality is firmly embedded in the normative Christian worldview and continues to shape advertising, legal treatment of rape victims, and many other features of the modern social world.[48] Other feminist work has made clear that both Jewish and Christian attitudes toward sexuality are rooted in a basic "energy/control paradigm" of sexuality, which understands sexuality as an independent and sometimes alien energy that must be held in check through personal discipline and religious constraints.[49] Since the perception of male sexuality as a distinct, powerful, and foreign force, triggered by women who are therefore responsible for it, is still our dominant cultural and religious model, it is especially difficult to see this paradigm as a social construction.

Feminist writing on sexuality has not stopped with trying to understand male images and institutions, however. Just as feminist work on other aspects of women's history has moved to reclaim a positive history, so feminist work on sexuality has both sought to uncover the experiences of women within and against patriarchal constructions and to create new frameworks for understanding and appropriating embodied, sexual life. Feminists have set out the dualisms that have shaped religious and cultural disgust at women's bodies, and also have tried to overcome these dualisms, reclaiming women's body experience in a conscious and affirming way. Sometimes feminist efforts to subvert dualisms have had the effect of simply reversing them, elevating women's body experience as a response to its devaluation. The consistent goal of feminist writing, though, has been to undercut dualisms, to find a way through and beyond the either/or thinking (either spirit or body, either virgin or whore) so central to western attitudes toward sexuality.[50] As Adrienne Rich argues in *Of Woman Born*—one of the richest and most profound feminist efforts to rethink dualism—women must resist the incarceration in the body that has been the legacy of patriarchy without either recoiling from our bodies or pretending we can live without them. In thinking of "our physicality as a resource, rather than a destiny," in imagining a world in which every woman can be "the presiding genius of her own body," women begin to work toward a society in which we can bring forth not only children but the visions and rethinking "necessary to sustain, console, and alter human existence."[51]

The project of challenging dualisms and reclaiming women's body experience is central to the female, sexual images for God that I discussed in the last chapter. When Naomi Janowitz and Maggie Wenig speak of God as the one who gives birth and whose womb covers the earth, they are not just suggesting new female metaphors for God but are also implicitly attacking modes of thinking that separate sexuality—particularly women's sexuality—from any contact with the divine.[52] Women's bodies are not snares and temptations, these metaphors proclaim; women's sexual functions are not to be degraded and feared. Women's sexuality is a source of life, a fitting image for the ultimate source of life who births the world and nourishes its being. Insofar as images of God are drawn from and reinforce what we value, imagining God in female sexual terms reflects and teaches a positive understanding of women's and human sexuality, disputing and dislodging the negative feelings and images that are so much part of the Jewish legacy.

Work that tries to bring together sexuality and the sacred is a minority strand in feminist writing, but it is a strand with considerable power not only to challenge traditional dualisms but also to generate alternatives to the energy/control paradigm of sexuality. A number of feminists concerned with the connections between sexuality and spirit have suggested a new model of sexuality that sees it as part of a continuum of embodied self-expression. From this perspective, our passions, including but not limited to our sexual passions; our self-identity as female or male, including but not limited to our capacity for sexual expression; and our capability of feeling generally, are all rooted in our being in the world as embodied persons. As ethicist Beverly Harrison argues in setting out the base points for a feminist moral theology, our whole relationship to the world is body-mediated. "All knowledge is rooted in our sensuality. We know and value the world, *if* we know and value it, through our ability to touch, to hear, to see." Without the capacity for feeling that is rooted in "our bodies, our selves," we would lose all connection to the world, all ability to act or to value. For Harrison, sexuality is an aspect of our embodiedness and inherent in it, the aspect that "represents our most intense interaction with the world." The intensity of sexuality, however, is not a function of its existence as a separate energy. Sexuality is one dimension of our body-mediated power, of the body space that is "literally the ground of our personhood." What makes sexuality special is that it is the part of ourselves that allows us to interact with others through touch, giving and receiving meanings that transcend our capacity for verbal communication.[53]

This understanding of sexuality as one dimension of bodily feeling finds its most powerful formulation in Audre Lorde's brilliant essay, "Uses of the Erotic: The Erotic as Power." Lorde defines sexuality as one expression of a spectrum of erotic energy that ideally suffuses all the activities in our lives.[54] The erotic is the life force, the capacity for feeling, the capacity for joy, a power we are taught to fear and ignore by a society that "defines the good in terms of profit rather than in terms of human need." The erotic can be experienced with another in the sharing of sexual passion, but it is not limited to this; it is also present in deep connection over any pursuit, "physical, emotional, psychic, or intellectual." Indeed, broadly speaking, the erotic is the joy that, every now and then, human beings find ourselves capable of. As such, it is a source of empowerment, because once we experience joy, the experience becomes a "lens through which we [can] scrutinize all aspects of our existence," honestly evaluating them in terms of their value and meaning within our lives. When we turn away from the knowledge the erotic gives us, when we accept powerlessness or resignation, we cheat ourselves of full life. And when we fail to understand sexual feelings as an expression of the power of the erotic, we reduce them to mere sensations that we then fear and seek to suppress.[55]

This view of sexuality as part of a spectrum of body/life energy rather than a special force or evil inclination has at least two important implications for understanding the place of sexuality in human life. One is that we cannot suppress our capacity for sexual feeling without suppressing our capacity for feeling more generally. If sexuality is one dimension of our ability to live passionately in the world, then in cutting off our sexual feelings, we diminish our overall power to feel, know, and value deeply. This connection does not imply that we must act out our sexual feelings—any more than we are compelled to act out any feelings. It does mean, however, that we must honor and make room for feelings—including sexual feelings— as "the basic ingredient in our relational transaction with the world."[56]

Second, insofar as sexuality is an element in the embodiment that mediates our relation to reality, an aspect of the life energy that enables us to connect with others in creativity and joy, sexuality is profoundly connected to spirituality, indeed is inseparable from it. "Sexuality is both a symbol and a means of communication and communion. . . . It is who we are as bodyselves who experience the emotional, cognitive, physical and spiritual need for intimate communion, both creaturely and divine."[57] It is that part of us through which we reach out to other persons and to God, expressing the need for relationship, for the sharing of self and of meaning. When we touch that place in our lives where sexuality and spirituality come together, we touch our wholeness and the fullness of our power, and at the same time our connection with a power larger than ourselves.[58]

Toward a New Theology of Sexuality

Feminist reconceptualization of the energy/control model of sexuality and affirmation of the profound connection between sexuality and spirituality provide directions for rethinking the ambivalent attitudes toward sexuality within Judaism. Acceptance and avowal of a link between sex and spirit is, as I argued earlier, by no means foreign to Jewish experience. In the mysteries of the marriage bed on Sabbath night; in the sanctity of the Song of Songs; for mysticism, in the very nature and dynamics of the Godhead, sexual expression is an image of and path to the holy.[59] Yet again and again in theology and practice, Judaism turns away from and undermines this acknowledged connection by defining sexuality in terms of patriarchal possession and control. Where women's sexuality is seen as an object to be possessed, and sexuality itself is perceived as an impulse that can take possession of the self, the central issues surrounding sexuality will necessarily be issues of control: Who has the right to control a particular woman's sexuality in what situation? How can a man control his own sexual impulses, given the constant bombardment of female temptation? How can the law control women and the relations between men and women so that the danger of illicit sexual relations (relations with a woman whose sexuality is owned by some other man) is minimized? All these questions make perfect sense as related aspects of a patriarchal system, but they are inimical to the mutuality, openness, and vulnerability in sexual relations that tie sexuality to the sacred.

Recognizing then that the role of women's sexuality in the institution of the family, the rules surrounding the relations of the sexes, and the energy/control paradigm of sexuality are all connected pieces of a patriarchal understanding of sexuality, the question becomes: What would it mean to develop a model of sexuality that is freed from this framework? How can we think about sexuality in a way that springs from and honors the experience of women? How can we develop a positive feminist discourse about sexuality in a Jewish context?

In line with the fundamental feminist insight that sexuality is socially constructed, a Jewish feminist understanding of sexuality begins with the insistence that what goes on in the bedroom can never be isolated from the wider cultural context of which the bedroom is part.[60] The inequalities of the family are prepared for by, and render plausible, larger social inequalities, and the task of eradicating sexual inequality is part of the wider feminist project of ending hierarchical separation as a model for communal life.[61] Thus a Jewish feminist approach to sexuality must take sexual mutuality as a task for the whole of life and not just for Friday evening, fitting its commitment to sexual equality into its broader vision of a society based on mutuality and respect for difference.

It is striking that one of the profoundest images of freedom and mutuality in sexual relations that the Jewish tradition has to offer is at the same time its central image of the connection between sexuality and spirituality. Unlike the Garden of Eden, where Eve and Adam are ashamed of their nakedness and women's subordination is the punishment for sin, the Garden of the Song of Songs is a place of sensual delight and sexual equality. Unabashed by their desire, the man and woman of these poems delight in their own embodiment and the beauty surrounding them, each seeking the other out to inaugurate their meetings, each rejoicing in the love without dominion that is also the love of God.[62] Since this book offers a vision of delight that is easier to achieve in a sacred garden than in the midst of the demands of daily living, it is perhaps no criticism of the institution of marriage that the couple in the Song of Songs is not married. Yet the picture of mutuality, and the sacredness of mutuality, offered by this book stand in fundamental tension with the structures of marriage as Judaism defines them. When the central rituals of marriage and divorce celebrate or enact the male acquisition and relinquishment of female sexuality, what are the supports and resources for the true reciprocity of intimate exchange that marks the holiness of *Shir Hashirim* (Song of Songs)? Despite the efforts of the tradition to legislate concern for women's sexual needs, the achievement of mutuality in the marriage bed is extremely difficult in the absence of justice for women in those institutions that legitimate and surround it.

A central task, then, of the feminist reconstruction of Jewish attitudes toward sexuality is the radical transformation of the institutional, legal framework within which sexual relations are supposed to take place. Insofar as Judaism maintains its interest in the establishment of enduring relationships both as a source of adult companionship and development and as a context for raising and educating children, these relationships will be entered into and dissolved by mutual initiative and consent. "Marriage" will not be about the transfer of women or the sanctification of potential disorder through the firm establishment of women in the patriarchal family, but the decision of two adults—any two adults—to make their lives together, lives that include the sharing of sexuality. Although, in the modern West, it is generally assumed that such a commitment is a central meaning of marriage, this assumption is contradicted by a religious (and secular) legal system that outlaws homosexual marriage and institutionalizes inequality in its basic definitions of marriage and divorce.

This redefinition of the legal framework of marriage, which accords with the feminist refusal to sanctify any hierarchical relationship, is also based on the important principle that sexuality is not something we can acquire or possess in another. We are each the possessor of our own sexuality—in Adrienne Rich's phrase, the "presiding genius" of our own bodies. The sharing of sexuality with another is something that should happen only by mutual consent, a consent that is not a blanket permission, but that is continually renewed in the actual rhythms of particular relationships. This principle, simple as it seems, challenges both the fundamental assumptions of Jewish marriage law and the Jewish understanding of what women's sexuality is "about." It defines as immoral legal regulations concerning the possession, control, and exchange of women's sexuality, and disputes the perspective that a woman's sexuality is her contribution to the family rather than the expression of her own embodiment.

But if one firm principle for feminist thinking about sexuality is that no one can possess the sexuality of another, it is equally the case that from a feminist perspective, sexuality is not something that pertains only or primarily to the self. Indeed, our sexuality is fundamentally about moving out beyond ourselves. As ethicist James Nelson puts it,

The mystery of sexuality is the mystery of the human need to reach out for the physical and spiritual embrace of others. Sexuality thus expresses God's intention that people find authentic humanness not in isolation but in relationship.[63]

Our capacity for intimacy, for sharing, for touch is rooted in our early relations with others; and throughout our lives, we seek genuine connection, longing for at least some relationship(s) that can touch the core of our being. The connecting, communicative nature of sexuality is not something we can experience or look for only in sexual encounters narrowly defined, but in all real relationships in our lives. We live in the world as sexual beings. As Audre Lorde argues, our sexuality is a current that flows through all activities that are important to us, in which we invest our selves. True intellectual exchange, common work, shared experience are laced with sexual energy that animates and enlivens them. The bonds of community are erotic bonds. The power that is generated by real community, that gives us access to a greater power that grounds and embraces us, is in part the power of our own sexual, life energy that flows through community and enlarges and seals it. We are all, women and men, embodied, sexual persons who respond sexually to the women and men among whom we live.

This erotic nature of community is by no means lost on Judaism; indeed, it is the subject of profound ambivalence in both the midrash and law. The story I described earlier in which the rabbis blind rather than kill the imprisoned *yetzer hara* concedes the vital role of the sexual impulse in the creation and maintenance of the world. A similar ambivalence underlies the extensive rabbinic legislation enforcing the separation of the sexes, legislation that tries to protect against the feelings it recognizes, even as it acknowledges the sexual power of community and the continuity of sexuality with other feelings. If the energy of community is erotic, there are no guarantees that eroticism will stay within prescribed legal boundaries rather than breaking out and disrupting communal sanctity. The strict "fence around the law" felt necessary when it comes to sexual behavior is itself testimony to the power of sexuality.

It is tempting for a feminist account of sexuality to deny the disruptive power of the erotic, and to depict the fear of it in rabbinic thought as simply misplaced. But it is truer to experience to acknowledge the power of sexuality to overturn rules and threaten boundaries. Then feminists can embrace this power as a significant ally. There is no question that the empowerment that comes from owning the erotic in our lives can disturb community and undermine familiar structures. On the level of sexual behavior, if we allow ourselves to perceive and acknowledge sexual feelings, there is always the danger we may act on them, and they may not correspond to group concensus about whom we may desire and when. The potentially disruptive effects of sexual feelings exist for communities with stringent sexual ethics that carefully restrict permitted behavior, but also for those with more open boundaries. Starhawk, in discussing the dynamics of political action and other small resistance and countercultural groups, formulates three pessimistic laws of group dynamics: (1) Sexual involvement in small groups is bound to cause problems. (2) "In any small group in which people are involved, sooner or later they will be involved sexually. (3) Small groups tend to break up."[64] Not only the values of a group can be trampled upon by unlooked-for sexual connections but—given the feelings of fear, vulnerability, pain, and anger that can accompany the birth and demise of relationships—sexual liaisons can threaten a group's ability to function cohesively as a community.

When the erotic is understood not simply as sexual feeling in the narrow sense but as our fundamental life energy, the owning of this power in our lives is even more threatening to established structures. In Audre Lorde's terms, if we allow the erotic to become a lens through which we evaluate all aspects of our existence, we can no longer "settle for the convenient, the shoddy, the conventionally expected, nor the merely safe."[65] Having glimpsed the possibility of genuine satisfaction in work well done, we are less likely to settle for work that is alienating and meaningless. Having experienced the power and legitimacy of our own sexual desire, we are less likely to subscribe to a system that closely and absolutely prescribes and proscribes the channels of that desire. Having experienced our capacity for creative and joyful action, we are less likely to accept hierarchical power relationships that deny or restrict our ability to bring that creativity and joy to more and more aspects of our lives. It may be that the ability of women to live within the patriarchal family and the larger patriarchal structures that govern Jewish life depends on our suppression of the erotic, on our numbing ourselves to the sources of vision and power that fuel meaningful resistance. It may also be that the ability of Jews to live unobtrusively as a minority in a hostile culture has depended on blocking sources of personal power that might lead to resistance that feels foolish or frightening. Obviously, from a patriarchal perspective, then—or the perspective of any hierarchical system—erotic empowerment is dangerous. That is why, in Lorde's words, "We are taught to separate the erotic demand from most vital areas of our lives other than sex,"[66] and that is why we are also taught to restrain our sexuality, so that it too fits the parameters of hierarchical control that govern the rest of our lives.

From a feminist perspective, however, the power and danger of the erotic are not reasons to fear and suppress it but to nurture it as a profound personal and communal resource in the struggle for change. When "we begin to demand from ourselves and from our life-pursuits that they feel in accordance with that joy which we know ourselves to be capable of," we carry with us an inner knowledge of the kind of world we are seeking to create.[67] If we repress this knowledge because it also makes us sexually alive, then we repress the clarity and creative energy that is the basis of our capacity to envision and work toward a more just social order.

It is in relation to this understanding of the power of the erotic that feminist insistence on seeing sexuality as part of a continuum of body/life energy is a particularly crucial corrective to rabbinic attitudes toward sexual control. As I have argued, the rabbis recognized the connection between the sexual impulse and human creativity. "The bigger the man, the bigger the *yetzer*," they said, and advised, "Hold him [the *yetzer hara*] off with the left hand and draw him nigh with the right."[68] Yet at the same time they acknowledged the role of sexuality as an ingredient in all activity, they apparently believed one could learn the fear of a woman's little finger without damaging the larger capacity to act and to feel. To love God with all the heart meant to love God with the good *and evil* impulses, and yet it was imagined one could rein in the so-called evil impulse without diminishing the love of God.[69] If we take sexuality seriously, however, as an expression of our embodiment that cannot be disconnected from our wider ability to interact feelingly with the world, then to learn fear and shame of our own bodies and those of others—even when these feelings are intermixed with other conflicting attitudes—is to learn suspicion of feeling as a basic way of knowing and valuing the world. We should not expect, then, to be able to block out our sexual feelings without blocking out the longing for social relations rooted in mutuality rather than hierarchy, without blocking out the anger that warns us that something is amiss in our present social arrangements, without blocking and distorting the fullness of our love for God.[70]

I am not arguing here for free sex or for more sexual expression, quantitatively speaking. I am arguing for living dangerously, for choosing to take responsibility for working through the possible consequences of sexual feelings rather than repressing sexual feeling and thus feeling more generally. I am arguing that our capacity to transform Judaism and the world is rooted in our capacity to be alive to the pain and anger that is caused by relationships of domination, and to the joy that awaits us on the other side. I am arguing that to be alive is to be sexually alive, and that in suppressing one sort of vitality, we suppress the other.

I mentioned above Starhawk's three laws of group dynamics that acknowledge the potential disruptiveness of sex to the creation of community. On the basis of more experience, she adds a fourth: A group that has survived one breakup between members is more likely to survive subsequent ones, and may experience a deepened sense of trust and safety because of what it has been through.[71] This fourth law points to the possibility that even the disruptions caused by sexuality can be a source of power if we refuse to look away from the feelings they evoke in us, maintaining our commitment to the building of community in full cognizance of its erotic bonds.

The question becomes, then: Can we affirm our sexuality as the gift it is, making it sacred not by cordoning off pieces of it, but by increasing our awareness of the ways in which it connects us to all things? Can we stop evicting our sexuality from the synagogue, hiding it behind a *mechitzah* or praying with our heads, and instead bring it in, offering it to God in the experience of full spiritual/physical connection?[72] Dare we trust our capacity for joy—knowing it is related to our sexuality—to point the direction toward new and different ways of structuring communal life?

While I am suggesting that the implications of a changed conception of sexuality go well beyond the sexual sphere, it is also the case that they shape that sphere. The ability to feel deeply in the whole of our lives affects what we want and are willing to accept in the bedroom, just as what we experience in the bedroom prepares us for mutuality or domination in the rest of our lives. A new understanding of sexuality and a transformed institutional context for sexual relationships will have significant impact on personal sexual norms. If the traditional models and categories for understanding sexuality are no longer morally acceptable from a feminist perspective, but sexuality is fundamentally about relationships with others, what values might govern sexual behavior for modern Jews?

It should be clear from all I have said thus far that rejection of the traditional energy/control model of sexuality and of ownership as a category for understanding sexual exchange is by no means synonymous with a sexual ethic of "anything goes."

On the contrary, I would argue—and the current move back toward sexual repression supports this—that the obsession with sexuality in US culture for the last twenty years, the pressures toward early sexual activity for women and men, the expectation that sex could compensate for dissatisfactions in every other area of life, all reflect a reversal of traditional paradigms that does not succeed in moving beyond them. If the Jewish tradition says sex is a powerful impulse that needs to be controlled, certain strains in modern culture say it is healthier to act out our impulses. If the tradition says men may have affairs but women may not, certain strains in modern culture give women "permission" to be promiscuous on male terms. If the tradition says sex has a place in life, but it must not be allowed to take over, modern culture offers sex as a panacea for all that ails us. But when sex is understood as a particular impulse that we act out instead of control, the result is an alienated sexuality that can never rescue us from the alienation in the rest of our lives. If greater genital expression were really the solution to our social miseries, says Beverly Harrison, we would expect ours to be the happiest society around. In fact, however, since, in Audre Lorde's terms, our "erotic comings-together . . . are almost always characterized by a simultaneous looking away," sexual encounters often leave us feeling used and abused rather than renewed and connected.[73]

To see sexuality as an aspect of our life energy, as part of a continuum with other ways of relating to the world and other people, is to insist that the norms of mutuality, respect for difference, and joint empowerment that characterize the larger feminist vision of community apply also—indeed especially—to the area of sexuality. If, in our general communal life, we seek to be present with each other in such a way that we can touch the greater power of being in which all communities dwell, how much more should this be true in those relationships which are potentially the most open, intimate, and vulnerable in our lives? The Song of Songs, because it unifies sensuality, spirituality, and profound mutuality, may offer us the finest Jewish vision of what our sexual relationships can be, a vision that at the same time points to the transformation of our common life. Beverly Harrison places the unification of these elements in a feminist framework:

A feminist moral theology requires that we ground our new ethics of sexuality in a "spirituality of sensuality." . . . Sexuality is indispensable to our spirituality because it is a power of communication, most especially a power to give and receive powerful meaning—love and respect or contempt and disdain. . . . The moral norm for sexual communication in a feminist ethic is radical mutuality—the simultaneous acknowledgment of vulnerability to the need of the other, the recognition of one's own power to give and receive pleasure and to call forth another's power of relation and to express one's own.[74]

It is important to note that this "spirituality of sensuality" and mutuality specifies and intensifies for sexual ethics what are also broader norms for interaction with the world.

The unification of sexuality and spirituality is a sometime gift, a measure of the possible, rather than the reality of everyday. What keeps this unification alive as a recurring possibility is the exercise of respect, responsibility, and honesty—commensurate with the nature and depth of the particular relationship—as basic values in any sexual relationship. In terms of concrete life choices, I believe that radical mutuality is most fully possible in the context of an ongoing, committed relationship in which sexual expression is one dimension of a shared life. Traditional insistence that sex be limited to heterosexual marriage might find its echo in support for and celebration of long-term partnerships as the richest setting for negotiating and living out the meanings of mutuality, responsibility, and honesty amidst the distractions, problems, and pleasures of daily life. Such partnerships are not, however, a choice for all adults who want them, and not all adults would choose them, given the possibility. To respond within a feminist framework to the realities of different life decisions and at the same time affirm the value of sexual well-being as an aspect of our total well-being, we need to apply certain fundamental values to a range of sexual choices and styles. While honesty, responsibility, and respect are goods that pertain to any relationship, the concrete meaning of these values will vary considerably depending on the duration and significance of the connection involved. In one relationship, honesty may mean complete and open sharing of feelings and experiences; in another, clarity about intent for that encounter. In the context of a committed partnership, responsibility may signify lifelong presence, trust, and exchange; in a brief encounter, discussion of birth control, AIDS, and safe sex. At its fullest, respect may mean regard for another as a total person; at a minimum, absence of pressure or coercion, and a commitment, in Lorde's terms, not to "look away" as we come together. If we need to look away, then we should walk away: The same choices about whether and how to act on our feelings that pertain to any area of moral decision making are open to us in relation to our sexuality.

The same norms that apply to heterosexual relationships also apply to gay and lesbian relationships.[75] Indeed, I have formulated them with both in mind. There are many issues that might be considered in reevaluating traditional Jewish rejection of homosexuality.[76] But the central issue in the context of a feminist reconceptualization of sexuality is the relationship between homosexual choice and the continuity between sexual energy and embodied life energy. If we see sexuality as part of what enables us to reach out beyond ourselves, and thus as a fundamental ingredient in our spirituality, then the issue of homosexuality must be placed in a somewhat different framework from those in which it is most often discussed. The question of the morality of homosexuality becomes one not of halakhah or the right to privacy or freedom of choice, but the affirmation of the value to the individual and society of each of us being able to find that place within ourselves where sexuality and spirituality come together.[77] It is possible that some or many of us for whom the connections between sexuality and deeper sources of personal and spiritual power emerge most richly, or only, with those of the same sex could choose to lead heterosexual lives for the sake of conformity to halakhah or wider social pressures and values. But this choice would then violate the deeper vision offered by the Jewish tradition that sexuality can be a medium for the experience and reunification of God.[78] Historically, this vision has been expressed entirely in heterosexual terms. The reality is that for some Jews, however, it is realized only in relationships between two men or two women. Thus what calls itself the Jewish path to holiness in sexual relations is for some a cutting off of holiness—a sacrifice that comes at high cost for both the individual and community. Homosexuality, then, does not necessarily represent a rejection of Jewish values but the choice of certain Jewish values over others—where these conflict with each other, the choice of the possibility of holiness over control and law.

Potential acceptance of gays and lesbians by the Jewish community raises the issue of children—for Judaism a primary warrant for sexual relations, and the facade that prejudice often hides behind in rejecting homosexuality as a Jewish choice. Again to place this issue in the context of a feminist paradigm for understanding sexuality, procreation is a dimension of our sexuality, just as sexuality itself is a dimension of our embodied personhood. If sexuality allows us to reach out to others, having children is a way of reaching out beyond our own generation, affirming the biological continuity of life and the continuity of Jewish community and communal values. Insofar as Jewish communities have an important stake in the rearing of Jewish children, it is in their interest to structure communal institutions to support in concrete ways all Jews who choose to have children, including increasing numbers of lesbians and gay men.[79] But, just as Judaism has always recognized that procreation does not exhaust the meaning of sexuality, so having children does not exhaust the ways in which Jews can contribute to future generations.[80] Recognizing the continuities between sexuality and personal empowerment strengthens the conviction of the inherent value of sexuality as an expression of our personhood and of our connection with and love for others.

The sense of integrity and self-worth that a loving sexual relationship can foster enhances the capacity to make commitments to the future, whether this takes the form of bearing and raising children or nurturing communal continuity in other ways.

Lastly, but underlying all that I have said, sexuality as an aspect of our life energy and power connects us with God as the sustaining source of energy and power in the universe. In reaching out to another sexually with the total self, the boundaries between self and other can dissolve and we may feel ourselves united with larger currents of energy and sustenance. It is also the case, however, that even in ordinary, daily reachings out to others, we reach toward the God who is present in connection, in the web of relation with a wider world. On the one hand, the wholeness, the "all-embracing quality of sexual expression" that includes body, mind, and feeling, is for many people the closest we can come in this life to experiencing the embracing wholeness of God.[81] On the other hand, the everyday bonds of community are also erotic bonds through which we touch the God of community, creating a place where the divine presence can rest. Feminist metaphors that name God not simply as female but sexual female—beautiful, filled with vitality, womb, birthgiver—seek to give imagistic expression to the continuity between our own sexual energy and the greater currents that nourish and renew it. Feminist images name female sexuality as powerful and legitimate and name sexuality as part of the image of God. They tell us that sexuality is not primarily a moral danger (though, of course, it can be that), but a source of energy and power that, schooled in the values of respect and mutuality, can lead us to the related, and therefore sexual, God.

6. Feminist Judaism and Repair of the World

This is a book about ideas, the central Jewish ideas of Torah, Israel, and God, and the related idea of sexuality, as they might be rethought from a feminist perspective. But it is also a book about the relationship between ideas and experience, and the connection of both to the world in which we live. In reformulating the major religious categories of Judaism from a feminist perspective, I have tried to be clear both about the ways in which patriarchal theology supports destructive institutions and religious structures, and about the concrete communal contexts out of which alternatives to that theology emerge. I have argued that patriarchal ideas reinforce patriarchy as a social system, but also that they are products of that system and must be understood in social, institutional, and historical context. I have suggested that feminist ideas may potentially alter, and at least no longer support, patriarchal structures, but also that feminist ideas and experiences will be able to develop fully only with the creation of feminist institutions.

Insofar as a feminist Judaism must be grounded in feminist modes of social relation, it is clear that such a Judaism can be just in its beginnings. While the partial emergence of feminist communities has made it possible for me to write this book or to imagine a feminist Judaism at all, it remains undeniably the case that the existence of feminist communities is far from a widespread reality. Any Jewish feminist program for change must grapple with the fact that not simply the shortcomings of individual education, imagination, and temperament, but also many of the structures of the world in which we live, militate against the creation and survival of communities based on feminist values. In 1981, when my Jewish feminist spirituality collective, B'not Esh, first met, we set as a central task for the weekend to share our spiritual pasts, presents, and futures. My small group found that we had no difficulty talking about the past and present. But when we came to the future, we ended up talking about relationships, children, work, community, politics—everything but "spirituality." Although at first we chided ourselves for evading a difficult subject, we soon realized that in speaking of these other issues, we were addressing the realities that stood between us and our capacity to imagine the futures we wanted to live. It became clear to us that if we wanted to create a feminist Judaism we would have to help to bring about a world in which such a Judaism would be possible. For me and for the group, this discussion marked the beginning of an increasingly active awareness of the connection between spirituality as the lived, experiential dimension of a feminist Judaism and the wider social and political contexts in which we would try to live our spiritual lives.[1]

The relationship between a feminist Judaism and larger social and political structures forms the subject of this last chapter. In ending my book with this theme, I hope to accomplish several things: to take up the relationship between spirituality and politics as a theological issue, to elucidate a connection implicit in all I have said thus far, and to place the feminist transformation of Judaism in its wider social context.

Like sexuality and the sacred, spirituality and concern for social institutions have often been viewed in American culture as polar opposites. Spirituality has been identified with ethereality, the presence of a place beyond the material world or deep within the self where the relationship to God is actualized. The assigned guardian of spirituality has been religion, which is itself relegated to the margins of society and expected to limit its interests to Saturday or Sunday mornings. As spirituality minds its otherworldly business, transformation of social structures is left to the often dirty work of politics, which catches us up in a realm of compromise, power seeking, struggle over what have been defined as limited resources, and confrontation with the distortions and disease in our social system.

This institutionalized separation of spirituality and politics, proceeding from the same hierarchy of mind and body that supports the disparagement of women, represents another dualism to be rejected. When spirituality is understood from a feminist perspective—not in otherworldly terms, but as the fullness of our relationship to ourselves, others, and God—it cannot possibly be detached from the conditions of our existence. Those ideologies and institutions that alienate us from ourselves and link us with others in relationships of domination and subordination militate against our spirituality on every level. In a sexist, heterosexist, anti-Semitic, class-ridden, and racist world, politics becomes the necessary work we do to make the world safe for the full realization and embodiment of spirituality.[2] In seeking to transform the ideas and institutions of Judaism, to live out our feminism, to overcome imperialism or class and race oppression, we attempt to create religious, social, and political structures that allow us to be present to each other in the fullness of who we are, and in doing so to experience the God who is with us in our personal and communal agency. As the vision and intuition of personal and communal wholeness guide our political goals and strategies, politics becomes an expression of spirituality in its intent to create more human institutions, and religion itself is transformed by politics. In understanding and living out the relation between politics and spirituality, Jewish feminists connect the transformation of the Jewish community with a multifaceted global struggle for social, political, and religious change.

Religion and Politics in Judaism and Feminism

In chapter 3, I discussed the centrality of community in human experience as an emphasis shared by Judaism and feminism. The connection between politics and spirituality is another issue on which at least some strands of Judaism and feminism come together. Just as Judaism—while it has not always construed action in political terms—has consistently refused to disconnect the relationship with God from the world in which it is manifest, so feminism—while it has not always understood itself as a religious movement—has tied a vision of women's wholeness to a broad program for social and political action. In theology or theory and their living stance in the world, Judaism and feminism provide models of a relationship between faith and action that are worthy of extended exploration.

Recent work in liberation theology has used the word orthopraxis (right action), contrasting it with orthodoxy (right belief), to signify a new mood in Christian theology that recognizes the importance of action and behavior as central measures of the Christian life.[3] The polemical edge to this definition highlights the fact that Judaism has always been a religion of orthopraxis, assessing spirituality through its manifestation in the deed. The enactment of faith in the world, a central Jewish imperative, has had at least two distinctly different meanings in Jewish theology and practice: social justice and obedience to halakhah.

The first meaning, spirituality as social justice, receives classical expression in the writings of the prophets, for whom the essence of human service to God is love, justice, and righteousness. Contrasting these virtues with the empty practice of the cult, the prophets affirm that the forms of worship are meaningless in the absence of social justice. Offerings brought by the wicked, feasts and solemn assemblies held by those who trample the poor, prayers said by people who traffic with injustice are all unacceptable and fruitless. The efficacy of worship "is contingent upon moral living"; in the absence of morality, worship becomes despicable.[4] "Your new moons and fixed seasons/ Fill Me with loathing," says Isaiah in the name of God. "They are become a burden to me,/ I cannot endure them" (1:14). "He has told you . . . what is good," says Micah. "And what the LORD requires of you:/ Only to do justice/ And to love goodness,/ And to walk modestly with your God" (6:8).

The prophets did not couch their concerns for justice in abstract generalizations that could be honored in principle and ignored in the particular. They described the social evils they saw around them in vivid and concrete terms. They repeatedly urged compassion for those on the margins of (patriarchal) society; the welfare of the widow and the fatherless is a refrain in their writings (for example, Isa. 1:17b; Ezek. 22:7b). They defended the rights of the poor in images as graphic as they are universal:

Listen to this, you who devour the needy, annihilating the poor of the land, saying "If only the new moon were over, so that we could sell grain; the sabbath, so that we could offer wheat for sale, using an *ephah* that is too small, and a shekel that is too big, tilting a dishonest scale, and selling grain refuse as grain! We will buy the poor for silver, the needy for a pair of sandals." (Amos 8:4–6)

The prophets were meddlers, troublesome busybodies. They were horrified by things that are daily occurrences all over the world, by abuses that are often taken for granted as normal, if regrettable, aspects of complex social relations. They were unwilling to mind their own business, to stay away from wrongs that did not involve them personally, or refrain from championing others' rights for lack of invitation.[5] Their meddlesomeness brought them into confrontation with their fellow citizens—and also with those in power, for the powerful were not exempt from the demand to act righteously, but rather were supposed especially to exemplify righteousness. When King David had Uriah killed in battle in order that David could marry Uriah's wife Bathsheba, the prophet Nathan appeared on David's doorstep with a parable of a rich man who steals from a poor one. Responding to David's anger at the rich man in the story, Nathan said to the king, "You are the man" (2 Sam. 12:7). This ringing indictment of specific injustice in high places stands as a splendid example of the prophetic fusion of spirituality and politics.[6]

The passion for justice in prophetic writing presupposes a view of the divine/human relation as enacted in human history and entangled in the world. To say that acts of worship and devotion, surely essential to religion, are less important to God than everyday righteousness is to make the sphere of human action the center of God's concern. The universe is finished, but history is still in the process of formation, and God needs human beings to create a just social order in history. As the covenant partner of Israel, God is a continuing participant in Israel's history, a participant who can be affronted, rejected, and humiliated by human cruelty and injustice. Israel's primary obligation to God is not to create a relationship to God that bypasses the material order, but to realize God's concern for human beings through interpersonal decency and the creation of social justice.[7] Attention to human relations and institutions, so far from conflicting with devotion to God, stands at its very center.

The prophetic identification of faith with social justice and its correlate, that God needs human beings to act justly, does not annul the militarism or patriarchal character of prophetic imagery; nor does it alter the prophets' religious intolerance or their lack of concern for justice for women. Prophetic writing is filled with contradictions. Thus, at the same time the prophets are concerned with widows as individual victims of a patriarchal culture, they help perpetuate that culture by using images of patriarchal marriage to symbolize faithfulness and apostasy. At the same time they call for a connection between religion and justice, they enforce a narrow and monolithic understanding of religion, condemning all who disagree with them as idolaters and whores. At the same time they presuppose the capacity of human beings to form or deform history, they depict God as the mighty warrior who holds all history in his hands. But the fact that the prophets failed to wholly live out their commitment to justice does not invalidate that commitment, any more than the commitment justifies its violation. Feminists can affirm our debt to and continuity with prophetic insistence on connecting faith and justice, even while we extend the prophets' social and religious critique beyond anything they themselves envisioned.

The second meaning of action in Jewish theology and practice, obedience to the law, is depicted in the prophetic writings as potentially in conflict with an emphasis on social justice. As the prophets see it, external obedience to the laws of sacrifice easily becomes the occasion for unwarranted self-righteousness that ignores the real demand of God, continuing justice. Unlike the passion for equity, which necessarily flows from a believing heart, cultic participation may be all outward sign, compatible with social evil and inner iniquity. While the prophets contrast true piety with observance of religious forms as they were known in that time, their contempt for empty ritual corresponds to some of the criticisms of halakhah that I raised in chapter 2. Just as the forms of sacrificial worship can become ends in themselves, so obedience to the law can become its own object, fulfillment of specific legal requirements replacing attention to the broader moral values that the law betokens but cannot demand.

Real and significant as the danger of empty legalism may be, however, it is not the *purpose* of the law to replace morality with formal obedience. The intention of prophetic and legal religion is the same: to connect faith with the concrete world, to express the relationship with God in the whole of life. Thus with reference to their goal, the two meanings of Jewish action—social justice and obedience to the law—are thoroughly interconnected. The law spells out the specific demands of justice; it regulates the *ephah* and the shekel that the prophets denounce as too small and too big. It takes ideals and shapes them to human measure, establishing a trajectory toward the righteousness that lies beyond the law's explicit claims. The rabbinic concept of *tikkun olam*, the right ordering of society, underlies many of the law's specific demands.[8] Even the purely ritual law proclaims the indivisibility of holy living; no detail of life is too small to escape the possibility of consecration. As Martin Buber says, applying his words immediately to the sacrificial cult:

Because God bestows not only spirit on man [sic], but the whole of his existence . . . man can fulfill the obligations of his partnership with God by no spiritual attitude, by no worship, on no sacred upper story; the whole of life is required, every one of its areas and every one of its circumstances.[9]

This consonance of purpose between law and prophecy represents the ideal without dissolving the tension between spirituality as law and spirituality as justice. Modern Jews involved in movements for social change have often intensified the dichotomies of prophetic invective, depicting the details of ritual observance as foolish distractions from the passion for justice. In modern times, the object of criticism becomes not simply the empty formalism of worship, but the particularity of legal obligation as contrasted with the pursuit of righteousness which is universal. Isaac Deutscher's "The Non-Jewish Jew," which expresses this conflict in the sharpest possible terms, sees the great revolutionaries of modern thought as Jewish precisely in the way they transcended the boundaries of Judaism, living their Jewishness in a universal arena. Heine, Marx, Luxemburg, Trotsky, all believed in human solidarity, and all saw solidarity as extending beyond Jewish borders. All believed that knowledge "to be real must be active," and all acted for the sake of a universal good. For them, Jewry was "too narrow, too archaic, and too constricting," and yet they betrayed a passion for justice and action that is rooted in the tradition they wanted to leave behind.[10]

Contemporary progressive Jews have tried to reconcile the prophetic and legal understandings of religious action by investing the Kabbalistic concept of *tikkun olam* with new political meaning. Isaac Luria's notion of the necessity of human action both to the repair of the world and the reunification of God seems to provide a basis for a Jewish political spirituality that is at the same time a religious politics. The idea of *tikkun* in Lurianic thought—restoration of the world to primal wholeness or the original intent of the creator—is part of a complex and esoteric mythological schema. Briefly, the possibility of creation is predicated on a withdrawal or contraction (*Tsimtsum*) of God from an area within Godself in order to make room for the existence of the world. Following this contraction, God sends out rays of light that constitute God's self-manifestation and creation, rays of light that are meant to be contained in special vessels. While the vessels containing God's first emanations function properly, the lower ones are too weak for the power of the divine effulgence and shatter and disperse. This breaking of the vessels (*Shevirath Ha-Kelim*) constitutes a cosmic calamity, releasing the forces of evil that are now at large in the world. *Tikkun* refers to the method through which repair is to be accomplished, and is largely a cosmic process preceding the creation of Adam. Not all the divine sparks held in captivity by the powers of darkness are able to free themselves by their own efforts, however, so a certain crucial aspect of this restoration is left in human hands. The religious acts of Jews who fulfill the commands of Torah accelerate the process of redemption, adding the "final touch to the divine countenance" and aiding the perfection of God and the world.[11]

This concept of *tikkun* as articulated in Lurianic Kabbalah is esoteric and elitist, but it undergoes transformation in a number of different hands. For Luria, restorative action is primarily ritual and contemplative action; the reunification of the divine sparks is initiated by the complex meditations of Kabbalists whose souls are first purified by a series of spiritual exercises. Hasidism, however, democratized the concept of *tikkun*, redefining it as attending to material needs with God in mind. In embracing the world while cognizant of the presence of the sacred in all aspects of reality, human beings can elevate the holy sparks present in the whole of creation.[12] Jewish radicals of the nineteenth century, while hardly meaning to respond to Luria, also helped rework Kabbalistic messianism. The task of repairing a broken world, the goal of which is redemption, for them is transferred entirely to human hands. Action means social action; evil is injustice; revolution repairs the material world which is the only world there is. In more recent Jewish writing, the Kabbalistic concept of *tikkun* with its eschatological dimension is united both with its older rabbinic meaning of just social order and with the universalism of nineteenth-century radicals.[13] Arthur Waskow's book *These Holy Sparks* calls for reunion of the separated projects of modern Jewry—Zionism, social justice, socialism, halakhah—as itself part of the process of reunifying God. Creating a just social order becomes a sustainable task when it is undertaken by communities rooted in Jewish practice and aware of the transcendent dimension of their work in the world.[14] This same meaning of *tikkun* as social, political, and religious transformation all reinforcing each other is found in the platform of New Jewish Agenda (a national Jewish organization seeking large-scale social change) and the progressive *Tikkun* magazine.[15]

The thread that winds through these sometimes conflicting notions of action and its social or cosmic effects is the refusal to disconnect religious belief from its practical expression or from human responsibility for the world. Whether action signifies just weights and measures, moral behavior, animal sacrifice, or daily prayer; whether its ramifications are purely mundane, covenantal, or cosmic in scope; faith is to be poured out in action which vivifies and embodies it. The maintenance of both social justice and sacred order emerges from the dialogue between God and humans, and thus rests partly on human shoulders, endowing our deeds with serious consequences.

The feminist contribution to the connection between politics and spirituality is for the most part more indirect than this forthright linkage of faith and practice. Yet many of the first arguments for women's rights emerged in a religious context, and religious rhetoric and concerns marked feminist commitment to women's emancipation from its very beginnings.

Church sewing circles, for example, provided an early seedbed for discussion of women's legal and social situation, and Quaker women, permitted a voice in church affairs denied by other denominations, early took the lead in the struggle for justice for women.[16] Prominent Quaker abolitionist and feminist Sarah Grimké, attacked in 1837 by the Council of Congregationalist Ministers of Massachusetts for giving antislavery speeches to mixed (male and female) audiences, defended her right to do so in the strongest religious terms. "Men and women were CREATED EQUAL," she said, alluding to Genesis 1; "they are both moral and accountable beings, and whatever is *right* for man to do, is *right* for woman."[17] The advertisement for the first Woman's Rights Convention, held at Seneca Falls in 1848, announced a meeting to "discuss the social, civil, and *religious* rights of woman." Among the eighteen grievances drawn up by Elizabeth Cady Stanton for the occasion were woman's subordination in the church as well as state, and man's usurpation of "the prerogative[s] of Jehovah."[18]

The use of religious vocabulary and interest in religious reform have also been features of the second wave of feminism. Mary Daly's *The Church and the Second Sex*, published in 1968, was a relatively early work that adopted the perspective of Simone de Beauvoir to illumine the subordination of women within Catholicism. Protestant and Jewish women also applied their feminism within a religious context, raising issues of sexist language, exclusion from ordination, and halakhic disenfranchisement as items for the feminist agenda. These concerns of religious feminists did not emerge in isolation from the wider feminist movement, but came out of and fed into a larger feminist vision. Christian feminist discussions of Jesus' "feminism" or the egalitarian tendencies in Pauline theology were meant to prod the churches back to what was perceived as a fundamentally liberating message, to call them to take the leadership in social change on women's issues, rather than dragging behind the secular society.[19] As feminist analysis and critique of traditional religion has become deeper and more sophisticated, there also has developed alongside it a grass roots women's spirituality movement that has found ways to express women's new sense of power and possibility in ritual and religious terms.

This focus on religion constitutes one significant dimension of feminism. Yet even where the women's movement has been indifferent or hostile to religious issues, it still has combined theory and practice in a way that parallels the Jewish connection of faith and politics. The consciousness-raising groups that marked the beginning of the contemporary feminist movement were seedbeds both for theory-making and for many concrete actions. Early feminist activities, from protesting Miss America pageants to working for abortion reform, projected a vision of a society in which women's humanity and dignity would be fundamental social and political values. Feminist theory developed side by side with organizations pressing for or making concrete changes, each feeding the other in an ongoing cycle. Thus women's claim to the right to direct our reproductive lives fed a struggle for abortion rights that in turn produced a clearer understanding of the forces aligned to control women's sexuality, and of the nature of feminist sexual values. Affirmation of women's right to physical safety and personal self-respect led to the establishment of shelters, rape crisis centers and hotlines; these then generating deeper theory that could name and address the sources of violence. Insistence on equalizing power relations in daily life led women to make new demands on their partners and children, demands that often exposed the connections between family dynamics and larger social structures and shaped the vision and practice of a more radical feminism. In thus placing deeds in the service of vision, feminism has linked political action to a fundamentally spiritual quest for new forms of relation to self, others, and the world.

It is this basic commitment to new modes of social relation, as much as any specifically religious language and concerns, that has led some feminists to define the women's movement as intrinsically religious. While, for some feminists, involvement in social change is a human project that lacks any transcendent referent, others experience feminism as having an underlying spiritual dimension, quite apart from its relation to particular religious projects or terms. I mentioned, in discussing feminist community, that the experience of personal empowerment that accompanies and enables participation in social change can also connect the individual and community to more embracing sources of power. Engaging in the process of transforming social structures and ideologies fosters awareness of structures of meaning that bind particular struggles for change to a larger past and future. It is this awareness that leads Mary Daly to call the women's movement an *ontological* revolution, which means that in fostering new ways of being and becoming in the world, the movement is part of a search for ultimate meaning and reality.[20] Other feminists have expressed the same insight in different terms. Nelle Morton, in a phenomenological discussion of consciousness-raising, describes the process of women's becoming as a religious transformation. The Goddess movement, in stressing the immanence of the Goddess in the world, sees the struggle for justice for women as serving the Goddess who is manifest in all social structures and relations. Jewish feminists have described women's liberation as an aspect of *tikkun*, an ingredient in the repair and transformation of the world that is part of its redemption.[21] These are all ways of insisting on the connection between social justice and the relationship to ultimate reality, of saying that social transformation is a spiritual process, that it points beyond itself.

The impulse to connect spirituality and politics does not annul the contradictions in feminist thought and practice, any more than is the case with prophetic notions of justice. Just as the prophets' passion for righteousness did not exclude religious intolerance or extend to abolishing patriarchy, so feminist commitment to the full personhood of women does not always encompass dismantling the race and class oppression that prevents most women's empowerment. In feminist practice as in prophetic thought, a politics unaware of its own privilege serves to highlight the relation between vision and social structures, even while it seems to separate them. Theory formulated by communities of white middle-class women often neglects issues crucial to minority feminists, just as lack of engagement in the concrete struggles of minorities limits the vision of white middle-class women. Insofar as feminism aims to make women the social equals of men, it emerges out of and reinforces race and class privilege. Lower-class and poor women, especially women of color, are more likely to emphasize a spirituality and politics of liberation than of equality, for they know that the men to whom they would be equal are in many ways not the equals of middle-class women.[22] While the vision of feminism as an ontological revolution theoretically incorporates the abolition of all forms of oppression, the absence of communal diversity at either the level of theory making or of action easily turns both into vehicles for domination.

Feminist Judaism and Its Social Context

If both Judaism and feminism, whatever their shortcomings, have propounded and practiced an ongoing connection between spirituality and politics, vision and social transformation, this connection must then be applied in the context of a feminist Judaism. What is a Jewish feminist politics, and how does it flow from the theological vision articulated in this book? In writing a Jewish feminist theology focused on the feminist transformation of Judaism, I have addressed myself largely to problems within the Jewish community, particularly to problems in the relationship between women and men. But while the creation of woman-affirming Jewish communities is an important element in the quest for social justice, it is just one piece of a larger struggle for justice that is being carried on in every corner of the earth. The Jewish community is a small one in the United States and a tiny one in the world. It would be foolish to expect that it could avoid entanglement in national and global structures of domination or forge its own way in creating new egalitarian forms of community in the absence of changes in the larger society. Jews have as often emulated and contributed to the inequality, domination, and injustice of their surroundings as modeled different ways of being. Only by keeping in mind the larger context of our efforts to create justice within Judaism can Jewish feminists avoid reproducing relationships of domination or turning our own liberation into a vehicle for the further oppression of others.

In chapter 3, in treating the role of difference in community, I discussed a series of overlapping failures on the part of various national, religious, and ethnic groups to create communities that honor diversity. The long history of persecution of the Jews and the failure of even modern liberal nations to make room for particularity finds its analogue and recapitulation in the Jewish community's subordination of women, the state of Israel's treatment of Arabs, and the (white middle-class) feminist community's neglect of minority women's issues and experiences. These failures are not coincidental, but rather each successive failure becomes the basis for the others. When we live in a world in which difference continually works itself out as domination and subordination, it becomes extremely difficult to create genuinely pluralistic communal forms. Not only do our imaginations often fail us, but, when they do not, larger social structures intervene to remind us that relationships of domination are not simply a product of faulty ideology but of institutional and political power.[23] Jewish feminists then, while we may want to begin with clearing our own house, must look beyond the Jewish community to the task of *tikkun olam*—repairing the world, creating a just society to which a just Judaism can contribute and flourish.

What repair of the world means concretely in the context of a feminist Judaism emerges most clearly from the contradictions between feminist vision and the realities of a profoundly unjust social order. The vision of the people of Israel as one among many overlapping nonhierarchical communities constitutes the living center of this book out of which other aspects of a feminist Judaism emerge. My reconceptualization of Torah, God, and sexuality arises out of, and seeks to make real, Jewish communities that respect and welcome their own diversity and nurture the full being of their members. A Torah that includes the Torah of women is the Torah of a community of Israel in which women are fully included. It is the Torah of a community that needs to remember the history of women because its new social and religious reality has altered the shape of memory. The God imaged in feminist theology and liturgy is God experienced and enacted in the mutual empowerment made possible by non-hierarchical communal structures. The beginnings of new language represent attempts to articulate experiences of God sustained within new communal forms and efforts to find language that can in turn nurture these forms. A new understanding of sexuality as part of a continuum of life energy can be lived only in a community that honors passion and in which the personal and political are thoroughly intertwined.

The attempt, however, to realize the kinds of communal structures and modes of being that a feminist Judaism requires and entails brings us up against opposing social, religious, and political realities. The structures of the Jewish community as it is for the most part constituted, the structures of our society and the global situation, are all obstacles to the formation of diverse, egalitarian communities that foster human empowerment.[24] To trace all the connections between the feminist vision of community and the forces that impede its realization would require a complex social, political, and economic analysis that goes far beyond the scope of this book. But even to begin to suggest some of the relationships between a feminist spirituality and its broader social context is to clarify the inescapably political dimension of spirituality and the necessary connection between theology and action.

I have already argued in discussing the state of Israel, for example, that Israeli failure to achieve equality for women in the context of a whole and integrated Jewish life cannot be separated from the wider issues of inequality in Israeli society. The particular texture and coloration of Israeli women's subordination is connected to the militarization of Israel as well as the role of Orthodoxy within it, and is interstructured with the control of the Arab population and the subordination of Mizrahi Jews. The development of Israeli society, however, in turn cannot be abstracted from the larger practice of statecraft in the twentieth century. Paula Rayman, in her study *The Kibbutz Community and Nation Building*, concretizes the connection between small-scale communal change and larger social forces by examining a particular kibbutz in relation to the process of state creation in Israel. She finds, not surprisingly, that the capacity of the kibbutz to realize its utopian values is constrained not simply by internal factors such as routinization and generational changes, but by the forces of nationalism, modernization, and industrialization in the surrounding culture.[25] The analysis she applies to the microcosm might also be made for the macrocosm. Jews were given the opportunity for "normalization" in the context of a nation-state system in which each country competes with others for its own aggrandizement and power and in which global economic forces shape individual national development. While Jews may not want to surrender the vision of many early Zionists that Israel would be a state different from others, the forces arrayed against this possibility are numerous and considerable. The complaint of many Israeli and non-Israeli Jews that Israel is singled out among the nations and held to a different and higher standard of justice than every country on earth points to the larger world order within which Israel came into being and reminds us that its injustices are "normal" indeed.

The conflicts between feminist demands and larger social forces, visible in the Israeli context, applies equally in the United States. As one of many ethnic/religious communities in a complex and diverse society, the Jewish community interacts with and is affected by structures of sexism, class inequality, racism, and homophobia that infect the society as a whole. It has to deal with problems of internal diversity in the context of a culture that professes respect for diversity while continually constructing difference as super- and subordination. Two issues can serve to illustrate the complex connections between particular aspects of feminist spirituality and broader social and political forces. Women's demand for equal participation in Jewish religious and communal institutions and the feminist understanding of the power of the erotic both have social and political ramifications that extend well beyond the borders of the Jewish community.

Women's full participation in leadership and decision-making, as well as in the ordinary activities of the Jewish community, presupposes not simply communal willingness to make certain positions available to women but a fundamental transformation of both structures of leadership and sexual roles. It is not enough for men in power to yield some of their power to women, or for educational institutions to prepare girls and women for equality and authority; the structures of Jewish communal and family life will have to change to make it possible for women and men to assume new tasks. The current hierarchical organization of most synagogues and Jewish communal institutions, for example, is uncomfortable and repugnant to many women, who have been socialized to other modes of interaction or have learned to value participatory leadership through involvement with feminism.[26] For an increasing number of women, assuming leadership in the Jewish community means struggling to redefine the nature of leadership to emphasize the catalytic and empowering functions of a rabbi or communal authority. Such redefinition, however, is itself contingent on greater participation and responsibility on the part of the "laity," a shift that in turn involves further communal changes. Women and men can function equally as active congregants or communal leaders only with changes in the sexual division of labor and the creation of communal institutions that promote new developments in community and family life. Otherwise, from early morning services to dinnertime meetings, Jewish activities presuppose a family structure in which women's responsibility for home and children frees men to fulfill their communal obligations. If the Jewish community is not to place the burden of equality on individual families that lack any external supports for their personal arrangements, it will both have to provide communal childcare and rethink its expectations of individuals in the light of new personal, family, and community roles.

Such changes in Jewish life cannot be separated, however, from parallel changes in the larger culture. Jewish models of religious leadership and organizational structure are often borrowed directly from analogous institutions in American society, institutions that provide few examples of female leadership or a female leadership style. The dearth of women in positions of authority in the wider culture is directly related to the sexual division of labor, itself sufficient to undermine women's full participation in the Jewish communal world. Despite the fact that the great majority of American women are now part of the paid workforce, salaries, the cultural definition of a committed worker, the (un)availability of childcare, and the unequal distribution of housework all continue to be based on the norm of husband supporting his family and wife working at home. The woman who labors all day in the marketplace is responsible both for making her own childcare arrangements and for a second job at home at night. How is she then to find the time and energy for taking on new roles in the Jewish community in the absence of changes in the nature of work, the division between home and workplace, and the accessibility of childcare?

The relationships between religious change and far-reaching changes in leadership and gender roles are not the only dimensions of the connection between spirituality and wider social issues. Within a social system in which the physical environment continues to be shaped to free men for "productive" work while women perform support services in the home, women can take on traditionally male roles only if they remain childless, have extraordinary energy, or pay someone else to act as housekeeper and child-tender.[27] It is possible for middle-class

women to take on expanded roles within Judaism without re-
negotiating family or social relations by compensating someone
else to play the role of "wife." But Jewish women's own freedom
then depends on the continued oppression of other women
who have fewer options within the social system. Women of
color and poor white women make up the overwhelming majority of domestic workers because a racist and class-divided
society presses certain groups into jobs that no one else wants.
While substantive changes in the sex role system would alleviate the burden of poor women by raising wages and providing childcare alternatives, it would not address the issues of
race and class that crucially affect job patterns and the range of
women's choices. If the feminist vision of social change is to
embrace all women, then any vision of equality within the Jewish community must address two questions: What communal
and social changes are necessary in order that *all* Jewish women
can enjoy full equality within the community? And what social
changes are necessary so that no Jewish woman's equality is
predicated on the individual or structural exploitation of other
women, but rather the struggle for equality in the Jewish community becomes part of a wider struggle for social justice?

If the feminist quest for equal participation in the Jewish community links up with larger issues of gender, race, and class,
the possibility of experiencing sexuality as a fundamental dimension of our embodiment is also dependent on a host of
social changes. I argued in the last chapter that equality for
women in the bedroom is not separable from justice for women
in the social structures that surround the bedroom. This means
that not only specific laws of marriage and divorce, but also the
more general discrimination against women in Jewish life and
the wider society foster patterns of domination and subordination that militate against mutuality and intimacy in sexual relationships. But beyond sexual connections in the narrow sense,
a feminist understanding of sexuality as part of a spectrum of
erotic energy also has striking ramifications for the world in
which we live. Truly to honor our bodies as the foundation of

our being or to experience the erotic as a current that flows through all our activities would necessitate profound changes in our relation to the world. The import of the feminist slogan "the personal is the political"—meaning that seemingly personal problems are often rooted in the wider social context, and that social change must bring changes in daily life—is nowhere clearer than in the challenge of the erotic to the devastation of the earth and to the ugliness and suffering in society.

First of all, to value our bodies means to value and care for the earth of which they are part; otherwise, this valuing has no relation to a material base that supports and sustains it. The increasing pollution of the environment, the dumping of toxic chemicals and nuclear wastes, the poisoning of the food supply through pesticides, and destruction of lakes and rivers all are rooted in denial of our embodied creatureliness, rejection of our embeddedness in the natural order. Feminist revaluation of the erotic entails an ecological consciousness and politics, an active awareness of, and responsibility to, the complex web of life.

Second, the capacity to open ourselves to the world, to allow the power of the erotic to quicken our lives, depends on creating a human world in which this is a possibility. In the world as it is, with its increasing numbers of hungry and homeless, the demand that we seek full life, take joy in our work, or live with our senses sharpened must come to many as a painful and irrelevant irony. For the privileged, there is only so long the senses can take in the sight of homeless and beggars, the city smells of urine and garbage, a constant barrage of sound. At least to live in a city and survive is to learn to shield oneself, to shut down feeling, to stop experiencing with the whole self. For those without privilege, the assault of hunger and the search for a quiet place to sleep take numbing precedence over the celebration of embodiment. It is not simply traditional attitudes toward sexuality that lead us to fear being alive, but also the world around us. To live with a full sense of our own erotic energy, then, entails not only dealing with natural environmental issues in urban as well as town and rural contexts, but also confronting the political questions that shape our total environment—the gentrification of inner cities that is leaving an increasing number of people homeless, the dearth of humane living spaces, the factory closings and relocations that are creating a new group of unemployed and homeless, the structures of racism and class domination as they affect housing, homelessness, and the distribution of government services.

Spirituality and Politics in a Feminist Judaism

When even sexuality—a matter that American culture has defined as intensely private—intersects with a wide range of issues of social justice, the connection between spirituality and politics becomes inescapable. Our visions of the way the world can be are articulated within and over against existing social structures, and everywhere we turn in seeking to realize these visions we come up against institutions that stand between us and our ability to live spiritually fulfilling lives.[28] Unless the quest for integration of our relationships to self, God, and others emerges out of and leads to the creation of forms of community that nurture our whole being, this quest remains marginal to our daily lives, and thus ineffective and irrelevant. For spirituality to matter, it must be poured out into the world in which we live, just as enduring social change must be rooted in some intuition of a richer and more humane future.

I have argued that both Judaism and feminism have tried to connect faith and vision with everyday realities—although often not in ways that are sufficiently self-critical. The prophets' insistence that love of God is to be manifest through justice is itself expressed in the language and thought forms of patriarchy, and in images that accept and perpetuate the existence of patriarchy. The rabbinic concept of *tikkun olam* (right ordering of society) demands that, "as a precaution for the general good," witnesses sign a bill of divorce.[29] But *tikkun olam* does not extend to reordering a society in which divorce is a male prerogative. The feminist vision of the liberation of women intends justice for all women, yet feminists often imagine the fruits of liberation in ways that presuppose continuing race and class inequity and domination.

For Jewish feminists to develop a theology and practice that is sensitive to the interrelation of different sorts of oppression, we will need to attend to the structural character of oppression and to address its structural forms. The complexity of modern society, the seeming intractability of certain social dilemmas, the global roots and ramifications of many political and economic problems force us increasingly to grapple with the systemic character of injustice and justice and to confront patterns of injustice that the tradition has taken for granted.[30] As emerging political and liberation theologies have made amply clear, the political and structural dimension of sin and salvation in the modern age requires the structural reformulation of many traditional values. In the contemporary context, concern for widows and orphans must express itself in dismantling the patriarchal structures that disenfranchise and marginalize women and children. Compassion for the poor must entail confrontation with corporate greed, arrest of imperialism, and the struggle against racism and class oppression that consign many to misery. Remembering the stranger must involve breaking down the barriers of nationality, religion, sex, race, and class that turn differences into occasions for domination. Apathy must be exposed as a primary form of wrongdoing, and with it the witting or unwitting collaboration with injustice that sustain destructive social structures.[31] Turning—*t'shuvah*—repentance must take place on an institutional level.[32]

Because certain key Jewish ideas and institutions are part of the unjust systems that need dismantling, the connection between politics and spirituality requires the transformation of Judaism itself. I have argued throughout this book that ideas and structures within Judaism that reflect and foster models of domination—a Torah that mirrors and reproduces the power of men over women, an Israel that in conception and communal form constructs difference as hierarchy, a notion of God as dominating Other, a legal structure that defines sexuality in terms of possession—must be reconstructed on the basis and for the sake of a different mode of relation. A spirituality that emerges out of the vision and sometime reality of diverse, egalitarian communities, that knows God as present within—not above—community as its binder, sustainer, and goad, can nourish and is nourished by the critique and transformation of all structures of oppression.

As Jewish feminists work for justice within the Jewish community and beyond it, the emergence of new communal forms becomes the vital foundation for shaping a feminist Judaism. Feminist spirituality collectives like B'not Esh, and many smaller-scale retreats and conferences attended by women around the country, provide spaces on the boundaries of the larger Jewish community for women to examine and enact our experience and our visions. In such contexts, feminists can pursue serious liturgical experimentation, discussions of spirituality, feminist text study and midrash-making with an intensity and freedom not often possible in other Jewish forums. Such special spaces are sources of new energy and resources for the larger community, and also provide models of leadership and community that may be translatable into broader contexts. B'not Esh, for example, as one small feminist community, has had to deal with many of the issues that arise within any Jewish institution: differences in members' expectations, diversity of class, education, sexual orientation, lifestyle, and religious upbringing. Moving from an initial focus on theological and historical questions to the realization that these differences are also an important part of our spiritual agenda, we have consistently tried to deal with difference in ways that can enrich us and move us forward. The work we have done together in B'not Esh, both as a talking community and as a praying one, we have taken into the wider Jewish community—in lectures, creative work, sharing of resources, and through the knowledge of what it is possible for communities to achieve.[33]

Certain broader-based Jewish communities and organizations have also begun to enact a feminist Judaism, connecting faith with their politics, and pursuing feminist goals. The havurah movement, for example, began in the late 1960s as an alternate to the hierarchical and often alienating structures of the traditional synagogue. Although it was not feminist in conception, the movement was influenced by feminism at an early stage, and it has consistently provided opportunities for women to take on roles closed to them in other quarters of the Jewish community. Today, few havurot have moved beyond a liberal model of egalitarianism to explore the deeper incorporation of women's experience into the Jewish community. Yet in their commitment to egalitarian community building, havurot have created models of rotating leadership and shared responsibility for teaching and worship that in many ways represent and embody feminist values.[34]

In contrast to the worship-centered havurah movement, New Jewish Agenda is focused primarily on political action. Founded in 1980 to counter a rising turn toward conservatism in the Jewish community, it links its commitment to left politics to a long history of Jewish involvement in social justice. Although, as a movement, Agenda's political work is not connected to any religious practice, its concerns are inspired by Jewish memory, both memory of the prophetic tradition and the long history of Jewish oppression and resistance to oppression. Moreover, in making concrete its commitment to "the complete equality of women and men," as well as its many other commitments, Agenda has often found ways to express its political aims through Jewish religious content.[35]

The creation of new kinds of community is one vital component of a feminist Judaism. Within Jewish communities seeking to connect faith and politics, new content poured into traditional Jewish ceremonies and forms often provides connections between visions of social and religious transformation and the basic rhythms of everyday life. The consonance of purpose between law and prophecy—to connect faith with the whole of reality—can be enacted in ritual and law attuned to the demands of justice. Thus, coming out of new Jewish communities, a number of Jewish feminists and other progressive Jews have called for a set of dietary laws (*kashrut*) that reflect the feminist value of connection to other persons and a wider web of life. *Kashrut* is already a system reminding us of the sanctity of animal life, and some have suggested that, for the sake of this sanctity as well as for the sake of preserving grain for the hungry, we extend this reminder to a full vegetarianism. *Kashrut* already tells us that "we are what we eat," and many values central to contemporary progressive food practices and to feminist concerns about sexuality and embodiment can be included in an expanded system of *kashrut*. Concern for protecting our bodies might take the form of prohibiting foods that are grown with pesticides or that contain carcinogens or hormones. Concern over the rise of hunger might be expressed in the form of a special blessing before or after meals and a commitment to set aside a proportion of the cost of all meals to feed the hungry. Concern about the exploitation of workers and planting of monocrops on lands needed for local agricultural production might lead to forbidding foods that are the product of exploitation and oppression. In these ways, *kashrut*, which has been a central dimension of Judaism as a system of separations and distinctions, can also be a vehicle for connecting Jews to others without losing its meaning as a marker of Jewish distinctiveness and identity.[36] Such a new *kashrut* would turn the simple everyday act of eating into an aspect of the continuing quest for justice.

Other ritual and legal forms provide different ways of concretizing the commitment to social and religious change and creating models of nonhierarchical difference. Shabbat, like *kashrut*, is a ritual central to Judaism and its system of hierarchical distinctions; but it is a ritual that can also be reworked to maintain its special quality in a nonhierarchical manner. Arthur Waskow has described the Sabbath as part of a rhythm of work and repose, labor and celebration that can provide time to examine the meaning and direction of our ceaseless production and consumption. Shabbat as celebration of creation, as a time for awareness of mystery, is a day both to enjoy the fruits of our work and to reflect on the values that could permeate all our days, so that Shabbat might guide the rest of the week even as it builds on our labor.[37] Ellen Bernstein has suggested turning Tu Bishvat, a minor holiday marking the new year of trees, into a major environmental holy day, celebrating the divine in nature and providing an occasion for taking stock of our responsibility to nature.[38] This proposal provides a way of expressing a feminist sense of connection with the natural world within a Jewish framework. Esther Ticktin has called for new halakhot that give concrete expression to the commitment to equality for women within the Jewish tradition. Her suggestion that Jews take on the obligation not to pray in any synagogue with a *mechitzah* and that male Jews refuse to go up to the Torah in congregations that do not call women to the Torah provides ways to act on feminist values that can sensitize and mobilize others.[39]

Each of these suggestions for ritualizing religious and political values—and each of the communities out of which they arise—represents an attempt to resist the forces that would separate faith from worldly involvement: the cultural opposition of religion and politics, the Marxist understanding of religion as a reactionary diversion from the battle against injustice, the lure of oases of spiritual experimentation in the midst of a world desperately in need of redemption. Each challenges us as feminists and as Jews to bring our spirituality and politics together in such a way that our religious lives change the way we live, and our political commitments shape our spirituality.[40] To build community, to work for political change, is to act out the spiritual vision of a world in which diverse communities can live together and learn from each other, each with the resources it needs to survive and mature. To celebrate and ritualize our visions is to locate our political projects in the context of the ongoing work of creation, to take our place in the eternal dialogue between God and creation through which the world develops and unfolds.

As we start where we are, addressing ourselves to particular constituencies and particular needs for healing or repair, we slowly build the institutions and communities that can begin to bring the future into being. As we create communities that can nourish and sustain us; as we work to transform the institutions that most deeply affect us; as we enact and celebrate together moments of commitment, clarity, and vision, we generate energy for further change that is rooted in what we have already envisioned and accomplished. Remembering women's history, writing new midrash, empowers us to create more inclusive communities and prods us to challenge all the institutions of the Jewish community to perpetuate and live out of a richer Jewish memory. Creating new, diverse, and egalitarian communities leads us to a new understanding of divinity, which in turn calls us to draw the circle of community ever wider and wider. Expanding the circle of community vivifies the erotic bonds of community, which in turn leads us to reclaim a suppressed part of Jewish history, and also reminds us of our responsibilities toward others. Just as structures of domination support each other, so do our efforts at justice. The sum of the changes that we seek eludes us as a total system, because those working for change have less power than the complex and entrenched institutions of hierarchical power that dominate our world.[41] But lured on by the ground already attained and by the Ground of that ground that empowers us, we remember the words of Mishnah *Avot* (2.16): It is not incumbent upon us to finish the task, but neither are we free to desist from it altogether. As we work toward the creation of a feminist Judaism as part of a larger struggle toward a more just world, we place our small piece in a mosaic that will finally provide a new pattern—a new religious and social order.

Notes

Introduction: It's Feminist, But Is It Jewish?

1. This story was told at a meeting of Jewish theologians in Denver, Colorado (July 1981), sponsored by the National Jewish Resource Center. See also Arthur Green's "Keeping Feminist Creativity Jewish," *Sh'ma* 16/305 (January 10, 1986): 33–35, which presupposes the same split between Judaism and feminism.

2. This was first printed in the special women's issue of *Response* (Summer 1973) and reprinted in *The Jewish Woman: New Perspectives*, edited by Elizabeth Koltun (New York: Schocken Books, 1976), 3–10. Compare Martha Ackelsberg, "Personal Identities and Collective Visions: Reflections on Being a Jew and a Feminist" (unpublished lecture, Smith College, March 8, 1983).

3. Mary Daly, *Beyond God the Father* (Boston: Beacon Press, 1973), 40–43.

4. B'not Esh met for the first time in 1981 and has been meeting annually since 1983. See Martha Ackelsberg, "Spirituality, Community and Politics: B'not Esh and the Feminist Reconstruction of Judaism," *Journal of Feminist Studies in Religion* 2 (Fall 1986): 109–20.

5. *Lilith* magazine (available from Lilith publications, 250 West 57th Street, New York, NY 10019) reflects something of this range. Four anthologies that together capture the diversity of issues discussed by Jewish feminists are Koltun, *The Jewish Woman*; Evelyn Torten Beck, ed., *Nice Jewish Girls: A Lesbian Anthology* (1982; reprint ed., Trumansburg, NY: The Crossing Press, 1984); Susannah Heschel, ed., *On Being a Jewish Feminist: A Reader* (New York: Schocken Books, 1983); Melanie Kaye/Kantrowitz and Irena Klepfisz, eds., *The Tribe of Dina: A Jewish Women's Anthology* (1986; reprint ed., Boston: Beacon Press, 1989).

6. The anthologies mentioned in note 5 cover most of these issues. Other examples in each category include: on ordination, Amy Stone, "Gentleman's Agreement at the Seminary," *Lilith* 1/3 (Spring 1977): 13–18 and Raye T. Katz, "Exploring the Link Between Womanhood and the Rabbinate," *Lilith* 14 (Fall/Winter, 1985–86): 19–24; on ritual, Penina Adelman, *Miriam's Well: Rituals for Jewish Women Around the Year* (Fresh Meadows, NY: Biblio Press, 1986); on communal institutions, Aviva Cantor with Reena Sigman Friedman, "Power Plays: Breaking the Male Monopoly of Jewish Community Leadership," *Lilith* 14: 7–13; on Jewish literature, Charlotte Baum, Paula Hyman, and Sonya Michel, *The Jewish Woman in America* (New York: Dial Press, 1976), chapter 7; on the family, Martha Ackelsberg, "Families and the Jewish Community: A Feminist Perspective," *Response* 48 (Spring 1985): 5–19 and Steven M. Cohen and Paula Hyman, eds., *The Jewish Family: Myths and Reality* (New York: Holmes & Meier, 1986); on Israel, Lesley

Hazleton, *Israeli Women: The Reality Behind the Myths* (New York: Simon & Schuster, 1977); on anti-Semitism, Elly Bulkin, "Hard Ground: Jewish Identity, Racism, and Anti-Semitism," *Yours in Struggle*, by Elly Bulkin, Minnie Bruce Pratt, and Barbara Smith (Brooklyn, NY: Long Haul Press, 1984); on history, Bernadette Brooten, *Women Leaders in the Ancient Synagogue*, Brown Judaic Studies 36 (Chico, CA: Scholars Press, 1982) and Paula Hyman, "Immigrant Women and Consumer Protest: The New York City Kosher Meat Boycott of 1902," *American Jewish History* 70 (Summer 1980): 91–105.

7. See my "The Coming of Lilith: Toward a Feminist Theology," in *Womanspirit Rising: A Feminist Reader in Religion*, edited by Carol P. Christ and Judith Plaskow (San Francisco: Harper & Row, 1979), 198–209.

8. Daly, *Beyond God the Father*, 8.

9. For example, Essenes, Sadducees, Kabbalists, Hasidim, Reform Jews, far-flung communities like Elephantine, everyday forms of popular religion—like women praying to Rachel at her tomb in Bethlehem—that exist in tension with or outright contradiction to ruling ideologies.

10. A few available sources are Hazleton, *Israeli Women*; Beck, *Nice Jewish Girls*, especially the section "Jewish Identity: A Coat of Many Colors"; and Kaye/Kantrowitz and Klepfisz, *The Tribe of Dina*, which contains a number of poems and essays by Sephardic women.

1. Setting the Problem, Laying the Ground

1. Carol P. Christ, "Spiritual Quest and Women's Experience," in *Womanspirit Rising: A Feminist Reader in Religion*, edited by Carol P. Christ and Judith Plaskow (San Francisco: Harper & Row, 1979), 229.

2. Simone de Beauvoir, *The Second Sex*, translated by H. M. Parshley (New York: Bantam Books, 1961), xv–xvii.

3. Dina's birth is mentioned in Gen. 30:21; her story is found in Gen. 34. In naming their anthology of Jewish feminist writing *The Tribe of Dina: A Jewish Woman's Anthology* (1986; reprint ed., Boston: Beacon Press, 1989), Melanie Kaye/Kantrowitz and Irena Klepfisz restore Dina to her rightful place.

4. The following discussion is based on my article, "The Right Question is Theological," in *On Being a Jewish Feminist: A Reader*, edited by Susannah Heschel (New York: Schocken Books, 1983), 223–33.

5. The fact that God takes Sarah's side does not alter the problematic nature of the relationship between Sarah and Hagar, which has been explored especially powerfully by black women. See, for example, Delores Williams, "Womanist Theological Perspectives on the Hagar–Sarah Story" (paper delivered at Princeton University, May 17, 1988).

6. See Savina Teubal, *Sarah the Priestess: The First Matriarch of Genesis* (Athens, OH: Swallow Press, 1984) and "Sarah and Hagar: Power in Ritual" (paper delivered at the 1985 Annual Meeting of the American Academy of Religion).

7. Jacob Neusner, *A History of the Mishnaic Law of Women*, 5 vols. (Leiden: E. J. Brill, 1980), 5: 13f., 271f.

8. Cynthia Ozick, "Notes Toward Finding the Right Question," in *Lilith* 6 (1979): 19–29; reprinted in Heschel, *On Being a Jewish Feminist*, 120–51; quotation, 149.

9. See T. Drorah Setel, "Prophets and Pornography: Female Sexual Imagery in Hosea," in *Feminist Interpretation of the Bible*, edited by Letty M. Russell (Philadelphia: Westminster Press, 1985), 86–95.

10. De Beauvoir, *The Second Sex*, 641–42. See Judith Plaskow, *Sex, Sin, and Grace: Women's Experience and the Theologies of Reinhold Niebuhr and Paul Tillich* (Washington, D.C.: University Press of America, 1980), chapter 1, for an extended discussion of "women's experience" and its relation to prevailing cultural role definitions.

11. Elisabeth Schüssler Fiorenza, *Bread Not Stone: The Challenge of Feminist Biblical Interpretation* (Boston: Beacon Press, 1984), 15ff.

12. *Ibid.*, 15. "Androcentric" and "androcentrism" refer to the assumption that maleness is constitutive of humanity. See Rita Gross, "Androcentrism and Androgyny in the Methodology of the History of Religions," in *Beyond Androcentrism: New Essays on Women and Religion*, edited by Rita Gross (Missoula, MT: Scholars Press, 1977), 7–21.

13. See my "The Jewish Feminist: Conflict in Identities," in *The Jewish Woman: New Perspectives*, edited by Elizabeth Koltun (New York: Schocken Books, 1976), 4.

14. Mary Daly, "Post-Christian Theology: Some Connections Between Idolatry and Methodolatry, Between Deicide and Methodicide" (address given at the Annual Meeting of the American Academy of Religion, 1973); for a more general reference see the paper of the same name in Joan Arnold Romero, *Women and Religion: 1973 Proceedings* (Tallahassee, FL: American Academy of Religion, 1973), 33. For Phyllis Trible's discussion of depatriarchalizing, see her *God and the Rhetoric of Sexuality* (Philadelphia: Fortress Press, 1978).

15. Schüssler Fiorenza, *Bread Not Stone*, 19–20.

16. See T. Drorah Setel, "Power and Pollution: The Ritual Purity/Impurity System in the Hebrew Bible" (paper delivered at the Annual Meeting of the American Academy of Religion, 1982); Merlin Stone, *When God Was a Woman* (New York: Dial Press, 1976), chapter 8.

17. Schüssler Fiorenza, *Bread Not Stone*, 19–20. The phrase in quotation marks is Johann Baptist Metz's.

18. See, for example, Richard Elliot Friedman, *Who Wrote the Bible?* (New York: Summit Books, 1987), chapter 14.

19. Emil Fackenheim calls this divided consciousness that characterizes modern faith "immediacy after reflection" (*God's Presence in History: Jewish Affirmations and Philosophical Reflections* [New York: New York University Press, 1970], 47–49), while Paul Tillich talks about "broken myths" (*Dynamics of Faith* [New York: Harper & Row, 1957], 50–51).

20. In editing *The Woman's Bible* (1898; reprint ed., Seattle: Coalition Taskforce on Women and Religion, 1974), Elizabeth Cady Stanton took advantage of the advent of biblical criticism to radically question biblical authority from a feminist perspective. Today the whole women's spirituality movement takes place outside the authority structures of Judaism or Christianity. See

Charlene Spretnak, ed., *The Politics of Women's Spirituality: Essays on the Rise of Spiritual Power within the Feminist Movement* (Garden City, NY: Anchor Books/Doubleday, 1982) for a range of examples. For a Christian response to the problem of authority, see Robin Scroggs, "Paul and the Eschatological Woman," *Journal of the American Academy of Religion* 40 (September 1972): 283–303, and Scroggs, "Paul and the Eschatological Woman: Revisited" and Elaine Pagels, "Paul and Women: A Response to Recent Discussion," *JAAR* 42 (September 1974): 532–49 for a small sample of the debate on Paul. Leonard Swidler was the first to propose the "Jesus was a feminist" argument which has been reiterated innumerable times; see "Jesus Was a Feminist," *Catholic World* 212 (January 1971): 177–83.

21. On the prophetic tradition, see Rosemary Ruether, *Sexism and God-Talk: Toward a Feminist Theology* (Boston: Beacon Press: 1983), 22–27 and "Feminist Interpretation: A Method of Correlation," in Russell, *Feminist Interpretation*, 118–22. On the themes of equality in creation and female God-language, see Trible, *God and the Rhetoric of Sexuality*. Russell's book provides a general overview of feminist hermeneutics, as does Adela Yarbro Collins, ed., *Feminist Perspectives on Biblical Scholarship* (Chico, CA: Scholars Press, 1985). Jewish feminist hermeneutics is in the earliest stages of development.

22. For example, at a major symposium on "Cultural and Religious Relativism," held at the 92nd Street YM-YWHA, January–February 1986, the issue of authority was presented as a conflict between communal imperatives rooted in divine sanction and individual choice. Martha Ackelsberg helped me to see and criticize this dichotomy.

23. See chapter 3, 76–81, for a fuller discussion of this point.

24. Martin Buber ("The Man of Today and the Jewish Bible," in *On the Bible* [New York: Schocken Books, 1968], 1–13 and *Moses: The Revelation and the Covenant* [New York: Harper & Row, 1958]) and H. Richard Niebuhr (*The Meaning of Revelation* [New York: The Macmillan Company, 1941]) are the two theologians who have most influenced my view of revelation.

25. See Norman K. Gottwald, *The Tribes of Yahweh* (Maryknoll, NY: Orbis Books, 1979), 685. "Yahweh's asexuality was apparently *not* invoked to challenge or shatter male dominance in the Israelite society as a whole—in the decisive way, for example, that class dominance was challenged and shattered by Yahweh's liberating action."

26. In this, I agree with Elisabeth Schüssler Fiorenza, *In Memory of Her: A Feminist Theological Reconstruction of Christian Origins* (New York: Crossroad, 1983), 29, 32 and *Bread Not Stone*, 3.

27. Both Louis Jacobs (*A Jewish Theology* [West Orange, NJ: Behrman House, 1973], 10–12) and Michael Wyschogrod (*The Body of Faith: Judaism as Corporeal Election* [San Francisco: Harper & Row, 1983], xiii) begin their Jewish theologies by addressing this point.

2. Torah: Reshaping Jewish Memory

1. Emil Fackenheim uses the term "root experience" in *God's Presence in History: Jewish Affirmations and Philosophical Reflections* (New York: New York University Press, 1970), 8–14.

2. Because of the importance of this story as a story, this is one of the places I consider the text as it has been received without regard to the historical problems it poses. See chapter 1, 15–18.

3. Judith Plaskow, "The Right Question Is Theological," *On Being a Jewish Feminist: A Reader*, edited by Susannah Heschel (New York: Schocken Books, 1983), 231. Compare chapter 1, 9.

4. Rachel Adler, "'I've Had Nothing Yet So I Can't Take More,'" *Moment* 8 (September 1983): 22f.

5. *Ibid.*, 23.

6. *Ibid.*, 22.

7. In the synagogue I belonged to in Wichita, Kansas, for example, the rabbi, after much discussion and argument, finally agreed to allow a woman to read the prayer for the congregation in English from below the *bimah* (elevated platform from which the Torah is read). When the *shammes* (synagogue beadle) threatened to have a heart attack, the rabbi withdrew the offer.

8. *Shabbat* 86a.

9. E. M. Broner, "Honor and Ceremony in Women's Rituals," *The Politics of Women's Spirituality: Essays on the Rise of Spiritual Power within the Feminist Movement*, edited by Charlene Spretnak (Garden City, NY: Anchor Press/Doubleday, 1982), 238.

10. *Ibid.*

11. Yosef Hayim Yerushalmi, *Zakhor: Jewish History and Jewish Memory* (Seattle: University of Washington Press, 1982), 9.

12. Martin Buber, *Israel and the World: Essays in a Time of Crisis* (New York: Schocken Books, 1963), 146.

13. Michael Walzer, *Exodus and Revolution* (New York: Basic Books, 1985); Esther Ticktin, "A Modest Beginning," *The Jewish Woman: New Perspectives*, edited by Elizabeth Koltun (New York: Schocken Books, 1976), 131.

14. Louis Ginsberg, *The Legends of the Jews*, 7 vols. (Philadelphia: Jewish Publication Society, 1909–1938), 5(1925): 235, note 140.

15. *Genesis Rabbah* 95: 3. Emphasis mine.

16. For example, in *The Body of Faith: Judaism as Corporeal Election* (Minneapolis: Winston Press, 1983), Michael Wyschograd talks about circumcision as a sign of the covenant as if Jewish women do not exist. See chapter 3, 83–84.

17. Elisabeth Schüssler Fiorenza, *In Memory of Her: A Feminist Theological Reconstruction of Christian Origins* (New York: Crossroad, 1983), xiv–xx. I am indebted to Schüssler Fiorenza for this whole paragraph and, indeed, much of my approach to the recovery of Jewish women's history.

18. Broner, "Honor and Ceremony," 238.

19. Gerder Lerner, *The Majority Finds Its Past: Placing Women in History* (New York: Oxford University Press, 1979), 160, 168f.

20. Phyllis Bird, "Images of Women in the Old Testament," in *Religion and Sexism: Images of Women in the Jewish and Christian Traditions*, edited by Rosemary Ruether (New York: Simon & Schuster, 1974), 41–42.

21. Just as Lerner says, *The Majority Finds Its Past*, 168.

22. The term "Godwrestling" comes from Arthur Waskow, *Godwrestling* (New York: Schocken Books, 1978).
23. H. Richard Niebuhr emphasizes the element of insight in revelation (*The Meaning of Revelation* [New York: The Macmillan Company, 1941], 101–2), while Martin Buber emphasizes the element of presence (*I and Thou*, translated by Walter Kaufmann [New York: Charles Scribner's Sons, 1970], 158–59). It seems to me these can be present to different degrees in different revelatory experiences.
24. See Norman K. Gottwald, *The Tribes of Yahweh* (Maryknoll, NY: Orbis Books, 1979), 685. Compare chapter 1, 20 and chapter 1, note 25.
25. Ginsberg, *The Legends of the Jews*, 1(1906): 3–4.
26. Gershom G. Scholem, *On the Kabbalah and Its Symbolism* (New York, Schocken Books, 1965), 37–65.
27. Thanks to Martha Ackelsberg for calling my attention to the theme of the relation between primordial and manifest Torah.
28. Gershom Scholem, "Tradition and Commentary as Religious Categories in Judaism, " *Judaism* 15 (Winter, 1966): 26.
29. Yerushalmi, *Zakhor*, 94.
30. Lerner, *The Majority Finds Its Past*, chapters 10–12, especially 168, 180.
31. Schüssler Fiorenza, *In Memory of Her*, 85–86; Ann D. Gordon, Mari Jo Buhle, and Nancy Schrom Dye, "The Problem of Women's History," in *Liberating Women's History: Theoretical and Critical Essays*, edited by Berenice A. Carroll (Urbana/Chicago/London: University of Illinois Press, 1976), 84–89. *In Memory of Her* is a good example of this method in action.
32. Lerner, *The Majority Finds Its Past*, 148, 178; Carroll Smith-Rosenberg, "The Female World of Love and Ritual: Relations Between Women in Nineteenth-Century America," *Signs: Journal of Women in Culture and Society* 1 (Autumn 1975): 1–29. The quotation is from Lerner, *The Majority Finds Its Past*, 178.
33. See, for example, Samson Raphael Hirsch, *Judaism Eternal*, vol. 2 (London: Soncino Press, 1960), chapter 2; Manachem M. Brayer, *The Jewish Woman in Rabbinic Literature* (Hoboken, NJ: KTAV Publishing House, 1986), 16; H. E. Yedidiah Ghatan, *The Invaluable Pearl: The Unique Status of Women in Judaism* (New York: Bloch Publishing Company, 1986), 3–13.
34. Bird, "Images of Women in the Old Testament," 67–68.
35. Rita J. Burns, *Has the Lord Indeed Spoken Only Through Moses? A Study of the Biblical Portrait of Miriam*, SBL Dissertation Series 84 (Atlanta, GA: Scholars Press, 1987), chapter 2, especially 40.
36. *Ibid.*, 20, 40.
37. See, for example, *Shemot Rabbah* I, 22, where Miriam's prophecy is described. Even her reproach of Moses is softened in the midrash; see, for example, *Sifrei Bamidbar*, 99 and *Avot d'Rabbi Natan* A, 9.
38. Compare Phyllis Trible, "Miriam, Moses, and a Mess" (address delivered at the Annual Meeting of the Society for Biblical Literature, December 5, 1987).
39. Schüssler Fiorenza, *In Memory of Her*, 41–56, especially 49 and "Women in the Early Christian Movement," in *Womanspirit Rising: A Feminist Reader in*

Religion, edited by Carol P. Christ and Judith Plaskow (San Francisco: Harper & Row, 1979), 92.

40. Carol Meyers, "The Roots of Restriction: Women in Early Israel," *Biblical Archeologist* 41 (September 1978): 101. See the whole article (91–103) and also her "Procreation, Production, and Protection: Male-Female Balance in Early Israel," *Journal of the American Academy of Religion* 51 (December 1983): 569–93. Meyer's new book, *Discovering Eve: Ancient Israelite Women in Context* (New York and Oxford: Oxford University Press) appeared too late for me to take account of it in this study.

41. David Bakan, *And They Took Themselves Wives: The Emergence of Patriarchy in Western Civilization* (San Francisco: Harper & Row, 1979); Savina Teubal, *Sarah the Priestess: The First Matriarch of Genesis* (Athens, OH: Swallow Press, 1984); Merlin Stone, *When God Was a Woman* (New York: Dial Press, 1976).

42. Teubal, *Sarah the Priestess,* 14. Also Bakan, *And They Took Themselves Wives,* 67.

43. Teubal, *Sarah the Priestess,* 42, 45.

44. J. Edgar Bruns, *God as Woman, Woman as God* (New York/Paramus/Toronto: Paulist Press, 1973), 21; Stone, *When God Was a Woman,* chapter 10; Theodor Reik, *The Creation of Woman: A Psychoanalytic Inquiry into the Myth of Eve* (New York: McGraw–Hill, 1960), chapter 9. Trible (*God and the Rhetoric of Sexuality,* chapter 4) sees these narratives as evidence of an egalitarian countertradition in the Bible, and Meyers accepts Trible's view. To my mind, however, the creation of woman from and after man is clear evidence that the intent of the stories is to justify patriarchy.

45. Raphael Patai's *The Hebrew Goddess* (New York: KTAV Publishing House, 1967) collects the extensive biblical evidence for this position.

46. William G. Dever, "Asherah, Consort of Yahweh? New Evidence from Kuntillet Ajrud," *Bulletin of the Schools of Oriental Research* 255 (1984): 21–37; Saul M. Olyan, *Asherah and the Cult of Yahweh in Israel,* SBL Monograph Series 34 (Atlanta, GA: Scholars Press, 1988); Patai, *The Hebrew Goddess,* 58–61.

47. The "foreign wives" of various kings are also repeatedly blamed for Israelite Goddess worship. See Carol P. Christ, "Heretics and Outsiders," in her *Laughter of Aphrodite: Reflections on a Journey to the Goddess* (San Francisco: Harper & Row, 1987), 37–40.

48. Stone, *When God Was a Woman,* chapters 7, 8; Judith Ochshorn, *The Female Experience and the Nature of the Divine* (Bloomington: Indiana University Press, 1981), chapter 4; R. Harris, "Woman in the Ancient Near East," *The Interpreter's Dictionary of the Bible,* supplementary volume (Nashville: Abingdon, 1976), 692.

49. Sheila Collins, *A Different Heaven and Earth* (Valley Forge: Judson Press, 1974), chapter 4.

50. Bernadette J. Brooten, *Women Leaders in the Ancient Synagogue: Inscriptional Evidence and Background Issues,* Brown Judaic Studies 36 (Chico, CA: Scholars Press, 1982).

51. Emil Schurer, *History* 2:435, quoted in *Ibid.,* 6.

52. Brooten, *Women Leaders*, 7–10, 15–29.

53. *Ibid.*, 141–44, 149.

54. Shaye J. D. Cohen, "Women in the Synagogues of Antiquity," *Conservative Judaism* 34 (November/December 1980): 27, 28.

55. Elaine H. Pagels examines this question for early Christianity in "What Became of God the Mother? Conflicting Images of God in Early Christianity" *Signs* 2 (Winter 1976): 293–303. She asks whether there may be a correlation between women's active participation in certain early Christian movements and the nonnormative status of such movements.

56. Lerner, *The Majority Finds Its Past*, 149. Schüssler Fiorenza makes this point repeatedly; see, for example, *In Memory of Her*, 60.

57. Lerner, *The Majority Finds Its Past*, 149.

58. Brooten, *Women Leaders*, 150.

59. Jacob Neusner, *A History of the Mishnaic Law of Women*, 5 vols. (Leiden: E. J. Brill, 1980), 5:13f., 271f.

60. Schüssler Fiorenza, *In Memory of Her*, 56–60.

61. Bernadette J. Brooten, "Could Women Initiate Divorce in Ancient Judaism? The Implications for Mark 10:11–12 and I Corinthians 7:10–11" (The Ernest Cadman Colwell Lecture, School of Theology at Claremont, April 14, 1981); published in German as "Konnten Frauen im alten Judentum die Scheidung betreiben? Uberlegungen zu Mk 10, 11–12 und Kor 7, 10–11," *EvTh* 42 (1982): 65–80; also Mordechai Friedman, "Divorce Upon the Wife's Demand as Reflected in Manuscripts from the Cairo Geniza," *Jewish Law Annual* 4 (1981): 103–26.

62. Chava Weissler, "The Traditional Piety of Ashkenazic Women," in *Jewish Spirituality*, edited by Arthur Green, vol. 2 (New York: Crossroad, 1987), 247–49; "The Religion of Traditional Ashkenazic Women: Some Methodological Issues," *AJS Review* (June/July 1987): 87–88; and "Voices from the Heart: Women's Devotional Prayers," *The Jewish Almanac*, edited by Richard Siegel and Carl Rheins (New York: Bantam Books, 1980), 544. I was also fortunate to be able to take a course with Weissler at the 1980 Havurah Summer Institute, on Yiddish literature for women. I am dependent on Weissler's work in this section. On Rosh Hodesh as a woman's holiday, see Arlene Agus, "This Month Is for You: Observing Rosh Hodesh as a Woman's Holiday," in Koltun, *The Jewish Woman*, 84–93.

63. Weissler, "Voices from the Heart," 541.

64. Sue Levi Elwell, *Text and Transformation: Towards a Theology of Integrity* (unpublished thesis, Hebrew Union College-Jewish Institute of Religion, 1986), 33; Weissler, "The Traditional Piety," 249, 266–67.

65. Merle Feld has been writing meditations for contemporary women in the style of the *tkhines*, trying to fill this gap. See her six poems in *Response* 14 (Spring 1985): 42–49.

66. Cynthia Ozick, "Notes Toward Finding the Right Question," in Heschel, *On Being a Jewish Feminist*, 129, 130. Ozick goes on, however, to accept the Jewish Encyclopedia's claim that all the *tkhines* are fraudulent. According to Weissler, this is incorrect.

67. See the articles listed for Weissler above, and also her "Women in Paradise," *Tikkun* 2 (1987): 43–46, 117–20.

68. Collins, *A Different Heaven and Earth*, chapter 4; Christ, "Heretics and Outsiders," 35–53.
69. See chapter 2, 35; Yerushalmi, *Zakhor*, 94.
70. Jacob Neusner, *History and Torah: Essays on Jewish Learning* (New York: Schocken Books, 1965), chapter 1.
71. Ginsberg brings together the midrash on these and many other questions in *The Legends of the Jews*.
72. Lynn Gottlieb, "The Secret Jew: An Oral Tradition of Women," in Heschel, *On Being a Jewish Feminist*, 273.
73. Some of the many poems on Miriam are Muriel Rukeyser, "Miriam: The Red Sea," *Breaking Open* (New York: Random House, 1973), 22; Chava Weissler, "Standing at Sinai," *Journal of Feminist Studies in Religion* 1 (Fall, 1985): 91–92; Chris Canaday "Miriam," in *Women in the Bible*, a study course compiled and edited by Marcia Cohn Spiegel (New York: Women's League for Conservative Judaism, n.d.), 41–43; Chava Romm, "Miriam Argues for Her Place as Prophetess," in Judith Stein, *A New Haggadah: A Jewish Lesbian Seder* (Cambridge, MA: Bobbeh Meisehs Press, 1984), 11. The quotations come from Canaday, Rukeyser, and Romm. Penina Adelman also names her book on women's rituals after Miriam and devotes the month of Nisan to her. See Adelman, *Miriam's Well: Rituals for Jewish Women Around the Year* (Fresh Meadows, NY: Biblio Press, 1986), especially 60–66.
74. See, for example, Jane Sprague Zones, et al., *Taking the Fruit: Modern Women's Tales of the Bible* (San Diego, CA: Woman's Institute for Continuing Jewish Education, 1981) and *Taking the Fruit*, new, expanded edition (1989). See Elwell, *Text and Transformation*, for a discussion of feminist midrash that both parallels and amplifies mine.
75. "The Coming of Lilith" first appeared in Ruether's *Religion and Sexism*, 341–43.
76. Ellen M. Umansky, "Creating a Jewish Feminist Theology: Possibilities and Problems," *Anima* 10 (Spring Equinox 1984): 133–34. For another feminist midrash on this passage, see Faith Rogow, "The Akedah: A Mother's Telling," *B'not Esh Newsletter* (Privately circulated, Spring 1984).
77. Gottlieb, "The Secret Jew," 273.
78. *Ibid.*, 273–77; Lynn Gottlieb, "Speaking into the Silence," *Response* 13 (Fall–Winter 1982): 19–33. Much of Gottlieb's work is unpublished. The quotation is from Broner; see chapter 2, page 31.
79. Presentation at the First National Havurah Summer Institute in 1980.
80. In a Women and Religion class at Wichita State University, Fall 1978.
81. Monique Wittig, *Les Guérillères* (New York: Avon Books, 1973), 89.
82. See Elwell, *Text and Transformation*, 62–90.
83. Adelman, *Miriam's Well*, especially chapter 10; Agus, "This Month Is for You," 84–93, was the first feminist piece on Rosh Hodesh.
84. Two published examples of feminist Haggadot are Aviva Cantor Zuckoff (now Cantor), "Jewish Women's Haggadah," in Koltun, *The Jewish Woman*, 94–102, and Broner, "Honor and Ceremony in Women's Rituals," 237–41. There are numerous Haggadot in private circulation and use.
85. These are just a few of numerous ceremonies in print and in private use and circulation: Judith Plaskow, "Bringing a Daughter into the Covenant,"

in Christ and Plaskow, *Womanspirit Rising*, 179–84; Rebecca Trachtenberg Alpert, et al., "The Covenant of Washing," *Menorah* 4 (April/May 1983): 5f; Ellen and Dana Charry, "Brit Kedusha," in *Blessing the Birth of a Daughter: Jewish Naming Ceremonies for Girls*, edited by Toby Fishbein Reifman with Ezrat Nashim (Ezrat Nashim, 1976), 5–8; Mary Gendler, "Sarah's Seed— A New Ritual for Women," *Response* 24 (Winter 1974–1975): 65–75; Sharon and Michael Strassfeld, "Brit Mikvah," in *Blessing the Birth of a Daughter*, 16–20.

86. Rachel Adler, "TUMAH and TAHARAH; Ends and Beginnings," in Koltun, *The Jewish Woman*, 63–71; Marcia Falk, "Notes on Composing New Blessings: Toward a Feminist-Jewish Reconstruction of Prayer," *Journal of Feminist Studies in Religion* 3 (Spring 1987): 39–53.

87. Blu Greenberg is the most prominent example. See her *On Women and Judaism: A View from Tradition* (Philadelphia: The Jewish Publication Society of America, 1981). Orthodox men who take feminism seriously have also focused on ways to halakhically address women's disabilities. See, for example, Saul Berman, "The Status of Women in Halakhic Judaism," in Koltun, *The Jewish Woman*, 114–28; also Eliezer Berkovits, *Not in Heaven: The Nature and Function of Halakha* (New York: KTAV Publishing House, 1983), 100–106.

88. See my "The Right Question Is Theological" as well as chapter 1, 8–9.

89. See chapter 1, 9.

90. Rachel Adler, "The Jew Who Wasn't There: *Halakhah* and the Jewish Woman," *Davka* (Summer 1972): 7–11 (reprinted in Heschel, *On Being a Jewish Feminist*, 12–18) and Paula Hyman, "The Other Half: Women in the Jewish Tradition," *Conservative Judaism* 26 (Summer 1972): 14–21 are two classic examples. See also Greenberg, *On Women and Judaism* and Rachel Biale, *Women and Jewish Law: An Exploration of Women's Issues in Halakhic Sources* (New York: Schocken Books, 1984).

91. Berman, "The Status of Women in Halakhic Judaism," 118, 121–22; Biale, *Women and Jewish Law*, 17. See Biale, chapter 1, for a presentation of the legal sources pertaining to this issue.

92. The exclusion of women from a minyan is actually argued on a number of grounds. See Biale, *Women and Jewish Law*, 21–23 and Moshe Meiselman, *Jewish Woman in Jewish Law* (New York: KTAV Publishing House and Yeshiva University Press, 1978), 135–36.

93. Adler, "The Jew Who Wasn't There," in Heschel, 13f.

94. Again, Biale, *Women and Jewish Law*, chapter 3 and Greenberg, *On Women and Judaism*, 125–45, are good sources.

95. Berkovits, *Not in Heaven*, 32–45.

96. See Biale, *Women and Jewish Law*, chapter 2.

97. Rachel Adler, "'I've Had Nothing Yet So I Can't Take More,'" *Moment* 8 (September 1983): 25.

98. *Ibid.*

99. See Anne Goldfeld, "Women as Sources of Torah in the Rabbinic Tradition," in Koltun, *The Jewish Woman*, 257–71.

100. See David Goodblatt, "The Beruriah Traditions," *Journal of Jewish Studies* 26 (Spring–Autumn 1975): 68–85 and Biale, *Women and Jewish Law*, 4.

101. Biale, *Women and Jewish Law*, 3.
102. *The Code of Maimonides*, Book 5: *The Book of Holiness* (New Haven and London: Yale University Press, 1965), XI, 4, 10.
103. Compare Shaye Cohen, "Menstruation and Purification: Women's Religion in Ancient and Medieval Judaism" (lecture presented at the Annual Meeting of the American Academy of Religion, December 6, 1987).
104. Charles G. Howard and Robert Summers, *LAW: Its Nature, Functions, and Limits* (Englewood Cliffs, NJ: Prentice–Hall, Inc., 1965), 6. H. L. A. Hart (*The Concept of Law* [London: Oxford University Press, 1961]) quoted in the same volume, 10–11, makes a similar point.
105. Carol Gilligan, *In a Different Voice: Psychological Theory and Women's Development* (Cambridge, MA: Harvard University Press, 1982), 10. Gilligan draws on studies by Janet Lever and Jean Piaget.
106. *Ibid.*
107. For example, Adelman, in *Miriam's Well*, 9, stresses that each group must create Rosh Hodesh rituals that answer its own needs.
108. At the National Havurah Summer Institutes, for example, there is often a Sabbath morning "feminist service" that is differentiated from the other services mainly by its very open structure and large amount of personal interchange.
109. Mary Daly argued many years ago that, insofar as ritual involves rigid repetition, the concept of feminist liturgy is a square circle. See her *Beyond God the Father* (Boston: Beacon Press, 1973), 145–46.
110. Nelle Morton emphasized this again and again. See her *The Journey Is Home* (Boston: Beacon Press, 1985), especially the second essay.
111. A few obvious examples include Gilligan, *In a Different Voice*; Nancy Chodorow, *The Reproduction of Mothering: Psychoanalysis and the Sociology of Gender* (Berkeley and Los Angeles: University of California Press, 1978); Carroll Smith-Rosenberg, "The Female World of Love and Ritual"; Paula Hyman, "Immigrant Women and Consumer Protest: The New York City Kosher Meat Boycott of 1902," *American Jewish History* 70 (Summer 1980): 91–105; Carter Heyward, *The Redemption of God: A Theology of Mutual Relation* (Washington, D.C.: University Press of America, 1982); Beverly Wildung Harrison, *Our Right to Choose: Toward a New Ethic of Abortion* (Boston: Beacon Press, 1983); Audre Lorde, *Sister Outsider* (Trumansburg, NY: The Crossing Press, 1984); Adrienne Rich, *Dream of a Common Language* (New York: W. W. Norton, 1978).
112. *Baba Metzia*, 59b.
113. Lynn Davidman points out in her doctoral dissertation, "'Strength of Tradition in a Chaotic World': Women Turn to Orthodox Judaism" (Brandeis, 1960), 89–90, that the socialization of *ba'alot tsuvah* (female returnees to Judaism) in a modern Orthodox synagogue revolves almost entirely around halakhah and explanation of particular observances. If individuals express too keen an interest in spirituality, that is, in focusing on their relation to God, they are referred to the Hasidim.
114. Indeed, Rabbi Joseph Soloveitchick argues that it is precisely this distance that characterizes "halakhic man" (sic). "Halakhic man" approaches the

world with the a priori ideal world of halakhah and sees and evaluates the concrete world in relation to that ideal one. *Halakhic Man* (Philadelphia: The Jewish Publication Society of America, 1983), 19–29.

115. Again, Soloveitchick sees this as part of the glory of "halakhic man"; *ibid.*, 23–24, 88.

116. Philip Selznick, "The Ideal of Legality," *Society and the Legal Order: Cases and Materials in the Sociology of Law*, edited by Richard D. Schwartz and Jerome H. Skolnick (New York: Basic Books, 1970), 20.

117. "Revelation and Law," *On Jewish Learning*, edited by Nahum Glatzer (New York: Schocken Books, 1965), 111.

118. The comments of Beverly Wildung Harrison at a New York Feminist Scholars in Religion meeting (Spring 1987) were very helpful to me in thinking about the place of law in community.

119. Though it seems incompatible with much else she herself has written, Ellen Umansky argues that a feminist Judaism, to be Jewish, must be halakhic; "What Are the Sources of My Theology?" *Journal of Feminist Studies in Religion* 1 (Spring 1985): 126.

3. Israel: Toward a New Concept of Community

1. The term "Israel" has two distinct meanings: the people descended from Jacob (Israel) and the nation-state. As should be clear from context, I will use the term only in its first sense for most of this chapter, then switch to the second sense in the last section.

2. For a thorough discussion and critique of the western patriarchal definition of selfhood as separation, see Catherine Keller, *From a Broken Web: Separation, Sexism, and Self* (Boston: Beacon Press, 1986).

3. Arthur Waskow, *Rainbow Sign: The Shape of Hope* (unpublished manuscript, 1987), 124.

4. Nelle Morton, *The Journey Is Home* (Boston: Beacon Press, 1985), 29. For fuller discussion of the dynamics of the consciousness-raising experience, see Morton's whole essay, "The Rising Woman Consciousness in a Male Language Structure," *The Journey Is Home*, 11–30, and my "The Coming of Lilith: Toward a Feminist Theology," in *Womanspirit Rising: A Feminist Reader in Religion*, edited by Carol P. Christ and Judith Plaskow (San Francisco: Harper & Row, 1979), 198–209.

5. Zillah Eisenstein, *The Radical Future of Liberal Feminism* (New York: Longman, 1981), passim, but especially chapters 1 and 8.

6. Keller, *From a Broken Web*.

7. See chapter 2, note 111 and pages 65–68.

8. Bell Hooks, *Feminist Theory: From Margin to Center* (Boston: South End Press, 1984), 10; the whole book is a critique of liberal feminism. See also Cherrie Moraga and Gloria Anzaldúa, eds., *This Bridge Called My Back: Writings by Radical Women of Color* (1981; reprint ed., Latham, NY: Kitchen Table: Women of Color Press, 1983); and Evelyn Torten Beck, ed., *Nice Jewish Girls: A Lesbian Anthology* (1982; reprint ed., Trumansburg, NY: The Crossing Press, 1984).

9. Delores Williams, "Women's Oppression and Life-Line Politics in Black Women's Religious Narratives," *Journal of Feminist Studies in Religion* 1 (Fall

1985): 60, 65–68; Carol B. Stack, *All Our Kin: Strategies for Survival in a Black Community* (New York: Harper & Row, 1974), especially chapter 6.

10. Everett E. Gendler, "Community," *Contemporary Jewish Religious Thought: Original Essays on Critical Concepts, Movements, and Beliefs*, edited by Arthur A. Cohen and Paul Mendes-Flohr (New York: Charles Scribner's Sons, 1987), 82. For the translations of Genesis see Phyllis Trible, *God and the Rhetoric of Sexuality* (Philadelphia: Fortress Press, 1978), 13, 89.

11. Gendler, "Community," 83; Martin Buber, *Israel and the World: Essays in a Time of Crisis* (New York: Schocken Books, 1963), 138; Jon D. Levenson, *Sinai and Zion: An Entry into the Jewish Bible* (Minneapolis: Winston Press, 1985), 38–39.

12. Martin Buber, *Moses: The Revelation and the Covenant* (New York and Evanston: Harper & Row, 1958), 131–33.

13. *Encyclopedia Judaica*, s.v. "Minyan"; Jacob Katz, *Tradition and Crisis: Jewish Society at the End of the Middle Ages* (New York: The Free Press of Glencoe, 1961), 176–77. Rabbi Johanan's words are quoted from *Berakhot* 6b by the *Encyclopedia Judaica*.

14. *Encyclopedia Judaica*, s.v. "Community"; Katz, *Tradition and Crisis*.

15. Phyllis Bird, "Images of Women in the Old Testament," *Religion and Sexism: Images of Women in the Jewish and Christian Traditions* (New York: Simon & Schuster, 1974), 49–50.

16. See chapter 1, 2–3.

17. Simone de Beauvoir, *The Second Sex*, translated by H. M. Parshley (New York, Bantam Books, 1961), xix, xvi.

18. Michael Wyschogrod, *The Body of Faith: Judaism as Corporeal Election* (Minneapolis: Winston Press, 1983), 33, 67, 23, 24.

19. Moshe Meiselman, *Jewish Woman in Jewish Law* (New York: KTAV Publishing House and Yeshiva University Press, 1978), 14.

20. Richard R. Niebuhr, *Experiential Religion* (New York: Harper & Row, 1972), 103.

21. See Introduction, xvii–xix, and chapter 1, 8–9.

22. There is an increasingly rich feminist literature dealing with this subject. Some of the important works are: Moraga and Anzaldúa, *This Bridge Called My Back*; Audre Lorde, *Sister Outsider* (Trumansburg, NY: The Crossing Press, 1984); Bell Hooks, *Feminist Theory* and *Ain't I a Woman: Black Women and Feminism* (Boston: South End Press, 1981); Gloria Hull, Patricia Bell Scott, and Barbara Smith, eds., *All the Women Are White, All the Blacks Are Men, But Some of Us Are Brave* (Old Westbury, NY: The Feminist Press, 1982); Elizabeth V. Spelman, *Inessential Woman: Problems of Exclusion in Feminist Theory* (Boston: Beacon Press, 1988); Adrienne Rich, "Disloyal to Civilization: Feminism, Racism, Gynephobia," in her *On Lies, Secrets, and Silence* (New York: W. W. Norton, 1979); Barbara Andolsen, *"Daughters of Jefferson, Daughters of Bootblacks"* (Macon, GA: Mercer Press, 1986).

23. Hooks, *Feminist Theory*, 1–3.

24. Beck, *Nice Jewish Girls*, xxiv–xxix; Elizabeth V. Spelman, "Theories of Race and Gender: The Erasure of Black Women," *Quest: A Feminist Quarterly* 5 (1982): 42–46. The "women and blacks" syndrome is exactly the point of the title of Hull, Scott, and Smith, *But Some of Us Are Brave*.

25. Spelman, *Inessential Woman*. The situation of Jewish women in the women's movement is not entirely analogous to that of women of color, since, as the case of Friedan makes clear, middle-class Jewish women have often written as if women of color do not exist. See my "Anti-Semitism: The Unacknowledged Racism," in *Women's Consciousness, Women's Conscience: A Reader in Feminist Ethics*, edited by Barbara Hilkert Andolsen, Christine Gudorf, and Mary Pellauer (San Francisco: Harper & Row, 1985), 75–84, for a discussion of the dynamics of racism and anti-Semitism.

26. Lorde, *Sister Outsider*, 118.

27. *Ibid.*, 115. Several essays in *Sister Outsider* deal powerfully with the issue of difference. See also Elizabeth V. Spelman, "I Think, Therefore You Are: Descriptive Struggles in Feminist Thought" (unpublished paper delivered as a Bunting Institute Lecture, Harvard University, December 2, 1986).

28. Paula Hyman, "Emancipation," *Contemporary Jewish Religious Thought*, 165.

29. Arthur Hertzberg, *The French Enlightenment and the Jews: The Origins of Modern Anti-Semitism* (New York: Schocken Books, 1968), 360.

30. Cited in Arnold M. Eisen, *The Chosen People in America* (Bloomington: Indiana University Press, 1983), 34. See Eisen, 33–35; also Hyman, "Emancipation," 165–66; Arthur Hertzberg, *The French Enlightenment and the Jews*, chapter 10.

31. Hertzberg makes the point that the Ashkenazi community in France relinquished its communal autonomy only with the greatest reluctance; *The French Enlightenment and the Jews*, 8, 325, 344, 348.

32. "The Assembly of Jewish Notables, Answers to Napoleon," *The Jew in the Modern World: A Documentary History*, edited by Paul Mendes-Flohr and Jehuda Reinharz (New York: Oxford University Press, 1980), 116.

33. Hyman, "Emancipation," 168; Arthur Hertzberg, *The Zionist Idea: A Historical Analysis and Reader* (New York: Atheneum, 1969), 22–23. See also Eisen, *The Chosen People*, especially chapter 2.

34. Quote from Hyman, "Emancipation," 170.

35. Lorde, *Sister Outsider*, 120; Martha Ackelsberg,"Towards a Feminist Judaism" (unpublished lecture delivered at the "Jewish Women's Conference, 1983: Challenge and Change," October 1983).

36. Riv-Ellen Prell, "The Vision of Woman in Classical Reform Judaism," *Journal of the American Academy of Religion* 50 (December 1982): 575–89, especially 585. While Prell focuses on Classical Reform, the dynamics of women's integration into the Conservative Movement are not essentially different.

37. The argument Zillah Eisenstein makes for feminism in *The Radical Future of Liberal Feminism*, I am now applying in a wider context.

38. T. Drorah Setel, "Feminist Reflections on Separation and Unity in Jewish Theology," *Journal of Feminist Studies in Religion* 2 (Spring 1986): 113–18; see also Marcia Falk's response, 121–25. It was Drorah Setel who, in conversation, first formulated this crucial issue for me.

39. See Setel's discussion of God, for example, or Falk's rewriting of *havdalah*, *ibid.*

40. Eisen, *The Chosen People*, 16–18; *Encyclopedia Judaica*, s.v. "Chosen People"; *The Encyclopedia of Religion*, s.v. "Election," by Ellen Umansky; Henri Atlan, "Chosen People," in *Contemporary Jewish Religious Thought*, 56–57.

41. *Ibid.*

42. Atlan, "Chosen People," 56.
43. Philip Birnbaum, trans. and ed., *Daily Prayer Book: Ha-Siddur Ha-Shalem* (New York: Hebrew Publishing Company, 1949), 136.
44. Wyschogrod, *The Body of Faith*, 60.
45. *Ibid.*, 60–65, 118; quotation on 65.
46. On this last point, see Richard Rubenstein, *After Auschwitz: Essays in Contemporary Judaism* (Indianapolis, New York, Kansas City: Bobbs-Merrill Company, 1966), chapter 2.
47. Eisen, 18–22 and passim.
48. The 1966 *Commentary* magazine symposium on the condition of Jewish belief phrased one its five questions in this way: "In what sense do you believe that the Jews are the chosen people of God? How do you answer the charge that this doctrine is the model from which various theories of national and racial superiority have been derived?" *The Condition of Jewish Belief* (New York: The Macmillan Company, 1966), 7.
49. T. Drorah Setel, "Prophets and Pornography: Female Sexual Imagery in Hosea," *Feminist Interpretation of the Bible*, edited by Letty M. Russell (Philadelphia: The Westminster Press, 1985), 86, 88–90.
50. *Ibid.*, 94–95.
51. *Encyclopedia Judaica*, s.v. "Chosen People"; Umansky, "Election"; Eisen, *The Chosen People in America*, 16, and 186, note 33.
52. Though they did not deal specifically with the issue of chosenness, Barbara Breitman and Drorah Setel sparked the ideas in this paragraph through a stimulating presentation on anti-Semitism and misogyny at the B'not Esh gathering, May 1987. Some of these ideas are contained in Barbara Breitman's letter, "Psychopathology of Jewish men," *Tikkun* 2 (1987): 5, 108 and in her "Lifting Up the Shadow of Anti-Semitism: Jewish Masculinity in a New Light," *A Mensch Among Men: Explorations in Jewish Masculinity*, edited by Harry Brod (Freedom, CA: Crossing Press, 1988), 105–9.
53. Emil Fackenheim, for example, says that modern Jews hear the "commanding voice of Auschwitz" telling them not to hand Hitler posthumous victories; *God's Presence in History: Jewish Affirmations and Philosophical Reflections* (New York: New York University Press, 1970), chapter 3.
54. In a 1986 survey of American Jewish attitudes, 94 percent of the respondents said that being a Jew is important to them because they they were born Jewish and that is their culture; Steven M. Cohen, *Ties and Tensions: The 1986 Survey of American Jewish Attitudes Toward Israel and Israelis* (Institute on American-Israeli Relations, The American Jewish Committee, 1987), 111.
55. Eisen criticizes Mordecai Kaplan for reductionism (*The Chosen People in America*, 78). While my position has a great deal in common with Reconstructionist rejection of chosenness and insistence on the self-justifying character of Judaism as a civilization, it rests on a very different understanding of God and spirituality.
56. Falk, response to "Feminist Reflections on Separation and Unity in Jewish Theology," 122. I have found Falk helpful in thinking through this whole paragraph.
57. This comment was made in a large group discussion at the 1986 B'not Esh gathering.

58. Martha Ackelsberg, "Personal Identities and Collective Visions: Reflections on Being a Jew and a Feminist" (unpublished lecture, Smith College, March 8, 1983) and "Toward a Feminist Judaism."

59. Hertzberg, *The Zionist Idea*, 17–18.

60. Hertzberg's *The Zionist Idea* provides an excellent discussion of and sourcebook on the important ideological differences among Zionist thinkers. See also Ben Halpern, *The Idea of the Jewish State*, 2d ed. (Cambridge, MA: Harvard University Press, 1969), chapter 2.

61. Dafna Izraeli, "The Zionist Movement in Palestine, 1911–1927: A Sociological Analysis," *Signs: Journal of Women in Culture and Society* 7 (Autumn 1981): 89; Deborah Bernstein, *The Struggle for Equality: Urban Women Workers in Prestate Israeli Society* (New York: Praeger, 1987), 4–5; Lesley Hazleton, *Israeli Women: The Reality Behind the Myths* (New York: Simon & Schuster, 1977), chapter 1; Natalie Rein *Daughters of Rachel: Women in Israel* (Harmondsworth, England: Penguin Books, 1979), 27–29.

62. Bernstein, *The Struggle for Equality*, 1, 2, 5.

63. Izraeli, "The Zionist Women's Movement in Palestine," 90–95; Bernstein, *The Struggle for Equality*, 16–20; Hazleton, *Israeli Women*, 15–17.

64. Vivian Silver, "Sexual Equality on Kibbutz—Where Did We Go Wrong?" (Unpublished paper delivered at the International Conference "Kibbutz and Communes—Past and Future," May 21, 1985); Naomi Fulop, "Women in the Kibbutz: A Jewish Feminist Utopia?" *Shifra* 3 and 4 (Dec. 1986): 33–35; Paula Rayman, *The Kibbutz Community and Nation Building* (Princeton, NJ: Princeton University Press, 1981), 53–54.

65. Tom Segev, *1949: The First Israelis* (New York: The Free Press, 1986), 249–52; Frances Raday, "Equality of Women Under Israeli Law," *The Jerusalem Quarterly* 27 (Spring 1983): 81–83; Hazleton, *Israeli Women*, 22–23. Thanks to Donna Robinson Divine for the Segev and other references.

66. Hazleton, *Israeli Women*, 137–51; Nira Yuval-Davis, "The Israeli Example," *Loaded Questions: Women in the Military*, edited by W. Chapkis (Amsterdam: Transnational Institute, n.d.), 73–77.

67. This term is used by Barbara Welter to describe the nineteenth-century American image of women's nature and role; *Dimity Convictions: The American Woman in the Nineteenth Century* (Athens, OH: Ohio University Press, 1976), chapter 2.

68. Yuval-Davis, "The Israeli Example," 76–77; Nira Yuval-Davis, "The Jewish Collectivity and National Reproduction in Israel," *Khamsin* 13 (July 1987): 86–87.

69. Segev, *1949*, 155–61.

70. Sammy Smooha and Yochanan Peres, "The Dynamics of Ethnic Inequalities: The Case of Israel," *Studies of Israeli Society*, vol. I, Migration, Ethnicity and Community (New Brunswick, NJ: Transaction Books, 1980), 167–73; Erik Cohen, "The Black Panthers and Israeli Society," *ibid.*, 147, 149–50.

71. Cohen, "The Black Panthers and Israeli Society," 160–61.

72. Ian Lustick, in *Arabs in the Jewish State: Israel's Control of a National Minority* (Austin: University of Texas Press, 1980), thoroughly analyzes these dynamics. See Lustick, chapter 3, for discussion of his analytic framework.

73. *Ibid.*, 93–94. Compare Anton Shammas, "The Morning After," *The New York Review* (September 29, 1988): 49.

74. Abba Eban, "The Central Question," *Tikkun* 1 (1987): 21.

75. *Ibid.*; Amnon Rubenstein, *The Zionist Dream Revisited: From Herzl to Gush Emunim and Back* (New York: Schocken Books, 1984), chapter 7; Uriel Tal, "Foundations of a Political Messianic Trend in Israel," *The Jerusalem Quarterly* no. 35 (Spring 1985): 42–45.

76. Mariam M. Mar'i and Sami Kh. Mar'i, "The Role of Women as Change Agents in Arab Society in Israel," in *Women's Worlds*, edited by Marilyn Sahr, Martha Mednick, Dafne Israeli, and Jessie Bernard (New York: Praeger Special Studies, 1985), 251–58.

77. Hazleton, *Israeli Women*, 143; Davis, "The Israeli Example," 76. Only 10 percent of Jewish Israeli men are exempted from military service.

78. Yuval-Davis, "The Jewish Collectivity and National Reproduction in Israel," 60–90, especially 85.

79. This analogy became clear to me in the course of a conversation with Paula Rayman on July 20, 1987. I am indebted to Paula both for pushing me to deal with the state of Israel and for helping me to organize my thoughts on many of the issues I discuss in this section.

80. I have in mind here the use of the Holocaust to justify almost everything and anything that Israel does.

81. Donna Robinson Divine, "Political Discourse in Israeli Literature," *Books in Israel*, vol. I, edited by Ian Lustick (Albany, NY: SUNY Press, 1988), 37–47.

82. See, for example, "The New Israel Fund: Annual Report, November 1987" (New York: New Israel Fund, 1987), 8–11, 20–23; Rein, *Daughters of Rachel*, part 2, deals with the emergence of the Israeli women's movement.

83. Good sources of information about such groups are "Shalom: Jewish Peace Letter" (published quarterly by the Jewish Peace Fellowship, Box 271 Nyack, NY 10960) and Jay Rothman with Sharon Bray and Mark Neustadt, "A Guide to Arab-Jewish Peacemaking Organizations in Israel" (New York: The New Israel Fund, 1988). (This and other publications and reports of the NIF are available from the NIF, 111 West 40th Street, New York, NY 10018.) See also Saul Perlmutter, "The Light at the End of the Tunnel" (unpublished paper, 1988) and "The Israel Palestinian Center for Research and Information (IPCRI)" (unpublished letter, May 26, 1988).

84. For news of such groups and their counterparts in the US, see the "Jewish Women's Peace Bulletin" (published by the Jewish Women's Committee to End the Occupation of the West Bank and Gaza, JWCEO, Suite 1178, 163 Joralemon St., Brooklyn, NY 11201).

85. Tal, "Foundations of a Political Messianic Trend in Israel," 36–45.

4. God: Reimaging the Unimaginable

1. A. Marmorstein, *The Old Rabbinic Doctrine of God*, vol. 1: *The Names and Attributes of God* (New York: KTAV Publishing House, 1927), 56, 90, 84.

2. Cynthia Ozick, "Notes Toward Finding the Right Question," *On Being a Jewish Feminist: A Reader*, edited by Susannah Heschel (New York: Schocken Books, 1983), 122. Ozick sees this clearly but denies its significance.

3. Phyllis Trible, "Depatriarchalizing in Biblical Interpretation," *Journal of the American Academy of Religion* 41 (March 1973): 32–35 and *God and the Rhetoric of Sexuality* (Philadelphia: Fortress Press, 1978), chapters 2 and 3.

4. On the tensions in the Jewish conception of God, see *Encyclopedia Judaica*, s.v. "God"; Louis Jacobs, "God," *Contemporary Jewish Religious Thought*:

Original Essays on Critical Concepts, Movements, and Beliefs, edited by Arthur A. Cohen and Paul Mendes-Flohr (New York: Charles Scribner's Sons, 1987), 291–98; A. Marmorstein, *The Old Rabbinic Doctrine of God*, vol. 2: *Essays in Anthropomorphism* (New York: KTAV Publishing House, 1937).

5. Arthur Green, "Keeping Feminist Creativity Jewish," *Sh'ma* 16/305 (January 10, 1986): 35.

6. In discussing feminist criticism of male God-language, I draw on my articles "The Right Question Is Theological," in Heschel, *On Being a Jewish Feminist*, 227–28 and "Language, God, and Liturgy: A Feminist Perspective," *Response* 44 (Spring 1983): 4–6.

7. See chapter 2, 42–43; Carol P. Christ, *Laughter of Aphrodite: Reflections on a Journey to the Goddess* (San Francisco: Harper & Row, 1987), chapter 3; Judith Ochshorn, *The Female Experience and the Nature of the Divine* (Bloomington: Indiana University Press, 1981).

8. Ochshorn, *The Female Experience*.

9. See T. Drorah Setel, "Prophets and Pornography: Female Sexual Imagery in Hosea," in *Feminist Interpretation of the Bible*, edited by Letty Russell (Philadelphia: Westminster Press, 1985), 86–95, for a discussion of the relation between God-language and the status of women in a particular historical period.

10. Mary Daly, *Beyond God the Father: Toward a Philosophy of Women's Liberation* (Boston: Beacon Press, 1973), 13. As if in confirmation of this view, a student of mine (in an Introduction to Religion class at Wichita State University) reported that when she asked her boss why there were no women executives in the company she worked for, he replied, "Because God is a man"!

11. Clifford Geertz, "Religion as a Cultural System," *Reader in Comparative Religion: An Anthropological Approach*, edited by William Lessa and Evon Vogt (New York: Harper & Row, 1965), 205, 207, 213, 215; quotation 215. See Carol P. Christ and Judith Plaskow, eds., *Womanspirit Rising: A Feminist Reader in Religion* (San Francisco: Harper & Row, 1979), 2–3 and Christ, *Laughter of Aphrodite*, 117–19 for the same use of Geertz.

12. I have in mind remarks like the one reported by my student (see note 10) as well as repeated use of this language to justify the exclusion of women from ordination. For the latter argument in a Jewish context, see Mortimer Ostow, "Women and Change in Jewish Law," *Conservative Judaism* 29 (Fall 1974): 5–12.

13. Maimonides, *The Guide of the Perplexed*, 2 vols., translated by Shlomo Pines (Chicago: The University of Chicago Press, 1963), Part I, chapters 55–59. Elizabeth Johnson makes this point for Christian philosophical theology in "The Incomprehensibility of God and the Image of God Male and Female," *Theological Studies* 45 (September 1984): 454.

14. Marcia Falk, "Notes on Composing New Blessings: Toward a Feminist–Jewish Reconstruction of Prayer," *Journal of Feminist Studies in Religion* 3 (Spring 1987): 44–45.

15. See Catherine Keller, *From a Broken Web: Separation, Sexism, and Self* (Boston: Beacon Press, 1986), 38–46, for an excellent discussion of the connection between male God-language and male ego ideals.

16. Louis Ginsberg, *The Legends of the Jews*, 7 vols. (Philadelphia: Jewish Publication Society, 1909–1938), 3 (1911): 81–82, 92. Since, as I have argued, the God of the tradition is thoroughly male, there is little point in not using the male pronoun in referring to traditional conceptions of God.

17. See, for example, Genesis 18: 22–33; Elie Wiesel, *Souls on Fire: Portraits and Legends of Hasidic Masters* (New York: Random House, 1972), 110–11 and *Gates of the Forest* (New York: Schocken Books, 1982), 197. Wiesel is the most powerful contemporary exponent of the view that God can be held accountable to the covenant.

18. Emil Fackenheim, *God's Presence in History: Jewish Affirmations and Philosophical Reflections* (New York: New York University Press, 1970), 28–29. For a contemporary version of the same response, see Elie Wiesel, *Night* (New York: Bantam Books, 1982), 61–62.

19. Alan Mintz, in "Prayer and the Prayerbook" (in *Back to the Sources: Reading the Classic Jewish Texts*, edited by Barry Holtz [New York: Summit Books, 1984], 407), implies that the experiences of intimacy and might are balanced. It seems to me this is rather like saying that God's masculine and feminine qualities are balanced. See Ellen Umansky, "(Re)Imaging the Divine," *Response* 41–42 (Fall–Winter 1982): 111.

20. Philip Birnbaum, *Daily Prayer Book: Ha-Siddur Ha-Shalem* (New York: Hebrew Publishing Company, 1949), 24.

21. The contrast between "power over" and power from within or empowerment is a common theme in feminist work. See, for example, Starhawk, *Dreaming the Dark: Magic, Sex, and Politics* (Boston: Beacon Press, 1982), chapter 4 and *Truth or Dare: Encounters with Power, Authority, and Mystery* (San Francisco: Harper & Row, 1987), chapter 1.

    Though I have drawn on the traditional prayerbook in describing the God of Jewish liturgy, the standard prayerbook of all denominations offers substantially the same picture. Congregation Beth El in Sudbury, Massachusetts, has produced an alternative prayerbook, *Vetaher Libenu* (Sudbury, MA: Congregation Beth El, 1980). Two new prayerbooks published too late to be considered here are *Kol Haneshamah: Shabbat Eve* (Wyncote, PA: Reconstructionist Press 1989) and *Or Chadash* (Philadelphia: P'nai Or Religious Fellowship, 1989).

22. Gordon Kaufman, *Theology for a Nuclear Age* (Manchester and Philadelphia: Manchester University Press and Westminster Press, 1985), 39.

23. *Ibid.*, 38.

24. For discussion of the "omni" attributes of God, see Grace Jantzen, *God's World, God's Body* (Philadelphia: The Westminster Press, 1984).

25. Sallie McFague, *Models of God: Theology for an Ecological, Nuclear Age* (Philadelphia: Fortress Press, 1987), 68.

26. *Ibid.*; Michael Wyschogrod, *The Body of Faith: Judaism as Corporeal Election* (San Francisco: Harper & Row, 1983), 106. It must be said that the Jewish tradition also contains conflicting images of God's parenthood. For example, at the end of the midrash cited in chapter 2, 69, God is delighted that his sons have defeated him.

27. Christ, *Laughter of Aphrodite*, chapter 5.

28. For a discussion of the religious use of political metaphors, see Davis Nicholls, "Images of God and the State: Political Analogy and Religious Discourse," *Theological Studies* 42 (June 1981): 195–215, especially sections 2 and 4.

29. Daly, *Beyond God the Father*, 114–22. In this paragraph, I have again drawn on my article "Language, God and Liturgy."

30. Rosemary Ruether, panel discussion on *Models of God: Theology for an Ecological, Nuclear Age* (Annual Meeting of the American Academy of Religion, December 7, 1987).

31. Rita Gross, "Female God Language in a Jewish Context," in Christ and Plaskow, *Womanspirit Rising*, 169. My view of theological language has been influenced by Gordon Kaufman's methodology as set out in *An Essay on Theological Method* (Missoula, MT: Scholars Press, 1975) and *The Theological Imagination: Constructing the Concept of God* (Philadelphia: Westminster Press, 1981). Yet I believe that theological construction, unless it is entirely arbitrary, must have a starting point in some commitment or vision that is rooted in a particular community. Thus, while the process of creating new imagery is imaginative and constructive, it is also less entirely rational than Kaufman seems to suppose.

32. Gross, "Female God Language," 167–73; quotation, 170f. In her "Steps Toward Feminine Imagery of Deity in Jewish Theology," in Heschel, *On Being a Jewish Feminist*, 234–47, Gross develops this argument further using the resources of Hindu Goddess imagery.

33. Gross, "Female God Language," 173.

34. Naomi Janowitz and Maggie Wenig, *Siddur Nashim: A Sabbath Prayer Book for Women* (privately circulated for the women's minyan at Brown University, 1976); selections are reprinted in Christ and Plaskow, *Womanspirit Rising*, as "Sabbath Prayers for Women," 175, 176. Since Janowitz and Wenig, there have been numerous attempts to rewrite the liturgy in feminine form, some changing the Hebrew as well as the English. *Vetaher Libenu* is the only congregational prayerbook I know of that, at least in English, alternates male and female pronouns for God.

35. Gershom Scholem, *Major Trends in Jewish Mysticism* (New York: Schocken Books, 1941), 229–30; Arthur Green, "Bride, Spouse, Daughter: Images of the Feminine in Classical Jewish Sources," in Heschel, *On Being a Jewish Feminist*, 254–57.

36. Lynn Gottlieb, "Speaking into the Silence," *Response* 41–42 (Fall–Winter 1982): 23, 27.

37. Rachel Adler, "Second Hymn to the Shekhinah," *Response* 41–42 (Fall–Winter 1982): 60. Many feminist uses of Shekhinah either emerge spontaneously or are found in material that circulates privately. For other published uses, see Penina Villenchik [Adelman], "Blessing for Kindling the Sabbath Lights," *Response* 41–42 (Fall–Winter 1982): 53; Penina Adelman, *Miriam's Well: Rituals for Jewish Women Around the Year* (Fresh Meadows, NY: Biblio Press, 1986), 22. Adelman has also written a beautiful song about the Shekhinah that says, "We have found rest under the wings of the Shekhinah."

38. T. Drorah Setel, "Feminist Reflections on Separation and Unity in Jewish Theology," *Journal of Feminist Studies in Religion* 2 (Spring 1986): 117.

39. Falk, "Notes on Composing New Blessings," 42; Gross, "Steps Toward Feminine Imagery," 242.

40. Raphael Patai, *The Hebrew Goddess* (New York: KTAV Publishing House, 1967), 201, 205. Patai accepts Matronit/Shekhinah as a male projection without reflecting on the implications of this for women. Compare Scholem, *Major Trends*, 37f.

41. Lynn Gottlieb, "A Psalm," *Response* 41–42, 21f.

42. Falk, "Notes on Composing New Blessings," 43–53. See also "What About God?" *Moment* 10 (March 1985): 32–36; response to "Reflections on Separation and Unity in Jewish Theology," 124f.; "Feminist prayer," *Sh'ma* 17/325 (January 9, 1987): 37–38. Her book, *The Book of Blessings: A Feminist Jewish Reconstruction of Prayer* is forthcoming from Harper & Row.

43. Falk, "Notes on Composing New Blessings," 52–53.

44. "Singleness/Community Group," *Women Exploring Theology at Grailville* (packet from Church Women United, 1972).

45. Daly, *Beyond God the Father*, 33–36; quotations, 34, 36.

46. See Sheila Greeve Davaney, ed., *Feminism and Process Thought* (Lewiston, NY: The Edward Mellon Press, 1981); Catherine Keller, *From a Broken Web*, chapter 4.

47. In *Diving Deep and Surfacing: Women Writers on Spiritual Quest* (Boston: Beacon Press, 1980), Carol P. Christ traces this theme in the work of several women writers and connects it to the women's spirituality movement.

48. Alice Walker, *The Color Purple* (New York: Harcourt, Brace, Jovanovitch, 1982), 164–68, 187–88; quotations, 164, 168, 167, 188.

49. See, for example, Starhawk, *Dreaming the Dark*, chapter 5; also Nelle Morton, "The Goddess as Metaphoric Image," in *The Journey Is Home* (Boston: Beacon Press, 1985), 147–75; Christine Downing, *The Goddess: Mythological Images of the Feminine* (New York: Crossroad, 1981).

50. Starhawk, *The Spiral Dance: A Rebirth of the Ancient Religion of the Great Goddess* (San Francisco: Harper & Row, 1979), 81. Compare Christ, *Laughter of Aphrodite*, 122.

51. Patai, *The Hebrew Goddess*, 49f; Saul M. Olyan, *Asherah and the Cult of Yahweh in Israel*, SBL Monograph Series 34 (Atlanta, GA: Scholars Press, 1988).

52. Jon Levenson, "Is There a Counterpart in the Hebrew Bible to New Testament Anti-Semitism," *Journal of Ecumenical Studies* 22 (Spring 1985): 252–60.

53. It must be said that Jewish feminists are by no means free from this contempt at the same time it has been used against us. On this point and on further parallels between Jewish anti-paganism and Christian anti-Judaism, see Lori Krafte-Jacobs, "A Comparison of Christian Anti-Judaism and Jewish Anti-Paganism" (unpublished paper, n.d.).

54. Ozick, "Notes Toward Finding the Right Question," 121. Ozick is, of course, a feminist criticizing a particular understanding of Jewish feminism, but her words are echoed by many anti-feminists. For a recent example, see Samuel Dresner, "The Return of Paganism," *Midstream* 34 (June–July 1988): 32–38.

55. See, for example, David Miller, *The New Polytheism: Rebirth of the Gods and Goddesses* (New York: Harper & Row, 1974).

56. I came to see the difference between these two conceptions of monotheism in the course of a conversation with Starhawk at the Women's Spirit Bonding Conference at Grailville, Loveland, OH, July 1982.

57. 21.6. *Pesikta Rabbati* is a ninth-century collection of discourses given centuries earlier in Palestinian synagogues and schools.

58. See Jo Ann Hackett, "Can a Sexist Model Liberate Us? Ancient Near Eastern 'Fertility' Goddesses," *Journal of Feminist Studies in Religion* 5 (Spring 1989): 65–76 and Tikva Frymer-Kensky, "The Bible, Goddesses, and Sex," *Midstream* 34 (October 1988): 20–23.

59. For an appallingly forthright statement of these issues, see Ostow, "Women and Change in Jewish Law," 5–12.

60. Daly, *Beyond God the Father*, 33.

61. Walker, *The Color Purple*, 166–67.

62. Christ, *Laughter of Aphrodite*, ix; Starhawk, *The Spiral Dance*, 77–78.

63. See chapter 3, 85–86.

64. Christ, *Diving Deep and Surfacing*, 23; also passim.

65. Martin Buber, *I and Thou*, translated by Walter Kaufmann (New York: Charles Scribner's Sons, 1976), 56–57, 172–73, 180–81.

66. H. Richard Niebuhr, *The Responsible Self: An Essay in Christian Moral Philosophy* (New York: Harper & Row, 1963), 84–89.

67. Lawrence Fine, "The Contemplative Practice of Yihudim in Lurianic Kabbalah" and Louis Jacobs, "The Uplifting of Sparks in Later Jewish Mysticism," both in *Jewish Spirituality from the Sixteenth Century Revival to the Present*, edited by Arthur Green (New York: Crossroad, 1987), 65–70, 107–8, 115–25. For a fascinating image of communal spirituality within Hasidism, see J. G. Weiss, "R. Abraham Kalisker's Concept of Communion with God and Men," *The Journal of Jewish Studies* 6 (1955): 87–99. Thanks to Martha Ackelsberg and Gershon Hundert for this last reference.

68. Falk, "Notes on Composing New Blessings," 48.

69. Arthur Green, "The Children in Egypt and the Theophany at the Sea," *Judaism* 24 (Fall 1975): 446.

70. Falk, "Notes on Composing New Blessings," 45, and "Toward a Feminist–Jewish Reconstruction of Monotheism," *Tikkun* 4 (July/August 1989): 53–54.

71. See McFague, *Models of God*, 79–84 for a very fine extended argument for personal God-language.

72. This last question comes out of a conversation with Marcia Falk, May 1988.

73. See Christ, *Laughter of Aphrodite*, 121–26.

74. Chapters 5 and 6. McFague also proposes the image of God as Mother. I do not discuss it here because it is an image drawn from family, and I want to focus on images that come from community.

75. Green, "The Children in Egypt," 453–55.

76. McFague, *Models of God*, 125–34. McFague talks about God as lover of the world as God's body; again, I want to focus on community. It may be no coincidence that the image of God as lover is important in the Jewish mystical tradition which also emphasizes human responsibility for the world.

77. Marmorstein, *The Old Rabbinic Doctrine of God*, vol. I, 86. *Ki Anu Amekhah* is a liturgical poem—my favorite since childhood—repeated many times on Yom Kippur, that provides a long series of metaphors for the relationship between God and Israel. While almost all the metaphors are metaphors of domination, the prayer is an excellent spur to imagistic inventiveness.

78. McFague, *Models of God*, 163–64.

79. "Brainstorm: The Meaning of the Grailville Conference," in *Women Exploring Theology at Grailville*.

80. In *The Responsible Self*, H. R. Niebuhr takes "responsibility" as the fundamental metaphor for understanding human life before God.

81. Falk, "Notes on Composing New Blessings," 46. "Wellspring" is Falk's more recent translation of *eyn ha-khayyim* (conversation, May 1988).

82. Marmorstein, *The Old Rabbinic Doctrine of God*, vol. I, 91, 92–93, 149.

83. I am aware that the image of God as king has been used to question the authority of any earthly king. (See, for example, 1 Sam. 8:7 and Rosemary Ruether, *Sexism and God-Talk: Toward a Feminist Theology* [Boston: Beacon Press, 1983], 64.) But the image is still problematic in its hierarchical understanding of the divine/human relation and is too easily reversed politically.

84. See Catherine Madsen and respondents, "If God Is God She Is Not Nice," *Journal of Feminist Studies in Religion* 5 (Spring 1989): 103–17.

85. H. Richard Niebuhr, *Radical Monotheism and Western Culture* (New York: Harper & Row, Harper Torchbooks, 1970), 122–24; Paul Tillich, *Systematic Theology*, 3 vols. (Chicago: University of Chicago Press, 1951–1963), 1: 110.

86. Niebuhr, *The Responsible Self*, 83, 86–87.

5. Toward a New Theology of Sexuality

1. See chapter 3, 83; and chapter 4, 149–50, 153–54.

2. See chapter 1, 4–6.

3. Phyllis Bird, "Images of Women in the Old Testament," in *Religion and Sexism: Images of Woman in the Jewish and Christian Traditions*, edited by Rosemary Ruether (New York: Simon & Schuster, 1974), 51. See also chapter 1, 4–5.

4. Bird, "Images of Women," 51.

5. Thus in *Chattel or Person? The Status of Women in the Mishnah* (New York and Oxford: Oxford University Press, 1988), Judith Romney Wegner argues that the Mishnah treats women as chattel precisely and only when a specific man has a "proprietary interest" in their sexual and reproductive capacities.

6. Rachel Biale, *Women and Jewish Law: An Exploration of Women's Issues in Halakhic Sources* (New York: Schocken Books, 1984), 148.

7. Jacob Neusner, *A History of the Mishnaic Law of Women*, 5 vols. (Leiden, E. J. Brill, 1980), 5:13–14, 268.

8. *Ibid.*, 271–272.

9. Louis Epstein, *Sex Laws and Customs in Judaism* (New York: KTAV Publishing House, 1967), 34–35, 46–47, 112–33, 115, 116, 120.

10. Leonard Swidler, *Women in Judaism: The Status of Women in Formative Judaism* (Metuchen, NJ: Scarecrow Press, 1976), 126–30.

11. Biale, *Women and Jewish Law*, chapter 6, especially 148, 154.

12. Rachel Adler, "*TUMAH* and *TAHARAH*; Ends and Beginnings," in *The Jewish Woman: New Perspectives*, edited by Elizabeth Koltun (New York: Schocken Books, 1976), 70.

13. Biale, *Women and Jewish Law*, 158–60, 168; Shaya Cohen, "Menstruation and Purification: Women's Religion in Ancient and Medieval Judaism" (paper delivered at American Academy of Religion Annual Meeting, December 6, 1987).

14. Swidler, *Women in Judaism*, 137; Blu Greenberg, *On Women and Judaism: A View from Tradition* (Philadelphia: The Jewish Publication Society, 1981), 115.

15. Samuel Glasner, "Judaism and Sex," *The Encyclopedia of Sexual Behavior*, edited by Albert Ellis and Albert Abarbanel, vol. 2, 575–84 (New York: Hawthorn Books, 1967). Cited in Joan Scherer Brewer, *Sex and the Modern Jewish Woman: An Annotated Bibliography* (Fresh Meadows, NY: Biblio Press, 1986), B-10.

16. Not surprisingly, many modern apologists cite only the positive side of Jewish attitudes toward sexuality, contrasting Judaism favorably with Christianity. See, for example, David M. Feldman, *Marital Relations, Birth Control, and Abortion in Jewish Law* (New York: Schocken Books, 1974).

17. Louis Epstein, *Sex Laws and Customs*, 1–11; Vern Bullough, *Sexual Variance in Society and History* (Chicago and London: University of Chicago Press, 1976), 74–75. Compare Steven Fraade, "Ascetical Aspects of Ancient Judaism," in *Jewish Spirituality from the Bible to the Middle Ages*, edited by Arthur Green (New York: Crossroad, 1987), 253–88; Bernard Prusak, "Woman: Seductive Siren and Source of Sin?" in Ruether, *Religion and Sexism*, 89–116.

18. Seymour Siegel, "Some Aspects of the Jewish Tradition's View of Sex," in *Jews and Divorce*, edited by Jacob Freid (New York: KTAV Publishing House, 1968), 168–69; Robert Gordis, *Love and Sex: A Modern Jewish Perspective* (New York: Farrar Strauss, & Giroux, 1978), 98, 105–7; Eliyahu Rosenheim, "Sexuality in Judaism," *Journal of Psychology and Judaism* 4 (Summer 1980): 249–59.

19. Gordis, *Love and Sex*, 87–88.

20. Biale, *Women and Jewish Law*, chapter 5; Feldman, *Marital Relations*, chapter 4.

21. Biale, *Women and Jewish Law*, chapter 5; Rosenheim, "Sexuality in Judaism," 256; Moses Maimonides, *The Guide of the Perplexed*, translated by Shlomo Pines (Chicago: The University of Chicago Press, 1963), part 3, chapter 8. Compare Steven Fraade, "Ascetical Aspects of Ancient Judaism," 269–77.

22. Biale, *Women and Jewish Law*, 137; Fraade, "Ascetical Aspects of Ancient Judaism," 275, 276.

23. Biale, *Women and Jewish Law*, chapter 6; Greenberg, *On Women and Judaism*, 112–17.

24. Epstein, *Sex Laws and Customs*, 167–70; Siegel, "Some Aspects of the Jewish Tradition's View of Sex," 175–77; Biale, *Women and Jewish Law*, 190–92.

25. This was the rabbinic perception, not necessarily the historical reality, which is much more difficult to judge. Many people today still see incest and homosexuality as extremely rare, despite massive evidence to the contrary.

26. Biale, *Women and Jewish Law*, 179–89, 192–97; Maurice Lamm, *The Jewish Way in Love and Marriage* (San Francisco: Harper & Row, 1980), 39–42, 65–68; Bradley Artson, "Judaism and Homosexuality," *Tikkun* 3 (March/April 1988): 52, 92.

27. Epstein, *Sex Laws and Customs*, 168–69.

28. Compare George Foot Moore, *Judaism in the First Centuries of the Christian Era and the Age of the Tannaim*, 2 vols. (Cambridge: Harvard University Press, 1958), 2:270.

29. Again here, I am discussing rabbinic assumptions, which may or may not have corresponded to reality. Compare note 25.

30. Epstein, *Sex Laws and Customs*, chapters 3, 4; Rabbi Solomon Ganzfried, *Code of Jewish Law: Kitzur Shulḥan Arukh*, 4 vols, translated by Hyman Goldin (New York: Hebrew Publishing Company, 1961), 4: 17–18, 20; Lamm, *The Jewish Way*, 40, 66–67; Biale, *Women and Jewish Law*, 195.

31. Epstein, *Sex Laws and Customs*, 13.

32. Ibid., chapter 2 and 114; Swidler, *Women in Judaism*, 129.

33. I put "religious" in quotation marks because, as should be clear from the previous discussion, the social order is itself religious, being the sphere of divine commandment and response. I am using the term here in its narrower modern sense.

34. See chapter 4, 148.

35. Compare Fraade, "Ascetical Aspects of Ancient Judaism," 262 and 281, note 35.

36. Mortimer Ostow, "Women and Change in Jewish Law," *Conservative Judaism* (Fall 1974): 5–12 and Samuel Dresner, "The Return of Paganism," *Midstream* 34 (June–July 1988): 32–38 both make this very clear.

37. Ostow, "Women and Change in Jewish Law," 7–8.

38. Cynthia Ozick, "Notes Toward Finding the Right Question," *On Being a Jewish Feminist: A Reader*, edited by Susannah Heschel (New York: Schocken Books, 1983), 121. See chapter 4, 149–50.

39. Gershom Scholem, *Major Trends in Jewish Mysticism* (New York: Schocken Books, 1941), 227–28 and *On the Kabbalah and Its Symbolism* (New York: Schocken Books, 1965), 104–5, 108.

40. Biale, *Women and Jewish Law*, 140–43; Scholem, *Major Trends*, 235.

41. Scholem, *Major Trends*, 8th lecture. In the case of Sabbatianism, this was not simply slander.

42. Laurence Fine, "The Contemplative Practice of Yihudim in Lurianic Kabbalah," *Jewish Spirituality from the Sixteenth Century Revival to the Present*, 77; Scholem, *On the Kabbalah*, 154–55.

43. Scholem, *Major Trends*, 37f. and *On the Kabbalah*, 154–55.

44. Feldman, *Marital Relations*, 101; Joan Timmerman, *The Mardi Gras Syndrome: Rethinking Christian Sexuality* (New York: Crossroad, 1984), ix; Alan Greene, *Sex, God, and the Sabbath: The Mystery of Jewish Marriage* (Cleveland, OH: Temple Emanuel, 1979), 29.

45. For an impressive array of documents on this issue, see Baruch Litvin, ed. *The Sanctity of the Synagogue*, 3d ed. (New York: KTAV Publishing House, Union of Orthodox Jewish Congregations, 1987), especially 189–91, 198–202.

46. Arthur Green, "A Contemporary Approach to Jewish Sexuality," *The Second Jewish Catalog*, edited by Sharon Strassfeld and Michael Strassfeld (Philadelphia: The Jewish Publication Society, 1976), 96–99; Arthur Waskow, "Down-to-Earth Judaism: Sexuality," *Tikkun* 3 (March/April 1988): 46.

47. The most important compendium of basic information on women's bodies and sexuality is The Boston Women's Health Book Collective, *Our Bodies, Our Selves* (New York: Simon & Schuster, 1973). On institutions shaping women's sexual lives, some examples of the massive literature include: Adrienne Rich, "Compulsory Heterosexuality and Lesbian Existence," *Signs: Journal of Women in Culture and Society* 5 (Summer 1980): 631–60; Andrea Dworkin, *Pornography: Men Possessing Women* (New York: Perigee Books, 1979); Suzanne Arms, *Immaculate Deception: A New Look at Women and Childbirth in America* (Boston: Houghton Mifflin, 1975); Linda Gordon, *Woman's Body, Woman's Right: A Social History of Birth Control in America* (New York: Penguin Books, 1974); Rosalind Petchesky, *Abortion and Women's Choice* (New York: Longman, 1984). For one set of explorations of a woman-defined sexuality, see Carol Vance, ed., *Pleasure and Danger: Exploring Female Sexuality* (Boston: Routledge and Kegan Paul, 1984).

48. Ruether's earliest work on this subject, "Motherearth and the Megamachine," is reprinted and discussed in *Womanspirit Rising: A Feminist Reader in Religion*, edited by Carol P. Christ and Judith Plaskow (San Francisco: Harper & Row, 1979), 21–22, 43–52. See also Ruether's "Misogynism and Virginal Feminism in the Fathers of the Church," in Ruether, *Religion and Sexism*, 150–83.

49. Martha Vicinus, "Sexuality and Power: A Review of Current Work in the History of Sexuality," *Feminist Studies* 8 (Spring 1982): 136.

50. Judith Plaskow, "Woman as Body: The History of an Idea," (unpublished lecture, 1979); Elizabeth V. Spelman, "Woman as Body: Ancient and Contemporary Views," *Feminist Studies* 8 (Spring 1982): 109–31.

51. Adrienne Rich, *Of Woman Born: Motherhood as Experience and Institution* (New York: W. W. Norton, 1976), 39, 285–86.

52. Naomi Janowitz and Maggie Wenig, "Sabbath Prayers for Women," *Womanspirit Rising*, 176; also chapter 4, 137–38.

53. Beverly Wildung Harrison, "The Power of Anger in the Work of Love: Christian Ethics for Women and Other Strangers," "Sexuality and Social Policy," and "Misogyny and Homophobia: The Unexplored Connections," all in *Making the Connections: Essays in Feminist Social Ethics* (Boston: Beacon Press, 1985), 13, 87, 149; quotations, pages 13 and 149. Compare Carter Heyward, *Our Passion for Justice: Images of Power, Sexuality, and Liberation*

(New York: Pilgrim Press, 1984), especially chapters 3, 6, 11, 17; and Starhawk, *Dreaming the Dark: Magic, Sex, and Politics* (Boston: Beacon Press, 1982), chapter 8.

54. Audre Lorde, "Uses of the Erotic: The Erotic as Power," in *Sister Outsider* (Trumansburg, NY: The Crossing Press, 1984), 53–59. Compare Vicinus, "Sexuality and Power," 136.

55. *Ibid.*, 55, 56, 57.

56. Harrison, "The Power of Anger," 14; Heyward, *Our Passion for Justice*, chapter 3.

57. James Nelson, *Between Two Gardens: Reflections on Sexuality and Religious Experience* (New York: Pilgrim Press, 1983), 6.

58. For this insight, and for all I will say in the next section, I am profoundly indebted to four years of discussion of sexuality and spirituality with my sisters in B'not Esh. See Martha Ackelsberg, "Spirituality, Community, and Politics: B'not Esh and the Feminist Reconstruction of Judaism," *Journal of Feminist Studies in Religion* 2 (Fall 1986): 115.

59. Green, "A Contemporary Approach," 98.

60. Harrison, "Sexuality and Social Policy," 83–114; Ruby Rich, "Feminism and Sexuality in the 1980s," *Feminist Studies* 12 (Fall 1986): 549–58.

61. See Mariana Valverde's insistence that the eroticization of equality is a central task of feminism, *Sex, Power, and Pleasure* (Toronto: The Women's Press, 1985), 43.

62. Nelson, *Between Two Gardens*, 7; Phyllis Trible, *God and the Rhetoric of Sexuality* (Philadelphia: Fortress Press, 1978), chapter 5; Arthur Waskow, *Godwrestling* (New York: Schocken Books, 1978), chapter 6.

63. Nelson, *Between Two Gardens*, 6.

64. Starhawk, *Truth or Dare: Encounters with Power, Authority, and Mystery* (San Francisco: Harper & Row, 1987), 153.

65. Lorde, "Uses of the Erotic," 57.

66. *Ibid.*, 55. Compare Starhawk, *Dreaming the Dark*, 141.

67. Lorde, "Uses of the Erotic," 57; compare Starhawk, *Dreaming the Dark*, 141.

68. Epstein, *Sex Laws and Customs*, 14.

69. Gordis, *Love and Sex*, 106.

70. Harrison, "The Power of Anger," 13–14; Lillian Smith, *Killers of the Dream* (New York and London: W. W. Norton, The Norton Library, 1978), 81–85.

71. Starhawk, *Truth or Dare*, 153.

72. See, for example, Waskow, *Godwrestling*, 59; Nelson, *Between Two Gardens*, 3–4.

73. Harrison, "Sexuality and Social Policy," 85; Lorde, "Uses of the Erotic," 59.

74. Harrison, "Misogyny and Homophobia," 149–50.

75. For a clear statement of this principle, see James Nelson, *Embodiment: An Approach to Sexuality and Christian Theology* (Minneapolis, MN: Augsburg Publishing House, 1978), 126 and chapter 8; and Artson, "Judaism and Homosexuality," 92–93.

76. The best consideration of this issue in a Jewish context that I am aware of is Artson, "Judaism and Homosexuality," 52–54, 92–93. See also Hershel

Matt, "Sin, Crime, Sickness or Alternative Life Style? A Jewish Approach to Homosexuality," *Judaism* 27 (Winter 1978): 13–24 and Arthur Waskow, "Down to Earth Judaism," 48–49, 88–89. *Twice Blessed: On Being Lesbian, Gay, and Jewish*, Christie Balka and Andy Rose, eds. (Boston: Beacon Press, 1989) appeared too late to be considered here.

77. I am grateful to Denni Liebowitz for putting the issue in this way; conversation, fall 1983.

78. Compare Waskow, "Down-to-Earth Judaism," 88.

79. Martha Ackelsberg, "Families and the Jewish Community: A Feminist Perspective," *Response* 14 (Spring 1985): 15–16.

80. Feldman, *Marital Relations*, chapters 2, 4, 5; Martha Ackelsberg, "Family or commmunity?" *Sh'ma* 17/330 (March 20, 1987): 76–78.

81. Green, "A Contemporary Approach," 98.

6. Feminist Judaism and Repair of the World

1. Compare Martha Ackelsberg, "Spirituality, Community, and Politics: B'not Esh and the Feminist Reconstruction of Judaism," *Journal of Feminist Studies in Religion* 2 (Fall 1986): 114.

2. This formulation was first suggested by Betsy Cohen and Martha Ackelsberg in leading a B'not Esh discussion on spirituality and politics in 1984.

3. For example, Gustavo Gutierrez, *A Theology of Liberation* (Maryknoll, NY: Orbis Books, 1973), 10.

4. Abraham Joshua Heschel, *The Prophets* (NY: Harper & Row, 1962), 195.

5. *Ibid.*, 3–4, 204–5.

6. For treatment of this story in a liberation theological context, see Robert McAfee Brown, *Unexpected News: Reading the Bible with Third World Eyes* (Philadelphia: The Westminster Press, 1984), chapter 3.

7. Heschel, *The Prophets*, 198, 199, 229–30.

8. Mishnah *Gittin*, 4.2–3. The Mishnah says that Hillel's *prosbul*, the practice of having witnesses sign a bill of divorce, and the practice of listing all names on a bill of divorce, are all for the sake of *tikkun olam*.

9. Martin Buber, *Israel and the World: Essays in a Time of Crisis* (New York: Schocken Books, 1963), 33.

10. Isaac Deutscher, *The Non-Jewish Jew and Other Essays* (London: Oxford University Press, 1968), chapter 1; quotations, 36, 26.

11. Gershom Scholem, *Major Trends in Jewish Mysticism* (New York: Schocken Books, 1941), 260–61, 265, 273–75, quotation, page 273; Lawrence Fine, "The Contemplative Practices of the Yihudim in Lurianic Kabbalah," in *Jewish Spirituality from the Sixteenth Century Revival to the Present*, edited by Arthur Green (New York: Crossroad, 1987), 65–70.

12. Fine, "The Contemplative Practices," 70; Louis Jacobs, "The Uplifting of Sparks in Later Jewish Mysticism," in Green, *Jewish Spirituality*, 108, 115–16, 124.

13. Thanks to Robert Goldenberg for helping me to sort out the different levels of meaning of *tikkun olam*.

14. Arthur Waskow, *These Holy Sparks: The Rebirth of the Jewish People* (San Francisco: Harper & Row, 1983), 3–6, 20.

15. New Jewish Agenda National Platform (adopted November 28, 1982), 1. Available from New Jewish Agenda, 64 Fulton Street, #1100, New York, NY 10038. *Tikkun* magazine, which integrates discussion of politics, culture, and religion from a progressive perspective, has on its back cover, "*Tikkun* . . . to heal, repair, and transform the world." Available from 5100 Leona Street, Oakland, CA 94619.

16. Eleanor Flexner, *Century of Struggle: The Woman's Rights Movement in the United States* (New York: Atheneum, 1970), 41–42, 44.

17. Sarah Grimké, *Letters on the Equality of the Sexes and the Condition of Woman* (1938; New York: Burt Franklin, 1970); reprinted in Elizabeth Clark and Herbert Richardson, eds., *Women and Religion: A Feminist Sourcebook of Christian Thought* (New York: Harper & Row, 1977), chapter 16. Capitals and emphasis in original.

18. Flexner, *Century of Struggle*, 74 (emphasis mine); Seattle Coalition Task Force on Women and Religion, *The Woman's Bible* (1898; Seattle: Coalition Task Force on Women and Religion, 1974), v.

19. Leonard Swidler's "Jesus Was a Feminist," *Catholic World* 212 (January 1971): 177–83 was the first of many books and articles pursuing the Jesus as feminist theme. Robin Scroggs, "Paul and the Eschatological Woman," *Journal of the American Academy of Religion* 40 (September 1972): 283–303, launched an extended debate about Paul.

20. See chapter 3, 86; Mary Daly, *Beyond God the Father: Toward a Philosophy of Women's Liberation* (Boston: Beacon Press, 1973), 6 and passim.

21. Nelle Morton, "The Rising Woman Consciousness in a Male Language Structure," *The Journey Is Home* (Boston: Beacon Press, 1985), 11–30; Starhawk, "Ethics and Justice in Goddess Religion," *The Politics of Women's Spirituality: Essays on the Rise of Spiritual Power within the Feminist Movement*, edited by Charlene Spretnak (Garden City, NY: Doubleday, Anchor Books, 1982), 418; Laura Geller and T. Drorah Setel's contributions to "What Kind of Tikkun Does the World Need?" *Tikkun* 1 (1986): 16ff.; 114–15.

22. For example, Bell Hooks, *Feminist Theory: From Margin to Center* (Boston: South End Press, 1984), chapter 2; Ada Maria Isasi-Diaz and Yolanda Tarango, *Hispanic Women: Prophetic Voice in the Church* (San Francisco: Harper & Row, 1988).

23. Sharon Welch, "Ideology and Social Change," in *Weaving the Visions: New Patterns in Feminist Spirituality*, edited by Judith Plaskow and Carol P. Christ (San Francisco: Harper & Row, 1989), 336–43.

24. Rosemary Radford Ruether has addressed this issue very powerfully in "Motherearth and the Megamachine: A Theology of Liberation in a Feminine, Somatic and Ecological Perspective," in *Womanspirit Rising: A Feminist Reader in Religion*, edited by Carol P. Christ and Judith Plaskow (San Francisco: Harper & Row, 1979), 44, 51–52 and *New Woman New Earth: Sexist Ideologies and Human Liberation* (San Francisco: Harper & Row, 1975), 196–211.

25. Paula Rayman, *The Kibbutz Community and Nation Building* (Princeton: Princeton University Press, 1981), chapter 5.

26. Of course, it is not only women who have criticized this aspect of Jewish life. Rejection of the hierarchical structure of the average synagogue has also been a central theme of the havurah movement; see page 235, below.

27. Ruether, "Motherearth and the Megamachine," 44.
28. Ackelsberg, "Spirituality, Community, and Politics," 114.
29. Danby translation of *Gittin* 4.2, 3.
30. I do not mean to suggest that the Jewish tradition is unaware of the systemic nature of justice and injustice. See, for example, Arthur Waskow and Rosemary Radford Ruether's discussions of the jubilee year as an instance of a structural solution to injustice. (Waskow, *Rainbow Sign* [unpublished manuscript, 1987], chapter 3 and Ruether, "Envisioning Our Hopes: Some Models of the Future," in *Women's Spirit Bonding*, edited by Janet Kalven and Mary Buckley [New York: Pilgrim Press, 1984], 334–35.) The tradition has taken certain systems of injustice for granted, however, and these must now be at the center of our awareness.
31. Dorothee Soelle, *Political Theology* (Philadelphia: Fortress Press, 1984), 89.
32. For example, Elisabeth Schüssler Fiorenza calls the Christian churches to repent of the sin of sexism. "Feminist Spirituality, Christian Identity, and Catholic Vision," in Christ and Plaskow, *Womanspirit Rising*, 145–47.
33. Ackelsberg, "Spirituality, Community, and Politics," 109–18.
34. More information on havurot is available through the National Havurah Committee, 9315 Southwest 61 Court, Miami, FL 33156. See also Waskow, *These Holy Sparks* and Chava Weissler, *Making Judaism Meaningful: Ambivalence and Tradition in a Havurah Community* (New York: AMS Press, 1988).
35. "New Jewish Agenda National Platform," especially 1–2.
36. For this paragraph, I am indebted to Marcia Falk's response to "Feminist Reflections on Separation and Unity in Jewish Theology," *Journal of Feminist Studies in Religion* 2 (Spring 1986): 123–24 and Arthur Waskow's "Down-to-Earth Judaism: Food, Sex, and Money," *Tikkun* 3 (1988): 21. Arthur Green also mentions *kashrut* in his inaugural address as president of the Reconstructionist Rabbinical College (printed and distributed by the College, November 15, 1987), 16. On Judaism as a system of distinctions and separations, see chapter 3, 96–97.
37. T. Drorah Setel, "Feminist Reflections on Separation and Unity in Jewish Theology," 117–18 and Falk's response, 124–25; Waskow, *Rainbow Sign*, chapter 3.
38. Ellen Bernstein, "The Trees' Birthday: A Celebration of Nature" (Philadelphia: Turtle River Press, 1987). Available from FRCH, Church Road and Greenwood Ave., Wyncote, PA 19095. Compare Green, Inaugural Address, 16.
39. Esther Ticktin, "A Modest Beginning," *The Jewish Woman: New Perspectives*, edited by Elizabeth Koltun (New York: Schocken Books, 1976), 129–35. Ticktin proposes other new halakhot as well.
40. This relationship was repeatedly urged by Hershel Matt at meetings of the New Jewish Agenda Theology Group that met irregularly from 1982–1984. Compare Ackelsberg, "Spirituality, Community, and Politics," 116–17.
41. Rosemary Radford Ruether, *Sexism and God-Talk: Toward a Feminist Theology* (Boston: Beacon Press, 1983), 233–34.

Glossary

Agunah. Lit., "bound" or "tied." A married woman separated from her husband who cannot remarry because the husband has disappeared, died without witnesses, or refuses to grant her a divorce.

Ashkenazim. Jews of German and Eastern European descent (as distinct from Sephardim and Mizrahim).

Bat Mitzvah. Lit., "daughter of the commandments." Refers to the age at which a girl reaches religious maturity (twelve or thirteen) and also the ritual at which this status is formally assumed.

Bimah. The raised platform in the synagogue from which the Torah is read and services are led.

Brit Milah. Lit., "covenant of circumcision." The ceremonial circumcision of a male child on the eighth day after his birth signifying his entry into the covenant of Abraham.

Get. Jewish bill of divorce.

Halakhah, halakhot (pl.), **halakhic** (adj.). Lit., "the way." Jewish law, encompassing both the oral and written Torah.

Hallah. Special bread for the Sabbath and festivals, generally braided.

Havurah, havurot (pl.). Lit., "fellowship." Refers to a recent movement among US Jews involving the formation of small, nonhierarchical—sometimes independent, sometimes synagogue-related groups—that meet for prayer, study, discussion, and celebration of holidays.

Imahot. Lit., "mothers." Refers to the matriarchs—Sarah, Rebeccah, Rachel, and Leah.

Kabbalah. General term for Jewish mysticism, especially as it developed from the twelfth century onward.

Kashrut. Jewish dietary regulations.

Kehillah. In the Diaspora, a local Jewish community that provided for the needs of its members and mediated their relationship to the outside world.

Kibbutz. In Israel, a primarily agricultural, voluntary collective community in which there is no private wealth and the community cares for the needs of its members.

Mechitzah. The partition separating men and women in traditional synagogues.

Midrash. A type of rabbinic literature involving the interpretation and elaboration of biblical texts and forming a running commentary on particular books of the Bible.

Mikvah. Ritual bath used for purification. Orthodox Jewish women go to the mikvah after each menstrual period and after childbirth.

Minyan. Quorum of ten, traditionally ten men, required for communal worship.

Mishnah. A second century rabbinic legal code that forms the basis of the Talmud.

Mitzvah. Commandment; also used for good deed.

Mizrahim. Jews of Asian and North African descent (as distinct from Ashkenazim and Sephardim).

Niddah. A menstruating woman; also refers to the laws surrounding menstrual purity and impurity.

Onah. The "conjugal dues" a husband owes his wife at specified intervals.

Sefirah, sefirot (pl). Important term in Jewish mysticism referring to the ten stages of emanation of the Godhead that constitute the realm of divine self-manifestation.

Sephardim. Jews of Spanish or Portuguese descent (as distinct from Ashkenazim and Mizrahim).

Siddur. Sabbath and daily prayerbook.

Shekhinah. The divine presence in the world. In Kabbalah, the Shekhinah is the feminine aspect of God immanent in the world.

Talmud. The central text of rabbinic Judaism, compiled at the end of the sixth century, consisting of the Mishnah and Gemara (commentary on the Mishnah).

Tanakh. The Jewish Bible, consisting of the Torah, Nevi'im (prophets), and Ketuvim (writings).

Tkhines. Petitionary prayers of Eastern European Jewish women written in Yiddish from the sixteenth to nineteenth centuries.

Torah. Lit., "teaching." The five books of Moses; the scroll containing the five books of Moses; the oral law; all of Jewish teaching.

Yetzer hara. The evil inclination, sometimes identified with sexual impulses.

General Index

Shavuot, 26, 57

Shekhinah, 124, 138, 139, 140, 146; as the presence of God, 165–66; sacred marriage with, 188

Shiphrah, 58

Siddur (prayerbook), 48, 130, 137, 257n

Silence, 1–10, 16, 23, 37, 39–40; in Genesis, 18; and the Jewish community, 84, 88; and the *Tanakh*, 13, 26–27; and women's experience, 1–2, 6, 8, 10–11, 12

Sin, 178, 183, 200

Sinai, covenant at, 21, 23, 60, 164, 169; as a central event, 25–27; and God's power, 129; and the idea of a secret Torah, 34; and the Jewish community, 79–80, 81, 85–86; and the law, 71; Miriam and, 54; souls at, 34, 105, 168

Sisterhood, 91

Sivan, month of, 57

Slavery, 14–15, 29–30, 221

Socialism, 220

Socialization, 11, 66, 77

Soul, 129; —s, at Sinai, 34, 105, 168

Spain, 96

Speaking/acting, as a mode of recovery, 56, 57–60

Stanton, Elizabeth Cady, 221, 241n

Starhawk, 146, 202, 204–5

Subordination, of women, 20, 41, 81–87, 116; and chosenness, 101; Eisenstein on, 78; and hierarchy. *See* Hierarchy; history of, 37; and Jewish history, study of, 28–29; and the law, 4–6, 8, 9, 20, 63; and male images of God, 132; and patriarchal theology, 22–23; and sin, 199. *See also* Marginalization, women's

Suffering, Jewish, 98, 101, 102; vindication of, 116

Suspicion/remembrance, hermeneutics of, 13–15, 17, 18, 71

Symbols, religious, 126–27, 134–36

Synagogue, 190–91, 205; ancient, 44–45; lack of decorum in, and the relational function of worship, 68; women's attendance at, 62

Talmud, 32, 46, 63, 138; and the laws of *onah*, 180–81; on the Sabbath, 190

Tammuz, 42

Tanakh, 13, 14, 16, 44; expanded notion of, 50; paganism in, 149; women's silence in, 26–27

Teubal, Savina, 41–42

Theology, 21–24, 76, 107–8, 211; Christian, 193, 214, 221; contemporary, extending the limits of, 51; and the finality of the Torah, questioning of, 32; and historiography, 37–38; liberation, 214; and memory, 75

Ticktin, Esther, 237

Tikkun olam, 217–20, 223, 225, 232

Tkhines, 48–49

Torah, 3, 22, 219, 226, 233, 237; dual attitude towards, 13, 15; expanded notion of, 28, 32–33, 50, 51–52, 55, 106; finality of, 32; as God's gift, 121; hidden, 136; historiography and, 32–52; /Israel/God, 121–23; and the issue of Israel, 75–76, 84, 87; as Jewish memory, 75–76; and the Mishnah, 46–47; partiality of, 6, 33–34, 85; preexistant, 34; primordial, 34–35; reading, 85; readings, annual cycle of, 26; and reshaping Jewish memory, 25–74; secret, 34; study, 85; translated as "law," 60; women and sexuality in, 170; women's, 9, 76, 136; woman's experience as visible in, 43; and women's silence, 6, 9. *See also* Bible

Trible, Phyllis, 14

Truth, 18, 53

Tu Bishvat, 237

Umansky, Ellen, 55

Unity, religious, 15–18

Universality, 18, 91

Value, standard of, 44

Values: Arab, 115; of the dominant group, internalization of, 93, 95; feminist, 212; Jewish, 23, 83, 84, 92

Virginity, 4, 172

Walker, Alice, 145–46, 155

War, 123, 124, 131

Biblical Index